ETHICAL THEORY

ETHICAL THEORY

From Hobbes to Kant

WILLIAM CURTIS SWABEY, Ph.D.

Formerly Chairman of the Department of Philosophy
in University College, New York University

THE CITADEL PRESS

New York

Printed in the United States of America

PREFACE

The problems of elementary ethics as a branch of philosophy tend to remain much the same over the centuries. The philosophers from Hobbes to Kant, whose views are to be analyzed and commented upon in this study, deal with a set of problems thoroughly familiar to teachers of ethics today. In the background there is the basic division between those who may be called naturalists and those who feel that morals must have a grounding in the realms of the transcendent. Neither Hobbes, Spinoza nor Hume literally denied the existence of God, but now, in a classification of systems, they are appropriately put with the naturalists, since, in one way or another, the concept of God has for them shifted its meaning. The others obviously accepted some form of traditional theism. Locke formulated ethics in terms of egoism and a God who sees men in the dark. Shaftesbury and Hutcheson established the existence of disinterested benevolence by considerations which have continued to be generally accepted down to the present day. Cudworth, Clarke, Balguy and Price state impressively the classic theory that we apprehend an eternal and immutable moral law by means of reason. Hutcheson propounded, with clarity, the theory of a moral sense, which causes us to approve of actions seemingly tending to the greatest good of the greatest number. Butler replaced moral sense by conscience, which had an eye to veracity and justice as well as the universal happiness. Hume and Adam Smith developed an emotive theory of the moral judgment, in which sentiment and sympathy played a great part. Bentham advanced a definition of right in terms of the hedonic consequences for all affected by the action. And lastly Kant dealt with the problems of ethical theory and of religion more radically than his predecessors and established the independence of ethics with reference to theology; Kant gave a wonderfully clear statement of the principle of ethical impartiality and of the supremacy of duty.

In general, in what follows, I have sought to discuss the points of ethical theory propounded by these men, in abstraction from their actual lives and contexts, as if they were contemporaries. I am here concerned with ethics rather than with history, although I have always had in mind the actual statements of these moralists of the age of reason. Hobbes and Locke, in writing of the natural law, had, each of them, a definite political purpose, while Bentham was concerned with the reform of law, especially in so far as it dealt with punishment. For the most part, the subject under discussion was the *foundation of morals* rather than some specific practical question; all accepted what we may call orthodox morality. Undoubtedly things were vastly simpler in those days before the French Revolution and the development of industrialism; philosophers did not feel called upon to discuss particular social problems; democracy had not yet been established and communism was, at most, considered, as by Hume, to be only an impractical dream. And yet the relevance of the arguments of Hobbes, Locke and Hume concerning natural law to present-day problems is obvious. All the ideas of these moralists have survived in the stream of culture, although their names are often forgotten, and yet these ideas are not fused into a single definite and coherent ethical theory. Perhaps such a synthesis is impossible. No one today would agree wholly with any one of these older moralists or with all of them put together. I have sought merely to discuss the various theories, without taking a strong stand for or against any one of them. It is clear enough that emotion is involved in the moral judgment as well as an attitude of impartiality. The rule of society, with its laws and customs, over our lives and thinking is obvious. Often our moral judgment is greatly influenced by our political and religious commitments. But whatever our ultimate allegiance, we shall not lose but only gain in clarity by comparing our ideas with those of the company discussed in this book.

ACKNOWLEDGMENTS

Acknowledgment is gratefully made to the following publishers for permission to reprint from their works:

The Clarendon Press, Oxford: *British Moralists* by Sir L. A. Selby-Bigge and *Review of the Principal Questions in Morals* by Richard Price.

Hafner Publishing Company, New York: *Adam Smith's Moral and Political Philosophy* by Herbert W. Schneider, in the Hafner Library of Classics.

The Liberal Arts Press, Inc., New York. Kant, *Critique of Practical Reason*, New York, 1956, and Kant, *Foundations of the Metaphysics of Morals*, New York, 1959, both translated and edited by Lewis White Beck.

Oxford University Press, Inc.: *Essay Concerning Human Understanding* by John Locke, *A Treatise of Human Nature* and *Enquiry Concerning Morals* by David Hume, and *Introduction to the Principles of Morals and Legislation* by Jeremy Bentham.

TABLE OF CONTENTS

ETHICAL THEORY

CHAPTER I

HOBBES

Hobbes is frequently referred to as a materialist. He did in fact exclude from the realm of existence the immaterial soul and such entities as forms, essences, universals and the like. On the other hand, he frequently implies the existence of such mental actions as sensing, imagining, desiring and choosing; he does not attempt to work out a consistent behaviorism. He may be more conveniently called a naturalist. A thorough-going materialism or naturalism would deny both the existence of God and the immortality of the soul. However, the *Leviathan* makes frequent mention of God and is full of scriptural quotations and references. Hobbes was primarily a political philosopher and his writings have reference to the period of Cromwell and the Stuarts. Nevertheless a fairly definite ethical theory can be found in the *Leviathan* and it is the foundation of Hobbes' political thinking. It would not be practicable to attempt to separate sharply Hobbes' ethical theory from his political theory, since, as he sees it, the details of right and wrong are inevitably determined by the state. Still, in this study, we can consider Hobbes, apart from his historical context, as an ethical theorist. A convenient

1

place to start is with his conception of human nature. Man aims at happiness and

> "felicity is a continual progress of the desire, from one object to another, the attaining of the former being still but the way to the latter. The cause whereof is that the object of man's desire is not to enjoy once only, and that for one instant of time, but to ensure forever the way of his future desire." [1]

> "The result of these restless and insatiable desires is a general inclination of all mankind, a perpetual and restless desire of power after power, that ceaseth only in death." [2] "Hence it is that kings, whose power is greatest, turn their endeavors to the ensuring it at home by laws, or abroad by wars; and when that is done, there succeedeth a new desire; in some of fame from new conquest; in others of ease and sensual pleasure; in others of admiration, or being flattered for excellence in some art, or other ability of the mind. Competition of riches, honor, command inclineth to contention, enmity and war; because the way of one competitor, to the attaining of his desire, is to kill, subdue, supplant or repel the other." [3]

In short, human life is the scene of a ceaseless struggle for power, the war of each against all; organized society is merely a more or less effective truce.

In constructing a theory of government, Hobbes commences with a hypothetical state of nature, which is a condition of anarchy, in other words, of an absence of government. The state of nature could conceivably be one of happiness, but, because of man's selfish desires and boundless will to power, it happens to be one of unrestricted warfare. The primeval struggle is natural but is far from desirable; the original state of nature was a situation in which the life

2

of man is "solitary, poor, nasty, brutish and short." [4]
In one sense, in the state of nature, there is neither
right nor wrong. Nevertheless, according to Hobbes,
even apart from any human government there are
certain everlasting laws of nature to guide one's
steps. Man's nature includes reason and reason demands that we claim for ourselves only the rights
which we grant to others. But where there is no government and a man finds that others are ready and
eager to rob and enslave him, reason also tells him
that it is permissible for him to rob and enslave others.
Hobbes' whole theory of government rests on the assumption that our fellow-men are not to be trusted
apart from the rule of some man or set of men who
force us to respect each other's rights.

The ancient and medieval doctrines of natural law
are lacking in precision; Hobbes substitutes a definite
statement of fifteen laws which do not, in so many
words, forbid us to deprive others of their lives, their
liberty or their possessions. This is in accordance with
his view that our specific rights are conferred on us
by the state. A law of nature, Hobbes tells us, is a
precept or general rule, found out by reason, by which
a man is forbidden to do that which is destructive of
his own life. This would, if taken literally, confine
the label "law of nature" to a prohibition of suicide.
Actually, Hobbes proceeds to give a list of things
which reason perceives to be destructive of our lives,
and which are, therefore, forbidden. Granted that all,
or almost all, living things seek to preserve their
being, there is still no logical connection between
this descriptive fact and an alleged moral law of self-
conservation. The second cannot be universally valid if
we accept the common opinion that, in certain circumstances, self-sacrifice is a duty. But leaving aside
this difficulty, a normative law of self-preservation,
if accepted as a foundation for ethics, would be impossible to prove. But one could hardly hope to prove
a first principle in any case. The principle would

3

have to be either a self-evident axiom or perhaps an inescapable postulate.

Hobbes' fifteen laws of nature are derived from the thought that "every man ought to seek peace, as far as he has any hope of attaining it; and when he cannot obtain it, he may seek and use all helps and advantages of war." In the state of nature, he may claim a right to everything, since he has a right to defend himself and he believes that all men are his enemies. But reason tells him, that he should be willing to enter a covenant and be content with the liberty which he allows to others. The covenant is the act of submission to a common ruler which sets up a government. A series of "laws of nature" follows, which are the consequences of the first two laws and the act of submission. We are to keep promises, show gratitude, strive to accommodate ourselves to others, forgive offences "upon caution of a future time" and punish only for the sake of future good. We are not to show contempt for others and are to acknowledge all as our equals by nature. The fifteen laws are condensed into the last one which forbids us to do that to another which we would not have done to ourselves. The first two laws, namely, that we are to seek peace and to be willing to enter a covenant on equal terms are unconditional but they bind us only to *seek* peace and *to be willing* to enter a compact; we are therefore only bound to try to be reasonable. If others do not seek peace and are not content with equality, we may defend ourselves by all means at our disposal. But what is equality? And who is to decide whether this condition is being observed or not? If we hand the decision over to the individual conscience, we can hardly avoid reverting to anarchy. Hobbes does not directly remove this difficulty, but rather places all emphasis upon promise-keeping.

The third law of nature, which tells us that promises are to be kept, only comes into play after a government has been set up. The duty of promise-keeping, he thinks, is conditional upon the existence of an enforcing power. This view is, however, extreme and difficult to maintain. It is no doubt true that in war violence and fraud are the rule and that a false promise may be used as a stratagem as well as any other; it does not follow that a promise has of itself no binding power. The view that, in the absence of an enforcing power, promises "are but words" would follow from the thought that nature teaches self-preservation, unless there exists some power to threaten punishment. However, if one admits self-preservation as a moral law, one can admit promise-keeping as a moral law of at least equal validity. Hobbes himself considers the arguments of the fool who has said in his heart, there is no justice, and answers the arguments of the fool as follows.[5] In the primeval war of each against all, no one can hope to survive without the help of confederates. He who breaks his word cannot be received into any society, which unites for peace and defense, save by error; it is therefore in accordance with reason to keep one's word. This however merely tells us that to break one's word is risky and does not prove decisively that there may not be a situation where treacherous behavior is more likely to be advantageous to the individual than keeping faith. The fact seems to be that the ability to promise is connected with belief in a moral world-order. When we swear we call upon God to witness that we have bound ourselves and we must expect punishment if we are false to our oath. There need not be a worldly enforcing agent; there may be merely a promise from A to B and A may feel that this promise is binding even to the sacrifice of his life. There may be a conspiracy against society by two or more individuals, but these individuals may feel bound to their confederates by honor. The obligation is only in their minds and yet may be of such a nature as to be regarded as sacred by an individual. The law of honor may supersede that of self-preservation. It would be rash to argue that the sense of honor is sufficient to make men keep their promises; unfortunately, we know that coercion must also be used. But there are numerous relations, involving small numbers of persons, where coercion plays little part. It is difficult to see how society could ever be organized were there not certain confederates who trust each other and are willing to sacrifice themselves to their sacred pledge. The idea of honor is woven into the foundations of society.

Hobbes' theory of governmental absolutism is that the king (or other ruler) is in a state of nature with reference to his subjects. Since there is no over-ruling authority save God to keep the king in line (since if there were such an authority, *it* would be sovereign) the king can do no wrong. The king can, it is true, sin against God, by violating the laws of equity, but he can do no unjust act against his subjects, since they have promised each other to render him absolute obedience. Common sense protests against this view. If the king violates the laws of equity (which are God's laws) his subjects may feel that they have a moral right to rise up against him and to overthrow his government. For most people, most of the time, fortunately, the *moral* and the *legal* coincide, but they need not always do so. The problem may be presented to the individual conscience whether one should do what he thinks is right even if it is contrary to the laws of the state and it would be rash to say that we should *always* do that which is legal in preference to what we think is right. The doctrine that a government, as such, can do no unjust action is a paradox which results from a simple identification of the legal and the just, since the actions of the supreme law-making authority can hardly be illegal. If the government is oppressive, there is still the right of revolution, which, although always illegal, may yet be recognized by an impartial spectator. We may take Hobbes as proclaiming a doc-

6

trine of unlimited obedience, which has the advantage of logical consistency, and yet is open to the obvious objection that even the most devoted loyalist must admit that there are possibilities of tyrannical atrocities which would render further acquiescence ridiculous.

At a risk of seeming to be arbitrary, let us ask, without any special reference to Hobbes, what *is* the essence of government? If we reduce it to the ultimate minimum, we find that the inescapable essential of government at all levels is that some person takes it upon himself to command others to do, or not to do, certain things. In part these commands are based on superior force and threats of violence, in part on persuasion and mere suggestion. To issue commands has always been regarded as a primary function of deity. The theory that the king is the viceroy of God is a natural one but it leads to the view that the church is somehow superior to the king and can determine his legitimacy. Hobbes substitutes the legalistic fiction of a universal covenant; the king derives his authority from the acquiescence of his subjects; he is by no means subordinate to the church but determines what religion shall hold sway within his domains and who shall be its priests. A leader assumes the right to rule and comes to be regarded as the incarnation of the national will; the people perceive that this man has a self-evident right to rule or, as Hobbes puts it, they find themselves bound by an implicit promise to each other to recognize this man and his heirs as their rightful rulers to the end of time.

The theory of the covenant by which we are bound to obedience may be understood to imply the absolute authority of the national will as expressed by its representatives. Each member of the group has somehow bound himself to conform to the decrees of the group as a whole. Here we may mention the famous bill of rights appended to the constitution. Our government voluntarily limits itself by granting certain rights, such as freedom of speech and assembly, to its citizens. However the same authority which granted these rights, the same individuals claiming to represent the people as a whole, could have taken them away. The constitution can be amended by the people; it cannot be legally abolished but actually the people, exercising the right of revolution, may set it aside altogether. A new constitution may be established giving us new rights and duties. This would imply that we are all in some sense slaves of the nation into which we happen to have been born; there may be laws and customs which seem to us to be unjust but we must still obey. But government necessarily claims the right to rule and cannot consistently be so liberal as to tolerate those who would destroy it; revolution must always be illegal. The colonists, in seceding from Britain, could only appeal to God and their inalienable rights; such an appeal is regarded as permissible in certain crises of history in which new governments are established; the right of disobedience and secession could be made a universal principle only at the cost of a total dissolution of society. Hobbes, by postulating a universal covenant, and defining justice in terms of promise-keeping, can regard all rebellion as unjust.

Hobbes was thus an advocate of governmental, and, ultimately, monarchical, absolutism. His theory may even be regarded as affording a theoretical basis for slavery. The slave promises to obey if his life is spared. He is not morally bound to obey, according to Hobbes, when in chains or directly threatened [6] but, at other times, Hobbesian justice demands that he fulfil his promise to obey. Against this one may argue that the slave was unjustly treated when first captured and, that, at any rate, he has inalienable rights to life and liberty. It is precisely these inalienable rights which are missing from Hobbes' theory. Hobbes did recognize a set of eternal

8

and immutable laws of nature, which include a principle of equality and are summarized in the golden rule; the application of these principles, however, is conditional on the existence of government; apart from a worldly enforcing agency, the laws, while to be regarded as expressing divine ordinances, still only bind us to wish to obey them; we need not actually obey them, if, as is often the case, we have reason to think that others hold them in contempt. It is important to note that, according to Hobbes, duty, in a practical sense, depends on a belief in the ethical character of those with whom we are dealing.

The fifteen immutable laws of nature, as we have seen, commence with the command to seek peace and to be willing to enter a covenant on equal terms; after a government has been set up, the third law, that promises are to be kept, comes into play. However, it is easy to see that this principle cannot be taken absolutely. Plato asked whether we must return his sword to a madman. Must a man keep his word to those who plan to kill or enslave him? A tyrannical government may demand a loyalty oath which later the cause of justice itself may demand that we repudiate. The remaining laws of nature are deduced by Hobbes from the basic duty of seeking peace, which is prescribed by reason as a consequence of the principle of self-preservation. However, the doctrine of peace at any price is hardly defensible; it would oblige us to submit to any unjust and shameful slavery. On the other hand, what is justice? While the institution of slavery is condemned by its name, it would be rash to regard all forms of inequality as unjust; a society will necessarily have leaders who will enjoy superior privileges. Hobbes rejected the Aristotelian doctrine of the natural inequality of men. The distinction of master and servant, he says, is introduced more by the consent of men than by difference of wit. Men think themselves equal "by nature" and will only enter into conditions of peace if

9

this equality is acknowledged. Hence it is a law of nature that every man acknowledge every other as his equal by nature; he is otherwise guilty of the sin of pride. In comment, we may say that it has hitherto frequently been the case that certain races or classes have regarded themselves as superior in nature and have only been willing to live peaceably when this superiority has been acknowledged. We can reconcile a claim of racial superiority with Hobbes' doctrine of equality by supposing that Hobbes meant to refer to a basic impartiality on the part of the spectator who functions as a moral judge. It may be for the greater good of all that some have greater privileges. If the system is one which meets with the approval of the impartial spectator as making for the greatest good on the whole, it may be called just, not as Hobbes defined the term, but in the sense of being fair and equitable and in accordance with the will of God, if we suppose God to be an impartial and benevolent being. Such differential treatment would still regard men as equal *in nature*.

The point of view of equity, in short, is that of any impartial spectator, who wishes well for mankind and approves of its acting in ways which are likely to produce a maximum of good for all. And yet the principle of equity does not tell us in detail how we should act; people differ passionately concerning the common good and frequently fail to distinguish their own good from the universal good. They are also much influenced by ancient custom and are inclined to cling to traditional privileges. It would not be practicable to live by equity alone, that is, by what is commonly called conscience. The state and its laws are a necessity and one would not be justified in setting out to put equity directly into practice. But the point of view of equity remains as a basis for criticism for every constitution and set of laws; that which cannot be approved by the impartial and benevolent spectator cannot be wholly satisfying, even though it may be impossible at the moment to establish a better set of laws.

The laws of nature, that is, the laws of equity, are considered by Hobbes to be the laws of God. At a risk of appearing to be dogmatic, I shall attempt to state briefly Hobbes' attitude on the nature and existence of God; this is not altogether easy since his language is often susceptible of more than one interpretation. In one sense, he seems to say, the word *God* is merely a traditional or poetic term for the ultimate and incomprehensible source of all things; God is a postulated explanation of the existence and nature of everything else. But men are emotionally and practically compelled to regard the inscrutable source of their existence and experience in personal terms. We may explain this, from an ethical point of view, somewhat as follows. The human being has a dual nature; in part he is an individual desperately struggling for his own survival and that of his family and friends; on the other hand, this same individual is capable of an outlook of impartial benevolence. He can look over the human scene and formulate certain laws, which, if universally obeyed, would tend to promote peace and the general good; these are the eternal laws of equity. In order to give these laws force over others and over himself the individual regards them as commands of God. He knows nothing of the nature of the first cause, but, for practical reasons, and under the sway of a powerful emotional prompting, he conceives of the first cause as a person, in fact, as a king issuing certain commandments, which are supposed to be enforced by weighty sanctions, which may be visited on the transgressor either in this life or in some future life. This is an emotional-practical view of God. If we think of God as merely the first cause, then his will, if we may speak of a will at all, is irresistible and never fails to be carried out, but in human life it is essential that God be regarded as a sovereign who has established cer-

11

tain laws for men to follow; he himself, however, is above all humanly comprehensible moral laws, and, without acting unjustly, inflicts suffering on innocent human beings, whom he has arbitrarily summoned from nothingness.

Ethical reason, that is, emotion surveying life with impartial benevolence, therefore, according to Hobbes, prescribes a proper conception of God. This is the traditional conception. We are to think of God as existing outside the world as its cause; we may not think of him as either identical with the world or as a world-soul. For, if we do not regard God as the creator of the world, we are actually denying his existence. We are likewise forbidden to deny that he concerns himself with human life; we may not properly ascribe to him figure, or parts, or place, or plurality, since such features would make him a part of nature and not its supernatural first cause. He is not to be conceived as possessing appetite or senses, although he is said to understand in a supernatural sense.[7] Enough has been said to make it clear that Hobbes regarded the traditional idea of God as a practical necessity. From this practical necessity we may deduce the desirability of institutions of public worship and a priesthood, etc. I shall not challenge this pragmatic conception of religion as an agency to cause men to restrain their natural egoism. It cannot satisfy those who demand that theology shall be true in the same sense that natural science is commonly thought to be true. On the other hand, it permits the naturalist or agnostic to regard the institutions of religion as justified by their social usefulness. From a naturalistic point of view the idea of God is a fiction, although it may be an indispensable fiction. God, in short, is the impartial well-wisher for humanity; such an "imaginary" being, conceived as loving all humans equally, would wish all men to act according to the golden rule and its corollaries. The naturalist is not obliged to be an indifferentist; he too can wish that men would act in accordance with equity and can feel indignation against them when they fail to do so. We may define Hobbes as a naturalist and agnostic, who, nevertheless, recognized a law of equity, which had at least the meaning that we were to obey it provided that others were equally fair-minded. Hobbes recognized the practical necessity of religious institutions as supporting a moral law superior to that of the state. At the same time, he granted to the state the function of determining right and wrong in detail and even of regulating religion in the sense of preventing religion from exercising a subversive influence.

According to Hobbes, man is a part of nature and his actions may be brought under the concept of necessity. But, at the same time, "liberty and necessity are consistent." [8] Just as water has both necessity and freedom in flowing in a certain channel, so man's voluntary actions are free in so far as they proceed from their choice, and yet are also determined in that they flow from some cause and ultimately from the first cause, which is the will of God. Liberty is defined by Hobbes as the absence of external impediment to motion.[9] Hobbes is no doubt to be classified as a determinist although our actions may possess a freedom which they share with inanimate objects, namely, the absence of external impediment. In terms of Hobbes' definition, a man who follows his animal appetites against his better judgment is still free. It is to be noted that the fact that our actions are causally necessitated does not prevent us from following the law of equity if we have a sufficiently strong desire to do so; neither does it excuse us from blame if our actions show that in fact we care nothing about our alleged promise to obey the laws and to respect the rights of our fellows. Determinism sheds no light on the questions, what is desirable? What ought we to do? These questions look to the future. The determinist merely says that whatever is to happen, must in any case

13

have a sufficient cause to bring it into being. Determinism is, however, a challenge to the theologian who must explain how it can be just for God to punish us for doing what he knew that we would do when he created us. Hobbes does not assert that our actions are humanly predictable. He merely asserts that whatever happens is necessary but in a sense which does not prevent necessary events from being also voluntary actions. All are necessary in the sense that whatever happens is in accordance with the will of God. But this is because the will of God, taken apart from the ethical concept of a supreme commander, is merely a name for fate, that is, for the power, however it may be conceived, which is the ultimate cause for all that has happened, is happening and is to happen in the future. Hobbes' necessitarianism merely tells us that every event has a cause. But in the class of causes there are human desires; we can feel that we too are parts of the universal will or fatality according to which everything happens. The reflection that whatever happens, happens in accordance with necessity would have a definite practical meaning only if it were taken to imply that no one was to be praised or blamed. But Hobbes had no doubt that men were to be controlled by rewards and punishments; he may be said to have believed in moral freedom in a practical sense, although it may be that from an ultimate point of view we are all equally blameless since we merely act as we have to act in the given circumstances.

Chapter II

I - Idetify

SPINOZA

The philosophy of Spinoza may be described as a combination of naturalism and rationalism. He sought to establish ethics without reference to the idea of God as a law-giver who dispenses reward and punishment. Spinoza elaborated a set of definitions of God, immortality and blessedness which, taken literally, are along lines of pantheism; they are, however, difficult to understand in any very literal sense. God is taken to be identical with the universe conceived as a totality and as self-existent, while immortality is defined in an impersonal sense rather than as implying the survival of our individual selves. From the standpoint of traditional theism, Spinoza appears to be an atheist who sought to conceal his position by speaking of a self-existent world-substance as God; it is not to be denied, however, that traditional theism contains various ambiguities and that Spinoza did little more than transform the ontological argument of Descartes into the thought that God is in essence a self-existent being. In what follows we need discuss his pronouncements only so far as they deal with theoretical ethics.

In accordance with an ancient tradition, Spinoza seeks to make self-preservation the basis of ethics. Reason demands, first of all, that every man should love himself and seek that which is useful to him.

"The foundation of virtue is the endeavor to preserve one's own being." The doctrine that the basic trait of human nature is an instinctive tendency to self-preservation is open to various criticisms. There is also an equally instinctive tendency to the perpetuation of the species, expressing itself in the reproductive urge and the parental impulses. The individual may freely sacrifice himself for his family, his friends or his country. But, in any case, self-preservation is a merely descriptive principle; it does not tell us how we ought to act but rather that as a matter of fact, men and animals do commonly seek to preserve themselves, either as individuals or as groups. Spinoza illustrates the age-old tendency to seek to ground the *ought* in the *is;* in other words, to deduce a normative principle from one which is merely descriptive. He lays great stress on the difference between activity and passivity; he implies that it is better to be active than passive but grants that no one of us can be completely free and self-expressive. The free man is the man who by virtue of his clear ideas and understanding of the world has gained a maximum of self-determination; he has escaped from human bondage as far as is humanly possible. The main purpose of Part 4 and indeed of the *Ethics* in general is to describe the life of the free man. Spinoza avoids saying that one *ought* to live in such and such a way; rather he says that a free man *will* live in a certain manner, since, by definition, his life is the life of reason. But, after all, the phrase "the free man" is a term of praise and it is implied or at least suggested that one *ought* to be rational, and hence free, and that one *ought* to desire for oneself only what one desires for others and to be "just, faithful and honorable."

If we regard Spinoza as a normative ethicist the supreme imperative from which he starts is apparent; we ought to fulfil our nature. But what is our nature? It is not something directly observable. If we under-

16

stand this imperative to mean that we are to gratify our strongest tendencies it is certainly a very dubious ethical principle. Looking at the matter in another way, the commandment to fulfil our nature is one which we cannot fail to obey, since, whatever we do, we shall be fulfilling our nature. This interpretation would render the principle wholly meaningless. Spinoza thought that our nature seeks primarily for self-preservation; this is an implication of the metaphysical generality which he propounds in Part 3, Prop. 7: the endeavor, wherewith everything endeavors to persist in its own being, is nothing else but the actual essence of the thing in question. Evidently, Spinoza is not here speaking of essence in the sense of genus and differentia (man is a rational animal, for example) since the striving for self-preservation, he thinks, belongs to everything and would not serve to distinguish one class from another. He may have been speaking of an individual essence (like Socraticity) which might be thought to be present in an individual and to guide the fulfilment of its destiny. Against this, one may urge that the individual as such does not have an essence; the distinction of essential and accidental belongs to things only as members of classes; all the properties and relations of an individual are equally essential. When we think of the individual essence as present in the thing and guiding its destiny we are indulging in metaphysical fancy, since we have merely taken the future and regarded it as somehow pre-existent in the present and as bringing itself to pass. Thus we know, in retrospect, that Caesar was destined to be assassinated and we may regard his life as progressively revealing the essence of an historical being; still we are merely illustrating the tautology that that which is to happen is to happen. But perhaps we are putting too much stress on the word *essence*. There is another question; how can we say that each thing strives to exist forever? Are not old age and death in accordance with nature?

17

May not a thing contain, in its essence, the seeds of its own destruction? It is true, as a matter of fact, that men strive to continue in existence but this is not the sole object of their desire, since they also seek for pleasant lives and for honorable lives. It cannot be said that all destinies are equally good. We are obliged to ask what do we regard as intrinsically good or desirable? Do we regard continued existence to be good even if without pleasure or combined with pain? In the same way, we may think the perpetuation of the species is a dubious good if we regard it as involving a miserable type of life for the majority of human beings.

There is a strain of hedonism in the *Ethics*. In one place,[2] good is defined as "every kind of pleasure and all that conduces thereto." It had been previously laid down [3] that we do not desire a thing because we think it good; rather we think it good because we desire it. This is deduced from the definition of desire, namely, desire is appetite with consciousness thereof. Appetite refers to an "endeavor" which follows from man's essence, which is said to be a striving for self-preservation. Hedonism is proclaimed on the basis of a simple definition of good in terms of pleasure. It is then asserted that we think a thing good, that is, find it pleasant because we desire it rather than *vice versa*. This remark, however, does not apply to pleasure itself, which is good by definition and not because it is desired. Other things, however, such as food, drink, wealth, fame, *etc.*, are good only because they are desired or because, alternatively, they produce pleasure. In contrast to Spinoza's definitional hedonism, ethical intuitionists adopt the view that good in general is that which is desirable, that is something which it is reasonable or fitting to seek to produce. It does not follow that we desire anything because it is good or desirable. But we might choose to produce something because we thought it desirable. Thus pleasure for ourselves or for others might be considered good in the sense of desirable. Food and drink, wealth and power might be declared not to be good in this sense but only in so far as they produce pleasure. This sort of normative hedonism would declare that pleasure is an intrinsic good in a special sense; it is debatable whether there may not be other intrinsic goods, such as continued existence, justice, virtue or knowledge. This form of hedonism, however, is not adopted by Spinoza who merely tells us that in one sense good and pleasant mean the same thing.

In certain passages, Spinoza attempts to give a definition of happiness. "Happiness consists in man's power of preserving his own being." [4] Do we not usually think that happiness is a pleasant state of mind? If happiness is a form of pleasure, it may either exist or not exist; if it does not exist, it may be possible; if it does exist, it is an *actuality* rather than a mere power, like the strength of one's arm, which fully exists as a power even when we are not using our muscles. We grant that knowledge of one's ability to survive may be a cause or ground of happiness. Pleasure is defined by Spinoza as "a passive state wherein the mind passes to a greater perfection." Part 3, Prop. 11, note. But, with all due respect, it may be urged that pleasure is an elemental experience and that the name of it is incapable of any definition other than a mere pointing to the experience itself. Spinoza has given us, not a true definition of pleasure, but a theory of the place of pleasure in life; it is, he says, an accompaniment of a process by which the body passes to a state of greater power to survive. This theory is open to various criticisms, since some pleasures are accompaniments of processes leading to enfeeblement and death. We may content ourselves merely with pointing out that Spinoza by no means succeeded in defining the word *pleasure*,

19

in such a way that it could be understood by a person who had never experienced pleasure, if such a being is thinkable.

We are told that "virtue is to be desired for its own sake and there is nothing more excellent or useful to us." [5] If virtue is to be desired for its own sake, then we have departed altogether from the view that pleasure and survival are the sole goods. Or did Spinoza mean merely that virtue is good because of its pleasurable consequences to the individual? What is virtue? We are told in Definition 8, Part 4, that by virtue and power Spinoza means the same thing, which is surely an odd definition of virtue. There are powers which are not virtues. The word *virtue* implies praise; virtues are commonly regarded as praiseworthy traits. Spinoza proceeds to render his definition somewhat more definite by telling us that virtue, "in so far as it is referred to man, is a man's nature or essence in so far as it has the power of effecting what can only be understood by the laws of that nature." [5] This clarification lays emphasis upon self-determination as opposed to determination by the environment; it is implied that true virtue is determination by our rational selves. The definition of virtue as power can be understood most easily with reference to the egoistic virtues; self-control is a character-trait which is useful to the individual in his effort to survive; it may, therefore, be considered a power, just as the strength of his muscles can be considered a power. On the other hand, the ability to sacrifice oneself for the sake of honor, that is, just because one has promised, has nothing to do with power to survive individually; it is a power to fulfil one's essence only if we include in our essence a will to be honorable. And this is a totally different conception of human nature than that which is implied in the *conatus in suo esse perseverare*. Still, such actions can be brought under the heading of rational self-determination, if we take *reason* in a distinctively

20

ethical sense rather than in the merely prudential sense implied in the original concept of self-preservation.

The individual, resolved to live and to survive, finds that he must join with others. Reason, which commences as a servant of egoism, becomes a mistress and obliges us to respect the rights of others. When a man has joined with his fellows, having noticed that "to man there is nothing more useful than man," he finds himself subjected to a law of impartiality and honor. "Men who are governed by reason . . . desire for themselves nothing which they do not also desire for the rest of mankind, and, consequently, are just, faithful and honorable in their conduct." Part 4, Prop. 18, note. In the sequence of propositions in the *Ethics* reason is at first prudential, formulating, guiding and imposing egoism; it suddenly becomes ethical and restrains egoism, granting to each only what it allows to all. The free man, we are finally told,[6] never acts fraudulently, but always in good faith.

"What should a man's conduct be in a case where he could by breaking faith free himself from the danger of present death? Would not his plan of self-preservation completely persuade him to deceive? This may be answered by pointing out that, if reason persuaded him to act thus, it would persuade men not to agree in good faith to unite their forces, or to have laws in common, that is, not to have only general laws, which is absurd." This passage is of interest, since the reasoning is precisely the same as that of Kant in the next century.

Egoism is to be regulated by the principle of impartiality. What reason demands of one it must demand of all; if reason demanded that we all deceive each other, co-operation would be impossible and the human race would perish. Reason, therefore, demands that we act in good faith, even at the risk of our

21

lives. Spinoza assumes that reason is an impartial faculty, interested in the common good, and, therefore, capable of forbidding the individual to seek survival at the cost of deceiving his fellows. The free man discovers an imperative in his own mind which supersedes the law of egoism. A group of men may "band together" for mutual defense and what was motivated by selfishness becomes an unwished-for opportunity for self-sacrifice. No doubt it is often true that had the banding together not taken place the individual would have lost his life or his life would have lost its value; still there is often a possibility of treachery which may seem to offer a more alluring prospect than stern self-sacrifice in fulfilment of a code of honor. To promise, therefore, implies a possibility of self-sacrifice which is at variance with the concept of man under the sole sway of self-preservation.

The specifically ethical parts of the *Ethics* are much along the lines of Hobbes. In the second note appended to Part 4, Prop. 37, Spinoza declares that sin is merely a violation of the laws of the state and that, in the "state of nature," that is, in the condition of man before a state has been established, there is no property and no justice. This doctrine is apparently contrary to the conception of ethical reason which we have just considered. An individual, it would seem, *can* sin, quite apart from the state, by not acting in good faith; in this sense he can act unjustly. It is true, however, that the establishment of the state and its laws introduces new conceptions of right and that, henceforth, there reigns a perpetual equivocation between the ethical and the legal. People tend to identify the two and to regard only those actions as wrong which are forbidden by the state.

Mention of the concept of sin reminds us that one of Spinoza's important doctrines is that virtue is its own reward and that there is no reward or punishment awaiting man after death. The teaching of

Spinoza on this point is quite incompatible with any literal acceptance of the conventional doctrines and there is a wide-spread tendency to believe that even if the traditional beliefs are fictitious still the preservation of social order demands that we pretend to believe in rewards and punishments after death. It is difficult to say to what extent people do actually believe in immortality. Men risk their lives and their earthly happiness in fulfilment of what they take to be their duty; it would be implausible to attribute such noble actions always to a cold-blooded desire for their own happiness in a future life. A man can perform an action involving risk of life or even sacrifice of life merely because he has promised, either explicitly or implicitly. He feels that he *must* do such and such a thing; this is an ethical necessitation utterly different from the sway of strong desire, in which we seem to ourselves to be slaves of fate. In keeping our word, even against our strong desires, we seem to ourselves to be free; we know that we are acting in accordance with reason even though risking our lives. The minimal account of self-sacrifice is that we act under an obscure compulsion, a sense that we *must* act in such and such a way, which we reconcile with our natural egoism, by means of the thought, which it is difficult to take literally, that we are to be compensated after death. Ultimately Spinoza must tell us that we *ought because we ought;* if we cannot be satisfied with ethics without supernatural sanction, we shall have to take refuge in the doctrine of a faith in a future life.

Spinoza was a rationalist, but not in the sense of one who believed in self-evident moral truths to be apprehended by an intuitive reason. How are we to understand the reason to which he frequently appeals? Let us, for a moment, consider how such philosophers as Hume and Adam Smith were to answer this question in a later century. They said that reason is a dynamic faculty, issuing commands and influencing our conduct. It is, therefore, more than merely cognitive. It clearly involves feeling, although it also involves detachment and impartiality. When we think of reason telling us to do so and so, we have put ourselves in the attitude of an impartial spectator. When reason demands that we be prudent, we have detached ourselves from our present impetuous desires and are asking ourselves what would be good for us on the whole. Ethical reason, as opposed to merely prudential reason, thinks of the common good of some social group and is impartial with regard to the desires of the members of that group. It ordains that we act in good faith, without necessarily binding us to promise-keeping in an extreme literalistic sense. This interpretation of the meaning of reason can claim the support of Spinoza. There are "desires which spring from reason." "Under desire which springs from reason, we seek good directly and shun evil directly." [7] "So a judge who condemns a criminal to death, not from hatred or anger, but from love of public well-being, is guided solely by reason." [8] It is relevant to mention that at the end of Part 3 Spinoza explains what he means by "actions" as opposed to "passions." The former are emotional expressions under the guidance of reason. Strength of character (*fortitudo*) is divided into courage (*animositas*) and high-mindedness (*generositas*). Courage is the desire whereby every man strives to preserve his own being solely in accordance with the dictates of reason. High-mindedness is the desire whereby every man endeavors, solely under the dictates of reason, to aid other men and to unite them to himself in friendship. These passages suffice to show that Spinoza does not take reason in separation from emotion; it was not a purely cognitive faculty like that involved in logic or arithmetic. The reason, he seems to be telling us, which ought to guide our steps, is itself contemplation plus emotion. This is conveniently

24

called practical reason, not in the sense of a faculty
which tells us how to achieve our ends, but more in
the sense of a regulative faculty which tells us to what
extent we should follow our own desires and to what
extent consider those of others.

25

CHAPTER III

LOCKE

Locke cannot be called a naturalist in the sense in
which Hobbes and Spinoza were naturalists; like Newton he combined an assertion of theism along with a
mechanistic view of nature. His *Essay on Human
Understanding* elaborates a system of dualistic realism
emphasizing the thought that all ideas are derived
from experience, which in turn could be resolved into
sensation and reflection (self-observation of the mind's
own operations). His outlook might perhaps be described as tending toward naturalism but as pre-
vented from reaching it by his belief that the existence
of God could be proved by a cosmological argument
and also by the thought that reason discovers a law
of nature which furnishes a basic criterion of right and
wrong. Locke did not write a treatise on the subject
of ethics; his views on the subject must be collected
from various passages in the *Essay on Human Understanding* and his treatises on government. The chief
elements of Locke's theory of ethics would seem to be:

1) a hedonistic definition of good;
2) denial of innate ethical principles;
3) founding of ethics on fear of divine punishment;
4) assertion of the existence of a law of nature
   which is also the law of God;

5) the possibility of a deductive science of ethics;
6) assertion of the freedom of man (rather than of the will) in the sense of "you can if you choose" but not in the sense of an explicit denial of divine omnipotence and universal causation.

1. *Hedonistic definition of good.* "That we call good, which is apt to cause or increase pleasure, or diminish pain in us; or else to procure and preserve us the presence of any other good or the absence of any evil." [1] This definition is not strictly an identification of good and pleasure; taken literally, it is a limitation of the word *good* to that which is good in an instrumental sense. Good is that which leads to pleasure; evil is that which diminishes pleasure or leads to pain. The doctrine that pleasure itself is good involves a conception of something good in itself, that is, something intrinsically good. Locke does not elaborate on this non-instrumental sense of the word *good*. In another context, Locke speaks of good and evil being drawn on us by the will and power of the lawmaker. [2] Here Locke identified good and pleasure. We may say that Locke defines the word *good*, in one of its several senses, as either pleasure or that which produces pleasure and evil as either pain or that which produces pain. There is another sense of good and evil, namely, moral good and evil which corresponds to what we commonly call right and wrong. Our actions are, according to Locke, subject to three laws: the divine law, the civil law and the law of reputation. Moral good and evil is the "conformity or disagreement of our voluntary actions to some law, whereby good and evil is drawn on us." We may say that Locke recognized two distinct meanings of good and evil; natural good and evil are identified with pleasure and pain (and what produces them); moral good and evil have always a reference to a law which

27

is imposed on us by some lawmaker, whether real or fictitious, by means of rewards and punishments.

2. *Denial of innate practical principles.* The denial of innate practical principles is in accordance with both empiricism and naturalism. But Locke was not a whole-hearted empiricist and naturalist. He believed that there was a natural moral law which was also God's law. The denial of innate practical principles was supported by anthropological data showing the prevalence of strange moral beliefs and practices in different places and ages. The reconciliation between the denial of innate practical principles and the assertion of natural law is accomplished by Locke, in so far as it is accomplished at all, by insisting that the natural law is not continuously present in the soul from birth onwards as a conscious possession; the natural law is discovered by reason in the course of the development of the individual and the race. Locke grants that there is an innate love of happiness. This is a tendency to act or to choose in a certain way but it is not an "inscribed" ethical principle in the sense which Locke had in mind. It is more like an instinct, such as the nest-building tendencies of birds, which is not what Locke meant to deny in denying innate practical principles. Locke was thinking of an innate knowledge of some set of laws similar to the ten commandments. There is no such innate knowledge, he says, and supports his position by reference to the fact that one can ask *why* one should obey the moral rules; this question is answered differently by different people. Why should we keep our promises? The Christian gives as a reason that God will punish us if we fail to do so. The follower of Hobbes refers to the punishments threatened by the Leviathan, the state, the mortal god. The ancient philosophers say that we must keep our word because to do otherwise is to act contrary to the dignity of human nature. It may be urged against Locke, that it might be the case that our duty is made known to us by some intuitive

perception that we *ought* to act in such and such a
way and that the demand for a selfish reason *why*
we should do our duty is an improper demand. It is
true, however, that human nature finds it difficult to
hold to the idea of duty for the sake of duty and necessarily seeks a reconciliation of duty and prudence.
With regard to the anthropological argument against
an innate practical law, there is the possibility that
there may be a universal law of a general character,
such as, Act according to principles which you think
tend to the universal good of mankind. The applica-
tions which we make of this general principle might
very well vary according to circumstances.

Locke felt that it was necessary to answer the in-
natists who insisted that "justice and the keeping of
compacts" are found in the "dens of thieves and the
confederacies of the greatest villains." Locke points
out that outlaws practice justice merely as a matter
of convenience within their own groups; they do not
acknowledge justice as an innate law since they are
ready to plunder and kill the first honest man they
meet. He grants that in all societies virtue is approved
because it is profitable. The moral rules are widely
accepted by mankind who often fail to perceive that
"the true ground of morality can only be the will and
law of a God, who sees men in the dark, and has in
his hands rewards and punishments and power enough
to call to account the proudest offender." [3] God has
joined virtue and public happiness together and made
virtue visibly beneficial to all those with whom the
virtuous man has dealings; it is therefore not surpris-
ing that everyone recommends these rules to others;
it is to everyone's interest to proclaim that to be
sacred without which he cannot himself be safe. Here
Locke intimates that moral codes are based on their
utility to the individual and to society. They are, in
short, conventions established for the common good
and then regarded as divine commandments enforced
by supernatural sanctions. Such a theory of morals is

29

naturalistic. But Locke's tendency to naturalism is concealed by the fact that he frequently speaks as one who accepted the conventional fictions of society as literal truth. The utilitarian turn of Locke's thought is in accordance with his denial of innate principles; if moral codes are merely conventions based on utility, it is natural that they should vary with circumstances; they cannot be innate or self-evident principles, since, if this were the case, they would be the same for everyone.

3. *The founding of ethics on fear of divine punishment.* We have seen that Locke regarded the true theoretical basis of morals to be the fear of a God who sees men in the dark. This, in short, is the final answer to those who ask why they should keep their word. However, let us consider the case of a man who is unpersuaded by either the ontological, the cosmological or the teleological arguments for the existence of God. Such a man might say, with Kant, that the existence of God, along with the immortality of the soul and the freedom of the will, is a postulate of practical reason. However, it may still be said that a convinced atheist can find a reason to keep his word if he is indeed an honorable man; if he is not an honorable man he will not be rendered honorable by a professed belief in God. He is likely to be able to persuade himself by some sophistry that he is doing the right thing or else that he can escape punishment by a timely repentance. The doctrine of a punitive God is perhaps defensible as a socially necessary fiction. It recognizes fear as the highest motive but the fear involved is the fear of God. Locke gives no reason why an unbeliever should keep his word save the usual fear of the vengeance or displeasure of his fellows. The Lockean doctrine does not convey a sense of freedom or of the fulfilment of a self-imposed law. The motive is always a prudent fear of bad consequences to ourselves; the opportunity of sacrificing ourselves to our own ideals is denied to us. Would

30

not an atheist and free-thinker who would sacrifice his life for what he regarded as truth be nobler than a follower of Locke could ever be, since the Lockean would always be guided by an anxious fear for his safety in the next life? The fact seems to be that the concept of belief in religious teachings is scarcely distinguishable from a practical commitment to a certain way of life and the man who sacrifices himself for what he regards as truth thereby attests his belief in something greater than himself.

4. *The law of nature.* Locke's doctrine of a law of nature was set forth in an *Essay concerning Civil Government* (1689) which is a classic statement of the philosophy underlying the British and American constitutions, that is, of the ideology of democracy. In this work, especially, Locke does not write as a detached theorist but rather as a theologically minded statesman setting forth authoritatively the law of God.

"The state of nature," he writes, "has a law to govern it, which obliges everyone; and reason, which is that law, teaches all mankind who will but consult it, that being all equal and independent, no one ought to harm another in his life, health, liberty or possessions. For men being all the workmanship of one omnipotent and infinitely wise maker—all the servants of one sovereign master, sent into the world by his order, and about his business—they are his property whose workmanship they are, made to last during his, not another's pleasure; and being furnished with like faculties, sharing all in one community of nature, there cannot be supposed any such subordination among us, that may authorize us to destroy one another, as if we were made for one another's uses, as the inferior ranks of creatures were made for ours. . . . Unless it be to do justice on an offender (we are not permitted) to take away the life, the liberty, health, limb or goods of another." [4]

31

We can understand this in a non-theological way by supposing the natural law to be the will of an imaginary disinterested and impartial spectator who loves all human beings with an impartial affection. Such a being, wishing for the good of all, would wish that humans would co-operate but at the same time should refrain from killing or enslaving each other; this is most easily expressed by supposing that there are, for each of us, certain things which we may do and with which it would be wrong, on the part of other humans, to interfere; these are called natural rights. Wrong actions are those which arouse a feeling of anger and resentment in such a spectator. The law of nature forbids us to commit suicide, to enslave our fellow-men, to kill them (save in self-defense or in defense of the rights of others), to deprive them of their possessions or to deceive them by false promises. The natural law is a set of ethical postulates which are, in fact, generally accepted in the society in which we live.

The chief difficulty has to do with the sanctity of property on which Locke lays great stress. It is fairly evident that this is not an *absolute* right. One can easily imagine a situation in which one man might own everything in a given country and be entitled to enforce starvation and death by exposure on all his fellow-citizens. The idea is indeed fantastic but everyone knows that those who own land and other natural resources can impose a tax (called rent) on those who are not so fortunate. The alleged natural right to own property may be criticized in this manner by a *reductio ad absurdum*. We know that the governmental right to tax destroys any pretension that private property may have to be an absolute right, since the government can take away an indefinitely large fraction of what we possess. It would seem, therefore, that perhaps Hobbes was right as against Locke. Property is merely granted us by the state and the sovereign authority can take back what it has conferred.

Locke's law of nature was later shown by Hume to contain at least two elements which may be called conventional: property and promises. It is an analytic truth that we ought not to deprive people of what is rightfully theirs. But frequently the title rests on some violent conquest or usurpation, which took place in the distant past, and is now regarded as beyond the scope of reasonable discussion. It is also analytically true that we ought to keep our promises, granted that the promise was valid in the first place. But there may have been an element of unjust extortion in the original promise. Who is to decide what property-titles are valid and what promises are to be kept? In reality, the government, whatever it is, will be the final authority on these questions. It is quite capable of nationalizing all the factories, stores, natural resources, etc., and the claims of individuals to their "natural rights" may come to be regarded as subversive, or, perhaps, anarchic, ideas.

The natural law is merely an outline of the basic conventions involved in the organization of society in non-communist lands. It cannot be truly claimed to be self-evident since it *might* be for the public good that the right of ownership be greatly restricted. Hobbes' fifteen laws of nature were an amplification of the idea of equity or fairness; Locke's laws are a statement of the ideal postulates involved in a society based on private property. Unlike Hobbes, Locke believed that there was a natural justice, which is logically prior to the establishment of a state; in the state of nature one does not have, as Hobbes supposed, a right to everything, but only limited rights and in passing to the condition of citizenship one does not give up a right to everything, but merely surrenders to the state his right of punishing offenders. The theory that there are certain natural rights prior to the establishment of government is an implication of the view that conscience is a cognitive faculty, which apprehends intuitively certain pre-existent rights and duties. But it may be said that at the basis of conscience, there is an *opinion,* based on common experience, that it would be for the common good for each person to respect the property-rights of each other person. This opinion, being empirical, is not truly self-evident. Furthermore, property-rights, apart from the laws of the state, are vague and indeterminate and therefore conducive to strife. The fact seems to be that Locke's natural laws are merely postulates presupposed in custom, which may be regarded as antecedent to the state.

These customs can be changed either for better or for worse. Consideration of the law of nature would lead a contemporary student of ethics to discussion of a number of controversial questions totally unknown to Locke, such as birth-control and euthanasia. Since the law of nature is supposed to be a divine law it may be used by various churches as a means of establishing certain views of right and wrong. In the end, the divine law, for any given church, is what the leaders of that church declare it to be. It follows that an appeal to the natural law is really an appeal to authority, that is, to what has generally been accepted in some tradition. A person who does not accept a given church as authoritative is not bound to abide by its decisions concerning the content of the law of nature. He can only be persuaded if appeal is made to some postulate which he accepts. Thus if both agree that rules of conduct concerning birth-control or any other matter should tend to the general happiness a rational discussion might take place. But, generally speaking, the question is regarded as settled in advance and principles of natural law are accepted, not because of their intrinsic self-evidence, but because they yield certain desired consequences. The conclusion is taken to warrant the premises.

5. *A deductive science of ethics.* Locke cautiously advanced the conjecture that morality might be a science capable of demonstration if men only applied

themselves to the task with sufficient zeal and disinterestedness. But Locke was not able to produce such a science himself and the examples which he cites are not encouraging.

He tells us that the statement "where there is no property, there is no injustice" is a proposition as certain as any in Euclid. This, however, means merely that Locke has commenced with a definition of justice in terms of property. If one defined justice in terms of promise-keeping, as Hobbes did, then there could be injustice between people who did not recognize property, namely, violation of promise. The second example "no government allows absolute liberty" is a truism or tautology. In short, Locke's examples are mere analytic propositions. The idea of a science of ethics, founded on self-evident axioms and clear definitions and leading to a set of demonstrated propositions, has continued to fascinate moralists through the centuries; we shall find it in the system of the rationalists such as Clarke and Price; the same doctrine is found, in more sophisticated form, in recent times, in the writings of Prichard, Ross and Ewing. It is quite contrary to the doctrine of utilitarianism which is strongly suggested by Locke's hedonistic definition of good.

6. *The freedom of man.* Locke devoted a lengthy discussion to what is commonly called the freedom of the will. He does not explicitly undertake to reconcile man's freedom with God's omnipotence; he regarded such a problem as beyond the scope of the human mind. He likewise does not deal directly with the relation between the free choice of the individual and universal causation, as stated, for example, in Kant's antinomies. It is evident that he did believe in the freedom of the individual in an empirical sense and as presupposed in moral responsibility, although he formally denied freedom of the will on the ground that liberty is one power and freedom another, and he thought it self-evident that one power cannot pos-

sess another. The point is not convincing, since we can quite intelligibly say that one potentiality has the power of increasing while another potentiality does not have such a power. But, at any rate, according to Locke, we are to think of the man as free rather than the will, since the phrase, the freedom of the will, tends to set up the will as a separate entity. However, the question is whether the man is free *in* his willing, that is, in his actions and the traditional phrase can at least be accepted as a manner of speaking.

The idea of freedom which Locke offers is much the same as that of Hobbes; it is a freedom which is compatible with necessity. It is "our being able to act or not to act according as we shall choose or will."[5] Thus we are free to jump from a precipice, if we choose, but we are not free to jump in the reverse direction, since this is not something which we could do if we chose. It is to be noted that the idea of power, for Locke, is a simple, indefinable, idea; it cannot be reduced to anything else, although it is true that a power cannot be a self-existent entity but must always be a power *of* something. "Volition or willing is an act of the mind directing its thought to the production of any action"[6] and includes forbearance, such as sitting still or holding one's peace. We are capable of being active; activity presupposes a mind which sets itself to do or not to do something. We are free when we can if we choose, although the action may be one which we do not choose to perform. Freedom belongs to us with reference to those actions which are commonly said to be physically possible; the choice is determined by desire. Locke had originally supposed that choice was always determined by the greater good in prospect; this was obviously contrary to the well-known fact of human folly (*video meliora, proboque, deteriora sequor*). He therefore replaced the theory of the determination of choice by the greater good in prospect by the theory that choice is always determined by the greater present uneasiness. The earlier theory is included in the later, since the thought of a future good is capable of producing an uneasiness sufficient to determine choice; it need not do so, however. What is it which determines whether or not we are to respond to the lure of the greater good? Locke does not tell us. Is it perhaps our temperament?

At any rate, Locke, in his later theory, affirms that choice is determined by the greatest present uneasiness, that is, by desire. He gives no further account of desire save that it is always determined by the thought of pleasure and pain. It evidently arises spontaneously in the individual. Locke's psychological hedonism is commonly rejected by later ethicists, who point to the existence of such desires as hunger and thirst, which seem to be directed on external objects such as food and drink rather than on pleasure and pain as such. In one sense of the word, desire is a readiness to receive uneasiness from the absence of a certain object (food) and pleasure in its presence or consumption. This sense of the word refers to the psycho-physical organism and does not seem to be quite the same as what Locke had in mind. He was thinking of what we may call "conscious desire." In "conscious desire" there is a thought of some possible future state of affairs. This sort of desire is not a propensity or instinct or habit; it is something which we can observe and analyse in ourselves. Locke believed that in fact we can only desire, in this sense, future states of ourselves; we are drawn toward what promises to be pleasant and away from what threatens to be painful. It is possible to reject this account of desire altogether, since it is something which can only be known by "reflection" or "introspection" but cannot be known by behavioristic observation. The Lockean doctrine is easily intelligible and highly plausible. On the other hand, there is the problem of the desire to produce happiness for others; this was

37

a matter to which Locke gave no consideration. He followed the tradition of the ancient and medieval philosophers who tended to think in terms of psychological egoism, according to which man is always seeking his own happiness. If we admit the possibility of altruistic desire, we have greatly modified Locke's theory; this was a path followed by Locke's successors, Shaftesbury, Hutcheson, Butler, Hume and Adam Smith and in fact by most later ethicists.

We are here concerned, however, with the problem of freedom. Choice is determined by desire and desire follows the prospect of happiness. Good or happiness is the proper object of desire in general

> "yet all good, even seen and confessed to be so, does not necessarily move every man's desire; but only that part of it as is considered and taken to make a necessary part of *his* happiness." [7]

In short, not all pleasure is actually desired, although all is good by definition. It is only desire, an actual uneasiness, which influences action.

> "All absent good does not at any time make a necessary part of our present happiness, nor the absence of it make a part of our misery. If it did we should be constantly and infinitely miserable; there being infinite degrees of happiness which are not in our possession." [8]

Locke is dealing with the difficult problem of contentment. We all know that a man can be content with something far less than the greatest possible happiness. This is a matter of an arbitrary limitation, which we place, for good or bad reasons, on our aspirations for happiness.

Man possesses liberty in the sense that he has a power to suspend his eager pursuit of some object; consideration of other and greater goods can raise a desire for them and change our whole course of conduct. Locke would insist that our actions are always determined by our desire for happiness and our judgment concerning the best means of gaining it, but determination of this sort, he would say, does not cancel liberty. Thus Locke gives an account of free will which seems in accordance with experience. It is not denied that our choice is always determined by desire. Locke does not bring out that when we suspend our action and pause to consider other possibilities, there is always a reason, some warning which flashes across the mind. We can suspend action if we choose and we can choose to suspend if there is a present uneasiness which prompts us to suspend; suspension is, therefore, no exception to the rule that action is always motivated. Locke is, therefore, to be listed among those who assert freedom in a sense which does not exclude determinism. He does not discuss the problem of the predictability of human actions; he would no doubt have taken the reasonable stand that only God is capable of knowing the future with certainty and in detail. Locke asserted determinism in combination with liberty in the sense that he held that choice is determined or necessitated by desire. This, however, is a peculiar form of necessitation. To choose to do a thing because we want to do it is not a type of necessitation to be found in inanimate objects; it is peculiar to beings who have reached a state of mental advancement sufficient to enable them to contemplate several alternative courses at once. It is, therefore, a necessitation within the domain of consciousness. But since we choose to do what we most want to do at the moment it is a type of necessitation which is, in a sense, identical with freedom.

Many comments can be made upon a theory of freedom such as Locke's. The following are perhaps worthy of consideration:

(i) The meaning of the saying "I had to." There may be a divided state of mind in which we act against our real desire. In such cases we have the feeling of being slaves of our habits and instincts. When we say "I couldn't help it; I had to" we know that we could have helped it and not done the thing if we had wanted not to strongly enough; the fact of our not having had a sufficiently strong contrary desire may reflect adversely on our characters. Generally speaking when we say "I had to," "I was forced to do so and so," we do not mean that we were forced physically; if a giant *had* seized our arm, the action would not have been ours; *we* would have done nothing. We mean rather that we were drawn astray by strong desires, especially by the desire to avoid pain. But it is still true that in such cases we act according to the desire which is supreme at the moment, although contrary to what we really want in the sense of "want in a calm or detached mood."

(ii) Locke's theory of liberty and human punishment. In defense of Locke's conception of freedom we may say that it is sufficient to justify human punishment. For we may think of human laws as rules attaching certain penalties to certain actions which are deemed undesirable by the law-making authority. These penalties offer motives for not doing certain things; the laws would be senseless if directed to inanimate objects or to animals incapable of understanding laws but they are not senseless if directed to intelligent beings whose actions are controlled by their conscious desires. Such beings cannot very well say "I couldn't help doing such and such an act" when the only sense in which they couldn't help it was that they lacked interest in the consequences of their actions, especially for others. For such lack of concern may be an expression of a sort of character deserving condemnation.

(iii) Lockean free will and divine punishment. But, although Lockean freedom may be in accordance with human justice, it is difficult to reconcile with divine punishment. An individual, we may say, is strong or weak according to his temperament, which may be a matter of heredity or else of mere chance; in any case, it is not something under the control of the individual. He necessarily acts according to his innate character, which has been modified by his past experiences and past deeds; he is responsible for his character only in so far as it is a product of his deeds; this cannot be the complete explanation, since no one wholly makes himself. One must always start with a certain innate temperament. God must ultimately take account of our given characters and, it would seem, extend forgiveness, since no one can be responsible for the character with which he was first provided. This line of reasoning may merely show that the subject of divine justice in its relation to human life is beyond our powers. Theologians use the concept of grace to cover what God confers and takes away arbitrarily, without regard to human rules of justice. The idea of God would lose its usefulness were we to explain all human suffering as due to the misdeeds of those who suffer.

(iv) Determination by desire is irrelevant to practical problems. The fact that choice is determined by the greatest actual desire or uneasiness is irrelevant to practical problems. When we choose we either look to the future and consider what action is likely to have the best consequences or we seek to fulfil some obligation which we feel to be binding. We know in advance that, however we choose, it will be in satisfaction of some desire, that is, for the relief of some uneasiness. This insight, however, has nothing to do with the question, What ought we to do?

(v) The fact of deliberation and choice excludes human foreknowledge of how in detail we are going to choose. This fact is, however, not relevant to Locke's type of determination, since he does not assert the possibility of human prediction. Furthermore, Locke's conception of liberty does justice to the fact that human choice cannot be indiscriminately classed with

41

the movement of inanimate objects. Furthermore, it presupposes a certain level of intelligence, since one who chooses must at least consider several alternatives; obviously choices can differ enormously in the range and complexity of the considerations involved.

In conclusion, one may say that Locke does not stress divine predestination to the extent that Hobbes and Spinoza did; he does not, however, assert the existence of freedom in any sense which denies divine omnipotence or universal causation. He rather describes the process of choice and asserts a psychological determinism, in the sense that choice is always in accordance with the stronger conscious desire. At the same time, he speaks the language of liberty rather than fatalism and had no doubt that his views were in accordance with any sense of moral responsibility that was practically important.

CHAPTER IV

CUDWORTH, CLARKE
AND WOLLASTON

I
Ralph Cudworth

The great tradition of ethical rationalism de-
scends from Plato and Aristotle, through the Stoics
and the medieval theologians and is carried on in the
18th century by Cudworth, Clarke, Balguy and Price.
This school assigns the guidance of human conduct
to reason, which is taken in the sense of an immediate perception of right and wrong rather than in the
sense of a process of reasoning, whether inductive
or deductive. The rationalists were mostly clergymen,
who were official spokesmen of morality; they did not
write from a psychological or sociological view-point
and did not seek to explain morality in a naturalistic
way; at the same time, they abstained from an appeal
to revelation. Rationalism was set forth, in a frame-
work of Platonic theology, by Ralph Cudworth, who
was especially interested in defending the existence of
"eternal and immutable morality" against the doctrines of Hobbes, which were taken as making right
and wrong entirely matters of governmental decree.
Moral good and evil, just and unjust, honest and dishonest, says Cudworth, cannot be arbitrary things,

but must have a reality of their own "since it is universally true that things are what they are not by will but by nature." [1] Things are white by whiteness, round by rotundity, *etc*. It follows that actions are just by participating in the nature of justice, which must, therefore, be an independent subsistent essence.

One can imagine a modern disciple of ethical relativism hastily interrupting Cudworth at this point to make the following criticism. It is true that everything is what it is by nature and not by will, save those things whose nature it is to be what they are by will. Thus a thing *is* commanded solely because it is in fact commanded; such *is* its nature. Cudworth has merely begged the question in assuming that justice is an independent and subsistent essence. But if we define justice as obedience to the will of God, then there must be a rational perception of the truth that God ought to be obeyed.

> "For it was never heard of, that anyone founded all his authority of commanding others, and others' obligation or duty to obey his commands, in a law of his own making, that men should be required, obliged or bound to obey him." [2]

The authority of the commander, whether divine or human, is founded on natural justice and equity. If it were not morally good and just in its own nature before any positive command of God that God should be obeyed by his own creatures, the bare will of God could not beget an obligation to do what he willed or commanded. [3]

Natural justice is illustrated by Cudworth by the usual example of keeping faith, i.e., of performing covenants. After we have promised to do something, an action, which was in itself indifferent, becomes obligatory. The foundation of morality was to be found in the nature of God; the great problem was the relation of the divine intellect to the divine will. Descartes had followed Duns Scotus in making the divine will absolute; Cudworth revives the Platonic doctrine that God is unable to change the nature of things, and, especially that even God could not, by an arbitrary decree, make an act right which was intrinsically wicked. God cannot change the eternal measures of right and wrong. This is, after all, an implication of the thought that moral truth belongs in the class of necessary relations. Cudworth thus maintains that at the basis of all duty, there must be a rational perception. One must *see* that promises are to be kept, or that God is to be obeyed or that a certain man has a right to command. This primary intuitive perception cannot itself be deduced from sensuous experience and nothing would be gained by deducing it from some prior intuitive perception. Cudworth does not discuss detailed questions of practical ethics; his chief interest was in a philosophical theism in the Platonic tradition and he seeks to make it clear that we must always presuppose an objectively existent right and wrong.

Cudworth's doctrine involves a rejection of the notion that the soul is a "mere *tabula rasa,* a naked and passive thing, which has no innate furniture or activity of its own." Cudworth's denial of the *tabula rasa* was in point of time before Locke made his famous attack on innate ideas. Even Cudworth denies that

> "the anticipations of morality spring merely from intellectual forms and notional ideas of the mind, or from certain rules or propositions, arbitrarily imprinted upon the soul as upon a book, but (rather) from some other inward and vital principle, whereby they have a natural determination in them to do some things and to avoid others, which could not be if they were mere naked passive things." [4]

45

This doctrine grants to the soul a certain eros or inner dynamism by which it strives toward what it regards as good. It might be thought that each soul has its own bias and that what was good for one was bad for another, but, if Cudworth's position is to be sustained, such relativism cannot be the whole truth. He was obliged to assume that human souls, at least, have a more or less common nature. The point may be made that when Cudworth ascribes to souls certain innate preferences he seems to grant that the power which claims the right to rule our lives is not purely intellectual or cognitive. But at the same time, he holds to the classic doctrine that there is one absolute truth, which includes moral truth as an important subdivision.

"It is the perfection of will, as such, to be guided by wisdom and truth." "Now all the knowledge and wisdom that is in creatures, whether angels or men, is nothing else but a participation of that one eternal, immutable and increated wisdom of God, or several signatures of that one archetypal seal, or like so many multiplied reflections of one and the same face, made in several glasses, whereof some are clearer, some obscurer, some standing nearer, some further off." [5]

Souls, then, share in varying degrees, the vision of goodness and truth, that is, the perception of "eternal and immutable morality" as a law which ought to be obeyed, however much it may be neglected in practice.

It may be relevant to compare briefly the position of Cudworth with that of Hobbes. The latter also recognized a law of nature, valid in all times and places, which was the law of equity. But, said Hobbes, considering human selfishness, we need not keep faith, unless forced to do so by governmental power, since we cannot be sure that others will not take advantage of us. It is obvious that no social organization is possible unless we postulate an elemental sense of honor and some degree of faith in our fellows. But after government has been established the follower of Hobbes would regard our paramount duty as obedience. The follower of Cudworth, on the other hand, might be informed by his guide, reason, that Hobbes was right in most cases and that we should practice conformity. However, in some unusual case, the intuitionist may be instructed by reason, which is only another name for conscience, that it is our duty to follow some supposedly divine law rather than human. The conclusion to be drawn is that the follower of Cudworth may believe that he is obeying "eternal and immutable morality" in taking part in a revolution against constituted authority; the follower of Hobbes would have to be a conformist as long as government protected him. The position of Cudworth would seem to be more acceptable in theory, although in practice no government can consistently recognize a right to attempt to overthrow it.

II
Samuel Clarke

In the Boyle Lectures of 1705, on *The Unchangable Obligations of Natural Religion,* Samuel Clarke, D.D. commences with the notion that there are

"certain unchanging relations of things to each other which determine the fitness of the application of different things or different relations one to another." [6]

The key word is *fitness.* It is fitting that the will of God should always act for justice, goodness and truth in order to promote the welfare of the

47

whole universe. God does what is fitting in each configuration of circumstances; the same pattern of conditions also determines how the wills of "all subordinate rational creatures" should choose to act. In a sense, the standard is relative, since what is right in one complex situation need not be right in some situation which is different in a relevant feature. This type of "relativism" is by no means contrary to the basic absolutism which Clarke means to proclaim. What is fitting is relative to a configuration of circumstances; the circumstances imply necessarily that something is our duty and place an obligation upon us apart from the positive will of God and from any prospect of reward and punishment.

The fundamental truths of ethics are, according to Clarke, self-evident, both with regard to God and man. It is manifestly most fitting that the ruler of the universe should always do what tends to the universal good of the whole creation; this is clearly more fitting than that he should strive to make the world miserable or that, in order to satisfy the desires of certain depraved natures, he should permit the world order to be perverted. It would be most contrary to fitness were God to inflict suffering needlessly on any innocent creature. In like manner it is most fit, in man's dealings with each other, that all men should seek to promote the universal good; it would be most unfit for them to be continually contriving each other's ruin and destruction. Even before any mutual covenant, it is more fit that men should deal with each other according to the rules of justice and equity than that every man should disappoint the reasonable expectations of his neighbors and seek to defraud or plunder with violence his fellow-men.

Clarke had in mind a contrast between his position and that of Hobbes, whom he regarded as denying an absolute right and wrong and as founding ethics on (1) the irresistible power of God and (2) on a compact into which men have entered. Against Hobbes, Clarke points out that the author of the *Leviathan* regarded the destruction of all mankind as an evil, and it is to avoid this evil that men enter into the covenant. Therefore, even before the covenant it was unfit and unreasonable in itself that all mankind should destroy one another. Those who teach that good and evil depend on positive laws, whether human or divine, run into the absurdity of supposing that one law cannot be better than another; they cannot give any reason why any law at all should be established. This argument can be used today against the doctrine of cultural relativism, which maintains that different values are valid in different cultures and that no comparison is possible between them. If Clarke had limited self-evident ethical truth to the goodness of public happiness and the badness of public misery, his position would have been rationalistic utilitarianism but he adopted the more generally accepted view that

> "keeping faith and performing equitable compacts receive not their obligatory power, from any law or authority, but are only declared, confirmed and enforced by penalties, upon such as would perhaps not be governed by right reason only." [7]

The statement that *equitable* compacts should be kept must remain unclear as long as the definition of *equitable* is lacking. One can imagine that a slave, or serf, or tenant farmer, or wage-slave or unemployed person today, might complain that the basic social compact is inequitable and not morally binding. The position of Clarke is substantially the same as that of Locke, namely, that there is a law of nature prior to all government and that this may be discovered by reason.

Against the existence of such a law of nature, one

may cite the variety of opinions to be found with regard to certain questions of justice and injustice and the many contrary laws and customs which have prevailed in different countries at different times. The situation, Clarke says, is similar to that found in the realm of color; black and white are clearly different, but there are shades of grey not easily distinguished from each other. In the case of the Spartan law, which permitted the youth to steal, one may argue that since every man has a right to his own goods, the members of any society may agree to transfer their possessions upon what conditions they see fit. This argument, we may say by way of comment, is comparable to those by which the right to tax is explained. Are we to cite the will of the majority? Is the will of the majority self-evidently the criterion of right and wrong? Is the majority any fraction over 50%? But (to return to the permitted stealing of the Spartan youth) Clarke declares that even though such a law can be defended, yet a law, whereby every man may rob whomever he meets and by which all equitable compacts may be violated, could not be accepted by any man possessed of reason. As a matter of common sense, one may agree that the law described by Clarke would be absurd and impossible. Still one may ask whether if all wished anarchy to prevail, how could it be wrong? But if only some persons preferred law to anarchy, are we to fall back on the will of the majority? Clarke's self-evident moral truth is by no means as definite as he seemed to think. There is always the question concerning what is fair and equitable and this does not seem capable of being reduced to any hard and fast rule.

But Clarke thought that the eternal fitness of things is manifest to all understandings, with the exception of those whose understandings are either "very imperfect or very much depraved." Just as it is absurd to deny that twice two is four, so it is absurd to deny moral truth. It is not in man's power to withhold his assent from a plain speculative truth, but by the natural liberty of his will he may fail to act as his reason tells him he should. "He that refuses to deal with all men equitably, as with every man as he desires they should deal with him, is guilty of the same unreasonableness and contradiction" as a man who should deny that things equal to the same thing are equal to each other. Those who depart from "the eternal and invariable rules of justice, equity, goodness and truth" and "suffer themselves to be swayed by unaccountable arbitrary humors and rash passions, by lusts, vanity and pride, by private interest or present sensual pleasures" are "setting up their own unreasonable self-will in opposition to the nature and reason of things" and seek "to make things be what they are not and cannot be." [8] Furthermore, our moral obligation to conform to the eternal fitness of things is not dependent on the existence of any external enforcing power.

> "For the reason and conscience of a man's own mind, concerning the reasonableness and fitness of the thing . . . is the truest and formalest obligation, even more properly and strictly so, than any opinion whatsoever of the authority of the giver of a law or any regard he may have to its sanctions by rewards and punishments. For whoever acts contrary to this sense and conscience of his own mind is necessarily self-condemned; and the greatest and strongest of all obligations is that which a man cannot break through without condemning himself." [9]

Rewards and punishments, although "absolutely necessary to the government of frail and fallible creatures" constitute only a secondary obligation.

Clarke's exposition of the self-evident fitness of

things tends to conceal the fact that the application of eternal moral truths is a matter of a more or less developed social system, which is itself the product of historical forces. Our duties are by no means self-evident but are impressed upon us by our parents and associates and especially by the state which establishes and enforces a system of property-rights. It may be that eternal reason tells us that it is for our own good and for the good of humanity in general that we should conform to the laws and customs of whatever society we happen to belong to; nevertheless, it is obvious that our rights and duties are not, in general, as clear as $2 + 2 = 4$; the latter is something that we could learn without being instructed by others but we could not possibly learn what was ours and what was not ours save by having it impressed upon us by society. Clarke's rationalism presents morality as something as clear and undeniable as the multiplication-table. The outcome of Clarke's exposition of morals was conservative in effect, since he tends to sustain the established order by presenting it as something intellectually unquestionable; the social order, however, can be regarded as self-evidently rational only by ignoring the large part played by tradition, custom and education.

Plato taught that all knowledge worthy of the name was based on recollection of something which had been seen by the soul in a state preceding the present life. Others have concluded that the ideas involved in primary truths are innate and belong to the mind in its essential constitution. Clarke formally denied both the pre-existence of the soul and the existence of innate ideas and yet agreed with Plato that the

"differences, relations and proportions of things, both natural and moral, in which all unprejudiced minds agree . . . are certain, unalterable and real

52

in the things themselves and do not at all depend on the variable opinions, fancies or imaginations of men prejudiced by education, laws, customs or evil practices." [10]

Reason, in short, discerns the eternal law when uncorrupted by education and custom. There are men, he tells, us, of vicious character, who have been corrupted by evil education, who deny any necessary difference between right and wrong. But even these men, the most abandoned of all mankind, who commit robbery and murder, would choose, if they could gain the same advantage without committing the crime, to avoid the crime even though they were sure of going unpunished. By way of comment, we may note that Clarke's assertion that people have a wish to respect the rights of others may spring from a desire to stand consistently on a principle which protects their own rights. Clarke overlooks the obvious fact that the definitions of both murder and robbery are matters of social convention. He sees no middle ground between the supposition that there is an intuitively discernible absolute moral law governing all the details of life and a total immoralism. It is probable that man has a predisposition to subordinate himself to the laws and customs of the society in which he finds himself; these laws are likely to appear to members of any given society as embodiments of eternal right, but in truth they lack altogether the strict cogency found in mathematics.

Rationalism cannot in truth deduce in detail an absolute moral code; nevertheless, it is able to state certain very broad principles which present an appearance of being true axioms of conduct and of being the foundation of all the specific rules. Our duty is brought under three headings, duty to God, to other humans and to ourselves.

I. *Duty to God*. With regard to God, the rule

of righteousness demands that we worship him as the supreme author, preserver and governor of all things and that

> "we employ our whole beings, and all our powers and faculties, in his service, and for his glory, that is, in encouraging the practice of universal righteousness and promoting the designs of his divine goodness among men, etc." [11]

It would be superfluous to discuss this axiom, since it is truly self-evident to those who believe in the existence of such a God. On the other hand, it would be rash to say that the proposition necessitates any particular form of worship. From the standpoint of naturalism, the image of an invisible king is a creation of a social instinct, which seeks a means of enforcing the laws of society beyond the reach of the officers of the law. From the standpoint of intuitionism, the existence of God and the necessity of worshiping him are self-evident.

II. *Duty to fellow-men.* With respect to our fellows, the law of righteousness has two parts: there is a law of equity and a law of love. The first tells us "to deal with every man, as in like circumstances, we could reasonably expect that he should deal with us"; the second that we endeavor "by an universal benevolence to promote the welfare and happiness of all men." [12] The law of equity, which is identical in meaning with the Golden Rule and the first formulation of Kant's categorical imperative, is undoubtedly the most plausible example of an absolute or a priori principle of morality in the arsenal of rationalism. The denial that what is right, *i.e.,* what may reasonably be expected of a man in a given set of circumstances, is right for any one else in that set of circumstances is a contradiction or absurdity. This rule holds, not only for social equals but for unequals as well, provided that we take account of the difference of circumstances; you should treat your superior (or inferior) as you would wish them to treat you if your respective circumstances were transposed. In comment upon this axiom, we may grant that it is truly self-evident that what is right for one is right for anyone in the same set of circumstances. Nevertheless the principle is empty and formal and presupposes a social system. Thus an action may be right for a father but not for a son. This implies that it is right for all fathers in the same circumstances. There is a course of conduct which is permissible or obligatory for a king, a nobleman, a judge, a priest, a soldier, a policeman, etc. The rules of morality apply to classes of individuals and to all members of those classes uniformly, but this fact does not tell us what those rules should be. Thus Clarke's law would not exclude serfdom or slavery if these are accepted institutions. The master should be a good master and the slave a good slave, in the sense that each should do what might reasonably be expected of him. It is logically implied in the concepts of the various categories which go to make up a social system that all members of these classes have certain duties which apply to them regardless of personal differences, that is, simply as members of these classes; it is this truism which is set forth in the law of equity. One may also remark that an ingenious mind, in applying the axiom, can generally find some difference in the circumstances which warrants, at least seemingly, some exceptional type of behavior. Thus the decision is thrown back to the individual conscience, which must decide whether in any given case the circumstances are sufficiently different to warrant a departure from some accepted rule of conduct. Nevertheless, the law of equity, like other formal truisms, holds without exception and even covers our treatment of animals, in the sense that if it is wrong for one man to torture an animal, it is also wrong for anyone else.

The second great law governing our dealings with our fellow-creatures is the principle of benevolence, which means that we are constantly to endeavor "to promote in general, to the utmost of our power, the welfare and happiness of all men." [13] "Every rational creature ought, in its sphere and station, according to its respective powers and faculties, to do all the good it can to all its fellow-creatures." [14] This law is supported by the fact that, after his love of self, every man has a natural affection for his children and for his relatives and friends. And since families cannot live comfortably by themselves, they must join in a friendship of families and this enlarges itself into a society of towns, cities and nations and finally into the community of all mankind. Every man is prompted by his uncorrupted affections

"to look upon himself as a part and member of that one universal body or community which is made up of all mankind, to think of himself as born to promote the public good and welfare of all his fellow-creatures." [15]

Evidence for this law is seen in the fact that action in accordance with it "affords a man an ample pleasure and satisfaction and gives him a comfortable sense of having answered best the ends of his creation and imitated as fully as possible the perfection of the creator." [16]

In comment upon the law of benevolence it may be noted that we are commanded "to will," "to endeavor" to promote the good of all men. In short it is a law of beneficence rather than merely a demand that we *wish* for the good of all. We note, in the second place, that the content of the law is vague. It might be that we could most effectively promote the universal good by looking out for ourselves, since we are in a much better position to help ourselves than to help others. There is also the question whether we are obliged always to forego a smaller good for ourselves in favor of a greater good for others. We normally think that we have certain rights as well as duties and that as long as we remain within the sphere of our rights, we are permitted to prefer ourselves, even though we thereby produce a smaller amount of good. The principle of benevolence was actually understood by Clarke to be limited by considerations of equity and means, at most, that we should act according to a system which tends to the universal good. It is conceivable that there should be a social situation in which no altruism or benevolence would be necessary and in which each person would follow only the demands of egoism. This is concealed from us by the fact that there will always be children and probably always poor people, as well as invalids and the aged, who cannot be expected to provide for themselves. This fact, namely, the universal existence of people who need our aid has given an opportunity for religious leaders to preach charity and in fact such preaching is one of the chief functions of religion. The law of benevolence, as stated by Samuel Clarke, if understood to mean that we should act according to a system which tends to the common good, and, at the same time, should give some aid to those who need help, is generally accepted and is one against which we can raise no protest. Ethical theory, however, has the alternative of regarding the principle as an expression of human emotion rather than a decree of pure reason.

III. *Duty to self.* The third part of the "rule of righteousness" has to do with our duty to ourselves. Every man is to preserve his own being and to take care of himself in order to perform his other duties. No man has a right to take his own life, because

> "what he is not the author and giver of, he can never of himself have just power or authority to take away. He that sent us into the world, and

alone knows for how long he appointed our station here, and when we have finished all the business intended we should do, can alone judge when 'tis fit for us to be taken hence." [17]

The prohibition of suicide has always been a primary point of religious ethics. No doubt there are many persons who would regard the necessity for such a prohibition as so important that they would, for this reason alone, accept theism. Nevertheless the religious argument against suicide is open to various criticisms. If we are forbidden to interfere to take our lives, it might seem that we are also forbidden to prolong them by medicine or even by taking food. The rationalist is obliged to appeal to the fact that we have a strong desire to live. But we have also a strong desire to escape from pain and anguish. The argument against suicide is not clear, since we may thereby injure no one, and in fact, even aid others by removing a burden. If, therefore, we wish to maintain the wrongfulness of suicide, we shall probably not be able to avoid an appeal to intuition.

The second branch of the rule of righteousness, applied to our duty to ourselves, is as follows: a man

"is obliged to attend to the duties of that particular station or condition of life, wherein Providence has at present placed him, with diligence and contentment, without being either uneasy and discontent, that others are placed by Providence in different and superior stations in the world, or so extremely and unreasonably solicitous to change his state for the future, as thereby to neglect his present duty." [18]

This rule shows how the doctrine of Providence tends to lend support to whatever system of caste is in existence at the time. The principle of being content with the station in which it has pleased Providence to place us, taken in an extreme way, would do away with ambition, which is often a cause of progress; it is also contrary to what we may call revolutionary equalitarianism. We cannot say that the rule is an absolute one, although it may be both wise and for the common good for people to be content with their humble stations in many cases.

In comment upon the above statement of the law of nature, we may say that only the law of equity is truly an absolute principle, since it expresses a truism, namely, that the ethical predicates, in their essential meaning, apply to all persons in a given configuration of circumstances. The principles of benevolence and duty to self are lacking in perfect definiteness. Duty to self is a difficult conception, since, in general, a man who neglects his own interest is guilty of folly rather than wickedness; his actions call forth pity from others rather than indignation. If we think of Clarke's prohibition of suicide and his rule of being content with our humble lot, it would seem that the third branch of the rule of righteousness is concerned with our duty to God rather than with duty to self. Such theological duties fall in a class by themselves and rest on special presuppositions. The principles of benevolence and prudence may be regarded as expressions of feelings found in most people; we sympathize with the striving for happiness seen in others and feel resentment against those whose actions thwart this striving, whether in others or in themselves. According to Clarke, the law of nature is the presupposition of all actual systems of law, although some correspond to it more perfectly than others.

"There never was any nation upon earth, but owned to love and honor God, to be grateful to benefactors, to perform equitable compacts, to preserve the lives of innocent and harmless men, and the like, were things fitter and better to be practiced than the contrary. In fine: This is that law of nature, which, being founded in the eternal reason of things, is as absolutely unalterable, as natural good and evil, as mathematical or arithmetical truths, as light and darkness, as sweet and bitter, as pleasure and pain." [19]

It is evident that as an historical generalization, this statement takes a good deal for granted. There remains also the question concerning the meaning of the phrase *equitable compacts*. It is easy to imagine people, in any age, and under any system of government, who would have reason to feel that whatever promises they made were extracted from them by force and were invalid. The eternal law of right may be a basis for revolution, although Clarke does not seem to have been of a revolutionary cast of mind.

But even if we grant the existence of such an absolute law the question remains why we should obey it. The answer of Clarke is that the law binds us by its own force, just as it binds God's will, and that rewards and punishments are a secondary consideration. But considering the weakness of human nature and the fact that the practice of virtue is often threatened with great calamities including death, God, in his goodness, established rewards and punishments after death. The position of Clarke is sufficiently familiar and thoroughly orthodox. An atheist, who nevertheless accepted the law of righteousness, in so far as it refers to fellow-humans, could only rely on natural sanctions, such as self-approval or self-condemnation, the approval or disapproval of others, etc. On the other hand, an orthodox thinker, like Clarke, would have to admit that our actions, so far as animated by a prudent regard for heaven and hell, really lack moral value. It is difficult to say in just how literal a sense such ideas were accepted in the 18th century or are accepted today by religious thinkers. We may be willing to say that God left us in a condition of uncertainty with regard to both his existence and to the reality of his rewards and punishments; the good man acts as if he believed in God and a future life; true faith is expressed by actions rather than words.

Clarke provides us with a vigorous statement of one of the alternatives of ethical theory, namely, ethical rationalism. The basic truths of ethics are, he holds, capable of being known by intuitive reason. They are self-evident as are also mathematical and logical axioms. It is only the unaccountable corruption of man's nature which keeps him from clearly grasping these truths and applying them in the conduct of his life. There are two possible interpretations of Clarke's ethical theory with reference to the social order. We may take Clarke's rationalism as upholding the established order in all its details, since all laws and customs can be regarded as based on the eternal fitness of things. Revolution and reform are an absurd rising up of the individual against the everlasting laws of God. On the other hand, we may conclude that the existing order is quite irrational, being largely based on tradition and prejudice, and that the eternal laws warrant a revolutionary attitude. But, in any case, the supreme principles stated by Clarke, the laws of equity and benevolence, are generally accepted as valid moral laws.

III
William Wollaston

William Wollaston (1659-1724) wrote a book which seems to have been widely influential in the 18th century, having gone through eight editions, namely, *The Religion of Nature Delineated*, which was first privately printed in 1722. He commences by noticing that moralists have not been able to discover the one rule of conduct which they have been looking for; he feels that such a rule may be easily stated. It is merely that we are always to act in accordance with truth. Wrong action is acting out a lie, since, for example, in taking your watch, I deny, by my action, that the watch is yours. The definition of truth is as follows: those propositions are true, which express things as they are; or "truth is the conformity of those words or signs by which things are expressed, to the things themselves." [20] Furthermore, a true proposition may be denied by deeds as well as by words. If A breaks his promise to B, he in effect declares by his action that he made no such promise.

The hypothesis is clever and even plausible, although it also has an air of triviality. Obviously it can shed no real light on any practical problem. Let us take the case of a Russian nihilist of the 19th century; should he throw a bomb designed to kill the Tsar? If he does do, he declares, by his deed, that the Tsar was not his rightful ruler or even a mere human being with a right to live; on the other hand, if he fails to do so, he denies that the Tsar was a frightful tyrant who deserved to die. The point may be made, by way of counter-argument, that no other ethical theory is able to give a definite answer to questions of this sort and that Wollaston may still be right in maintaining that the essence of wrong-doing is that it is contrary to truth.

The nature of truth has always been a primary topic of philosophy, but is generally treated in another context. In one sense, we may say that in general truth follows existence as its shadow. If I exist, it is true that I exist; if I shall exist in the future, it is true that I shall exist in the future. If the earth is round, it is true that the earth is round, etc. A moral truth, however, such as "Promises should be kept," is not a description of existence in this sense. If one is to uphold Wollaston's point of view, one must suppose that there are certain self-existent moral truths; one may act either in accordance with these truths or contrary to them, either knowingly or by accident. Action which is knowingly contrary to a moral truth is wrong and morally bad. Action in accordance with moral truths or facts is identical with action in accordance with the eternal fitness of things. This general description of rightness is not to be rejected because it does not of itself tell us what is right in any given set of circumstances. The point may be made, however, that truth as a mere description of existence is not a complete moral guide; Wollaston's theory can only be defended if one admits a special class of truths which are not so much descriptions of existence as statements of what ought to be.

A difficulty was felt by Wollaston with regard to the question whether all wrong actions are equally wrong. The case of stealing a book is compared with that of defrauding a man of an estate worth ten thousand pounds. The "truth" involved is that in the first case, one man is deprived of a certain amount of happiness while in the case of the estate another man is deprived of a great deal more happiness and his heirs and dependents are likewise injured in the same manner. If the book was worth one pound, then in the fraudulent gaining of the estate, the wrong must be multiplied by ten thousand. "Thus the degrees of evil or guilt are as the importance and number of truths violated." [21] This thought, namely, that we must consider the number of truths violated seems unsound. How can we count truths? We must admit, it seems, that certain truths or moral facts are more important than others. This strongly suggests that the amount of moral evil is proportional to the amount of suffering or deprivation of happiness caused by the act.

Our natural concern with the consequences of actions with regard to happiness or misery suggests that the key to the problem of morality is to be found in the idea of happiness rather than in that of truth. An early utilitarian, John Brown, writing *On the Motives to Virtue* in 1751, compares happiness to the sun. The uninstructed marvel at the varying positions

63

of the rainbow, but when it is noted that the position of the rainbow varies with the position of the sun, the inquirer is convinced that this "gay meteor (does) but shine with a borrowed splendor derived from the influence of that mighty luminary." [22] In the same way, right and wrong are determined by happiness and misery. Wollaston had mentioned the impropriety of treating a man like a post. But the impropriety of treating a post like a man, while ridiculous, could never be compared to the former offense, yet both are equally contrary to the nature of things, or, in Wollaston's language, in both cases we act against truth. But when we treat a man like a post, or when we deprive a man of ten thousand pounds, we act in ways likely greatly to diminish the happiness of some person or persons. It seems then that happiness is the sun of the moral universe and that the beauty of virtue is derivative.

Let us attempt to answer this objection from the standpoint of Wollaston and Clarke. (1) Truth, or the nature of things, demands that when the general happiness is alone at stake, we should act in a manner likely to produce a maximum of happiness. (2) When a promise or human rights are at stake, and there is no contrary consideration from the standpoint of the general happiness, then we are to keep this promise or respect the rights involved. (3) But if there is a conflict between a promise which we have given and the general good, then we must act according to the paramount obligation. In other words, truth, or the nature of things, ordains that in some cases we should keep our word and neglect the general good, and that, in other cases, we promote the general good at the cost of breaking our word. "It is not in man's power," says Wollaston, "to promise absolutely. He can only promise as one, who may be disabled by the weight and incumbency of truths not then existing." [23] It is true that all wrong action is contrary to truth and in, this sense, all such actions are equally bad. On the other hand, we may have a choice between two actions both of which are formally contrary to the nature of things but one of which is more contrary to truth than the other; that is to say, one is contrary to a more weighty truth than the other. One cannot say that happiness alone determines what we ought to do. Reason may tell us, on some occasion, that our obligation to respect the rights of individuals is greater than our obligation to promote the universal happiness.

For Wollaston, the religion of nature is inseparably connected with the existence of moral distinctions; if acts can be divided into good, bad and indifferent, there must be religion. It is evident that he had in mind a far simpler religion than any which has actually held sway in the world, namely, one defined by Kant, later in the 18th century, by the postulates of practical reason: the existence of God, the immortality of the soul and the freedom of the will. We cannot suppose, Wollaston tells us, that if we follow truth we shall fail to be happy. If this were to happen it would imply some defect in the divine nature, either weakness or an evil disposition. Wollaston's religion of nature bypasses all forms of traditional religion and bases itself solely on an appeal to what is self-evident to pure reason. Like the doctrine of Clarke, it may be interpreted in either a conservative or revolutionary manner. In the former interpretation, it endorses the whole existing system of things; it suppresses all naturalistic or historical explanation of the origin of laws and customs. With a slight shift of emphasis, the religion of nature can become a violent revolutionary force, namely, with the perception that the traditional religious beliefs and social practices were contrary to reason. Wollaston does not seem to have taken this step. What he added to Samuel Clarke's position was the idea of truth as a synonym for "the eternal fitness of things." The idea of truth is not genuinely enlightening as a formula for morality. There are many truths which are not directly relevant to action. We know that in seeking to accomplish certain ends we must consider the nature of the things we have to deal with. Nevertheless, the only truths which directly apply to action are what we may refer to as categorical imperatives. These would be such sentences as "You ought to tell the truth," "You ought to consider the general good," "You ought to keep your word," etc. These can be regarded, if we choose, as self-existent moral facts. These moral facts have the peculiarity that they cannot be discovered by sensuous observation. A conventionalist, like Hume, would say that they can be discovered by reason only when they are involved in some previously adopted convention, as when we say that we should not take what is not ours. The rationalists say that we simply perceive such truths and that no further explanation is possible.

CHAPTER V

SHAFTESBURY

The third Earl of Shaftesbury's *Enquiry concerning Virtue* (1699) was followed, in the course of the 18th century, by a series of writings by men who held, as Shaftesbury himself did, that morals can be founded, more or less completely, on human nature. These writers may be listed as Hutcheson, Butler, Hume and Adam Smith. They represent, in an early form, what has now come to be known as the emotive theory of ethics. Their views are in contrast with the teachings of the rationalists, such as Cudworth and Clarke, and with the attitude of Locke, who stressed the power of God and rewards and punishments after death. Butler is to some extent between the rationalists and the humanists and shares some traits with each school. Shaftesbury and Hutcheson work out a theory of the moral sense and of benevolence as the motive of virtue; Butler replaces the moral sense by conscience; Hume and Adam Smith speak of the moral sentiments.

Shaftesbury's attitude is not wholly clear. He was a free-thinker and a devoted student of the Greek and Roman moralists. Although a pupil of Locke's he was not satisfied with the theological authoritarianism and prudential attitude implied in Locke's doctrine of the God who sees men in the dark and has sufficient power to punish the proudest offender. He seeks to make clear, as did the ancient moralists, the thought that a man has in his own mind a power to discern the unchanging standards of right and wrong and to judge himself and others. This he combines with a doctrine of teleology which asserts that the universe is a great system of things in which each creature has a part to play. A human being is good or bad according as the affections of benevolence and self-love are present in the right proportion to produce the greatest good for the species.

> "Affection toward self-good may be a good affection or an ill one. For if this private affection be too strong (as when the excessive love of life unfits a creature for any generous act) then it is undoubtedly vicious." [1]

If this selfish creature is accidentally led to do good he is no more a good creature than one who fights for a just cause for a fee. We can see the profound difference between Locke and his pupil, since, for Locke, the motive of all our actions is the desire for our own happiness (or, what comes to the same thing, the desire to escape from some present uneasiness). For Shaftesbury, on the other hand, the goodness of the action is a matter of the unselfish character of the motive.

Actions, says Shaftesbury, and the affections of pity, kindness, gratitude and their opposites, are brought before the mind by reflection. And just as the shapes, colors, motions and proportions of sensible objects appear clothed in beauty or deformity, so behavior appeals to our feelings and seems to be beautiful or ugly.

> "In these vagrant characters or pictures of manners, which the mind of necessity figures to itself

68

and carries still about with it, the heart cannot possibly remain neutral; but constantly takes part, one way or the other. However false or corrupt it may be with itself, it finds the difference as to beauty and comeliness between one heart and another, one turn of affection, one sentiment and another; and accordingly, in all disinterested cases, must approve in some measure what is natural and honest and disapprove what is dishonest and corrupt." [2]

Virtue is conceived as a species of beauty; the mind perceives what is "natural" and "honest" in feeling and action. This is not merely a matter of education and custom, which are quite capable of perverting and falsifying our moral judgment; the mind can penetrate the mask of conventional untruth and perceive the unchanging values. The following is a weighty ethical pronouncement showing that Shaftesbury, like the rationalists, believed that there was an "eternal and immutable" moral law of higher authority than mere custom.

"And thus if there be anything which teaches men either treachery, ingratitude or cruelty by divine warrant; or under color and pretense of any present or future good to mankind; if there be anything which teaches men to persecute their friends through love; or to torment captives of war in sport; or to offer human sacrifice; or to torment, macerate or mangle themselves, in a religious zeal, before their God, or to commit any sort of barbarity as amiable and becoming; be it custom which gives applause or religion which gives a sanction, this is not, nor can ever be, virtue of any kind or in any sense; but must still remain horrid depravity, notwithstanding any fashion, law, custom, or religion, which may be ill or vicious

69

itself but can never alter the eternal measures and immutable independent nature of worth and virtue." [3]

This doctrine of an absolute moral law could only be justified by the thought that man has a faculty of ethical reason or moral intuition which can distinguish between social convention and the eternal measures of virtue. On this matter there is agreement between Shaftesbury and the rationalists, and yet the emphasis is different. Shaftesbury stresses the importance of having the right affections, which means having the right amount of altruism as well as a proper love of virtue for its own sake. If we do the right thing merely out of fear of punishment in this life or the next, we have no claim to the title of virtuous.

There is a right degree of concern for the good of others which should regulate our conduct. There is an "unequal affection" which is wicked and wrong.

> "Wrong is not such action as is barely the cause of harm (since at this rate a dutiful son aiming at an enemy, but by mistake or ill-chance happening to kill his father would do wrong) but that anything is done through insufficient or unequal affection as when a son shows no concern for the safety of a father; or, where there is need of succor, prefers an indifferent person to him, this is the nature of wrong." [4]

What is unequal affection? The "equal affection" which Shaftesbury has in mind does not mean that we are not to love members of our own families more than we love strangers; it means rather that we are to have that degree of affection for them which our minds or hearts tell us is right and proper. A sociologist would tell us that this is a matter of convention and that it is quite conceivable that there might be a society in which family relations were entirely ignored. Different societies have discovered rules which work for survival and these rules are communicated to the young by education. The same authority which dictates the rules of conduct, namely, custom, also ordains what are the proper feelings and tells us that we are to love members of our own families more than we love strangers. Shaftesbury merely tells us that our minds perceive what is natural and right and sometimes set aside as perverse and corrupt the teachings of society. The "equal affection" which we are to cultivate can only be that degree of affection which our hearts perceive to be right and proper in consideration of our place in the world.

Virtue, Shaftesbury tells us, is not merely a matter of doing deeds which have an external rightness or legality; it involves, as we have just seen, having the right affections. This involves not only having a love for our fellows but also a love of virtue for its own sake. We are told that if we are excessively selfish, we are vicious; if we have the right amount of altruism we escape censure; we are to be called virtuous only if we love virtue for its own sake.

> "So that if a creature be generous, kind, constant, compassionate; yet, if he cannot reflect on what he does or sees others do, so as to take notice of what is worthy or honest; and make that notice or conception of worth and honesty to be an object of his affection, he has not the character of being virtuous." [5]

The thought of loving virtue for its own sake involves difficulties. It may be objected that we really seek only happiness for ourselves and that we are incapable of loving virtue save as a means to our own happiness. Shaftesbury clearly teaches that we have disinterested affections directed either on the good of others or on virtue for its own sake. However,

71

whether virtue for its own sake is a necessary requirement for the title of virtuous is a matter of definition. It is safe to say that actions done solely because they are thought to be right, without any motive of either egoism or altruism, are very rare if they occur at all. Furthermore, society may judge such actions to be wrong and deserving of punishment in cases where an individual has an unorthodox conception of what is right.

Locke had believed that a denial of God would deprive morality of its ultimate foundation; he had also believed that reason was capable, by itself, of establishing the existence of God. Shaftesbury disavowed atheism but did not believe that the existence of a punitive God was the primary basis of morality. False opinions as to religion, one of which was atheism, can have a bad effect on morals only in three ways: (1) by taking away a just and natural sense of right and wrong; (2) by creating a false sense of the same and (3) by creating contrary affections. With regard to (1) atheism does not remove our concern for what we think makes for the common good. With regard to (2) custom and education can indeed corrupt the moral sense; there is no reason to suppose that

> "atheism should of itself be the cause of any estimation or valuing of anything as fair, noble or deserving, which was the contrary. But false religion or superstition can cause many unnatural and inhuman things to seem good." [6]

It is impossible to conceive, he tells us, that a rational creature, on being introduced to justice, generosity, gratitude and other virtues should have no liking for them. The soul

> "must needs find a beauty and deformity in actions, minds and tempers. If there is no real amiableness or deformity in moral acts, there

72

is at least an imaginary one of full force. Though perhaps the thing itself should not be allowed in nature, the imagination or fancy of it, must be allowed to be from nature alone." [7]

We may interpret Shaftesbury as teaching that man perceives what makes for the common good and that he is naturally interested in this inclusive good; this causes him to view with favor actions which illustrate justice, generosity, gratitude and the like. Morals are, he thinks, in essence independent of religion save in so far as the latter affects opinion with regard to the consequences of actions. Men would still approve and disapprove even though they believed that there were in fact no rewards and punishments after death. Even among those who are indifferent to religion there are, he thinks, some who are modest, kind and friendly.

The following may be said in comment on Shaftesbury's position. The question is not fundamentally concerning the good or bad consequences of either religion or atheism; it is rather whether or not atheism is logically excluded by man's moral consciousness. Let us start with a definition of right action; it clearly consists in doing what we ought to do and must be something within our power. Our affections, on the other hand, do not seem to be entirely, or even, mainly matters of free choice; we may happen to have a love for our fellows or for virtue or, again, we may lack these affections. Shaftesbury speaks as if virtue consisted in a happy or fortunate emotional constitution, a kind of mental health, which would render us agreeable to others and to ourselves. Virtue

"is a certain just disposition or proportionable affection of a rational creature towards the moral objects of right and wrong." [8]

But let us suppose that we happen not to have this fortunate moral constitution; it is still true that we

73

ought to act according to principles which tend to the common good. We ought, for example, to do what we have promised to do. The traditional argument is that a theist who believes that there is a God who will punish him if he does wrong has a motive for doing right which the atheist lacks. Against this the point may be made that belief in an impersonal moral order which brings it about that wrong-doing is inevitably punished in the long run would be equally effective. This is a postulate of practical reason which can be accepted by the atheist but, like theism itself, demands an act of faith.

But let us continue with Shaftesbury. There are, in such a creature as man, affections which tend to the interest of the species and others which tend toward the good of the individual. Since pursuing the common interest involves hazards and hardships, it may appear that self-interest involves an absence of any public-spiritedness. Against this "extraordinary hypothesis," which makes moral rectitude the ill, and depravity the good, of the individual, Shaftesbury must try to show that moral rectitude or virtue is for the advantage of the individual in this life. The problem is very similar to that with which Plato dealt in the later books of the *Republic*, where he seeks to show that virtuous conduct, taken in the usual sense of honesty, justice and generosity, is truly in the interest of the individual. Salient points in Shaftesbury's argument are as follows: The pleasures of the mind are superior to those of the body. He means, apparently, as a recent advocate of a similar philosophy has taught,[9] that mental satisfactions make a greater contribution to the happiness of the individual than do what are called physical enjoyments. The natural affections are in themselves, the "highest" satisfactions in the sense of making the greatest possible contribution to happiness. The honest man can enjoy and compare both kinds of satisfaction; the immoral man is, however, not able to judge of social pleasure, to which he is a stranger. There is a genuine intellectual pleasure in the mastery of a mathematical demonstration, but an even greater satisfaction in the exercise of benignity. In the passion of love between the sexes, there may be manifested a genuine self-sacrifice which is, at the same time, a source of great and noble satisfaction to the individual. In such satisfaction, the hereafter of the theologians is ignored "for who has ever thought of preparing a heaven of future recompense for the suffering virtue of lovers?" [10] In addition to the immediate satisfaction of altruism, we participate, by sympathy, in the good which we produce; we can also enjoy "the pleasing consciousness of actual love, merited esteem or approbation of others." [11] The objection occurs that perhaps we can profit by substituting an "imperfect partial regard" in place of the "entire, sincere and truly moral attitude." But, says Shaftesbury, a "partial affection" is a contradiction. A person conscious of such a partial affection can be conscious of no moral worth. Such a passion will be highly variable and will undergo frequent successions of hatred and love and thus produce continual disturbance and disgust. But "entire affection" or integrity is "answerable to itself, proportionable and rational" and hence is "irrefragable, solid and durable." Conscience, in a religious sense, is more than a mere fear of the deity; it must be "an apprehension of what is wrong, odious, morally deformed and ill-deserving." [12] And if we attempt to escape from this argument by picturing a man without conscience we are reminded that such a man will be incapable of all social affection and must be subject "to all manner of horrid, unnatural and ill-affection." [13] Neither chivalrous honor nor religious zeal can take the place of moral integrity.

"For 'tis impossible that a cruel enthusiast or bigot, a persecutor, a murderer, a bravo, a pirate or any villain of less degree, who is false to the society of mankind in general, and contradicts natural affection, should have any fixed principle at all, any real standard or measure by which he can measure his esteem or any solid reason by which to form his approbation of any one moral act." [14]

This phase of Shaftesbury's argument can be summarized by saying that when we act in accordance with "entire affection" we act according to principles which we wish to be universally applied and therefore enjoy the approval of our own minds; when we act in a contrary manner we must necessarily condemn ourselves. The argument is more convincing with regard to the unjust; there is always the possibility that the just are unhappy for various external reasons. In fact, experience suggests, when we consider the heroes and martyrs of mankind, that the nobler types of human being are likely to suffer greatly from the cruelty and injustice of others. If we think of the unjust man as a man who acts contrary to his own standards, we may suppose that he will be unhappy in so far as he has any concern for the common good. The just man will *tend* to be happy but may fail to achieve happiness because of ill-fortune or social hostility.

The ideal of Shaftesbury, like that of Plato, is the health of the soul, which is a state of emotional balance conducive to the greatest happiness of both society and the individual. All would agree that this is a desirable thing, although it is not what we usually mean by moral goodness. We are told that we may fall short of this state of spiritual perfection in three ways: (1) through lack of the social affections; (2) through excessive strength of the self-regarding passions, especially love of life, desire for sensuous pleasure, love of praise and indolence; and (3) through unnatural affections, such as delight in

76

watching torments. The latter passions, being contrary to man's natural benevolence, cannot produce happiness for those who indulge them. But even if we grant that virtue is, in some sense, as Plato said, the health of the soul, it is still true that the individual cannot remold his character at will. Our characters, at any given moment, are the result of an innate disposition, which has been modified by various influences, which have been brought to bear on us. Let us consider a man who is unusually selfish; how is he to blame, since he did not fundamentally make himself? Or, again, granted that a man is good in the sense of being generous and public-spirited, still this would seem to be due either to a fortunate original pre-disposition or else to favorable environmental influences. Our characters may be socially useful or socially injurious, but, in any case, although we are responsible for our actions, we do not seem to be responsible, to any great extent, for being the kind of beings that we are. What society demands of us is, after all, in the language of Hobbes, obedience; our actions are said to be right if they conform to the rules of the society in which we live, whatever our emotions may be. Furthermore, heroic virtue, self-sacrifice in the full sense of the word, is not suggested by the phrase "the health of the soul" which normally denotes a state making for the happiness of the individual.

John Brown,[15] writing a half-century after the publication of Shaftesbury's *Enquiry*, brings an effective criticism to bear on Shaftesbury's doctrine that a life of virtue tends, of itself, to produce happiness for the individual in this life. He proceeds by dividing mankind into three groups. The first and largest group is made up of those in whom the senses are dominant and, who, therefore, have no appreciation of the beauty of virtue for its own sake. The second group is smaller and is composed of people in whom the imagination predominates and who devote themselves to the elegant refinements of the polite arts such as painting, music, architecture, poetry, sculpture or else to the false delicacies of dress, furniture and equipage. These aesthetes will not be greatly interested in the alleged beauty of pure virtue. There remains a third class in whom the passions (in some limited sense) are the chief sources of pleasure and pain. Now the "passions" may be either those contrary to universal happiness, such as selfishness, jealousy, pride, hatred, envy and revenge or they may be the benign passions of hope, faith, candor, pity, generosity and good-will. Only the small group in whom these generous passions are dominant can appreciate the beauty of virtue. These few will perform noble deeds because such is their nature; the majority can be swayed only by hope of heaven and fear of hell. Furthermore, experience affords a clearer argument that vice leads to misery than that virtue, in the sense of heroic self-sacrifice, leads to happiness. It seems rather that what most leads to happiness is mere innocence, an absence of vice rather than an attitude of ethical strenuosity. Brown's own opinion was that nothing could persuade men of the universal profitableness of virtue save the "lively and active belief in an all-seeing and all-powerful God, who will hereafter make them happy or miserable, according as they designedly promote or violate the happiness of their fellow-creatures." [16] According to Brown, the nobler types of men do not need the belief in ultimate retribution for good and bad deeds; the majority are to be led to do the right thing by a belief in God which will presumably be instilled in them in childhood. Brown thus formulates a familiar type of religious pragmatism, which gives a very important role to the Church. The point may be made that in so far as the majority do the right thing out of fear they are still lacking in nobility; what matters is, apparently, simply our obedience. In practice, no clear line can be drawn between action out of fear of God and action for the sake of righteousness; this is because belief in either the existence of God or of an impersonal moral order can only be faith, not knowledge.

CHAPTER VI

MANDEVILLE AND HUTCHESON

Bernard de Mandeville, author of the *Fable of the Bees,* gave a systematic account of his theory of morals in his *Enquiry into the Origin of Moral Virtue,* which was published in 1723. No creature, he tells us, is naturally less capable of living with his fellows than man, since he is an extraordinarily selfish and headstrong as well as a very cunning animal; he may be momentarily subdued by force but force alone is not sufficient to render him susceptible of civilization. We must therefore assume the existence of certain wise law-givers who invented a means for subduing man in his natural wildness. Whether these legislators were animated by a desire to benefit society or merely by a selfish interest in maintaining order to enjoy the advantages of their position is not made clear by Mandeville; he need not deny strictly all altruism. His theory does demand, however, that men shall be conceived as predominantly egoistic. The means which the legislators invented for subduing the selfish impulses of human nature, consisted above all of flattery. They extolled the excellency of our nature above other animals and set forth the "wonders of our sagacity and vastness of understanding" and made it seem shameful for men to gratify the impulses which they have in common with brutes. They divided men into two classes; on the one hand, there were the low-minded masses, who were incapable of self-denial and had no regard for the good of others, and, on the other hand, there were "lofty, high-spirited creatures," who took the improvements of the mind as their fairest possessions and, making a constant war on themselves, aimed only at public welfare. By thus glorifying rationality, the clever lawmakers were able to cause men to relinquish their own good and to subordinate themselves to the good of the group. In short, a subtle appeal to pride was made and thus self-sacrifice was rendered palatable. As Mandeville put it "the moral virtues are the political off-spring which flattery begot upon pride." [1]

Mandeville's theory exercised some influence on later moralists, who recognized both its cleverness and its superficiality. Subsequent writers pointed out that the leaders of men could not put into people's minds totally new ideas; the common man's ability to understand such ideas as noble and base, duty and justice, presupposes a moral sense. He must already have possessed some understanding of right and wrong, although society and its leaders may be necessary to give this indeterminate feeling a specific form. Mandeville's theory obviously gives too great a role to the conscious scheming of the rulers. He assumes that man has an innate tendency to pride; one may as well assume that the human being possesses a latent pre-disposition to morality, which can be appealed to and shaped, in various ways, by astute leaders. The individual learns from experience that he can only survive along with other members of the tribe, never as a solitary individual. He also learns that he often gains in the long run when he consults reason and restrains his desires. He is, therefore, ready to accept the thought that law-abiding actions are noble and he

81

is prepared to accept, as compensation for his sacrifice, the social recognition of his nobility, or even a bare self-knowledge of his own nobility. The wise legislators of Mandeville, in rewarding actions of self-sacrifice with what we may call "verbal medals" were appealing to an inborn disposition without which the individual could not have been rendered a social being. Mandeville's theory of flattery as the basis of morality stresses the role of fiction in the control of men and may be regarded as a forerunner of Hume's theory that justice is an artificial virtue.

Hutcheson's *Inquiry into the Original of our Ideas of Beauty and Virtue*, 1725 (later called *An Inquiry into Moral Good and Evil*) had, as its announced purpose, a defense of the teachings of the Earl of Shaftesbury against what seemed the cynicism of Mandeville. The *Inquiry* is directed to establishing two theses:

(1) That some actions have an immediate goodness perceived by a moral sense, and,

(2) That the motive of virtue is not an intention to gain the pleasure which accompanies virtuous actions, neither is it an intention to gain the reward, which may be given to the virtuous person by society or by God.

We commonly think of a "sense" as a faculty which apprehends some pre-existent quality in objects; an example would be sight and color. However, Hutcheson does not think of a sense in this naive realistic way; he was inclined to agree with Locke that such qualities as color, in the primary sense of the word, have only a subjective existence; the moral qualities which we ascribe to actions and persons, while they have an objective basis, just as colors have, are still only in the mind of the spectator. Hutcheson defines a "sense" as follows: a sense is a "power of receiving" a class of "perceptions" from objects independently of our will. In the case of the moral sense, we are continually praising and blaming actions and the persons who do them, even though we personally derive neither profit nor injury from them. What Hutcheson had in mind is represented by the following passage:

> "As soon as any action is represented to us as flowing from love, humanity, gratitude, compassion, a study of the good of others and a delight in their happiness, although it were in the most distant part of the world, or in some past age, we feel joy within us, admire the lovely action and praise its author. And on the contrary every action represented to us as flowing from hatred, delight in the misery of others or ingratitude raises abhorrence and aversion." [2]

It is evident that the moral sense is a matter of feeling and that what it judges is also, in the end, feeling, since actions are judged by the feelings from which they flow. It deserves to be called a sense, however, since, like sight, hearing, smell and taste, it is a source of a distinct class of ideas, namely, of all those perceptions which express "moral" praise and blame. A thing can be regarded as "naturally" good or evil, that is, as useful or injurious but this does not involve the distinctively moral praise or blame. The latter refers, primarily, only to acts which have intentions and which spring from certain motives, and, in the second place, to the persons who perform the acts which are praised or blamed.

As a comment on Hutcheson it may be said that we have feelings of praise and blame for the actions of others as well as of ourselves. The fact that we do judge morally proves that we have a faculty for doing so. The question remains whether this faculty is properly described as a sense. Hutcheson thinks of the moral sense as especially concerned with motives, since it leads us to approve of altruism. But if we turn our attention from the region of motives to the practical problem of what is right we find that it is difficult to separate the respective contributions of intelligence and the moral sense. Thus the moral sense alone could not very well decide on monogamy vs. polygamy or free-enterprise vs. socialism, since, obviously, psychological, sociological and economic considerations are involved. The same observation holds also in the case of truth-telling and promise-keeping; we know from experience that these are practices which make for the good of society in most cases. We must suppose Hutcheson to mean that the moral sense merely approves of altruism whenever it occurs. But some altruistic actions are socially injurious. It would seem that the moral sense could safely extend its approval merely to a will for the universal good, however it might express itself. But such a will to universal good is far more abstract than the love of our friends, our relatives, or our country. Intelligence tells us that such and such practices are for the general good; the function of the moral sense would have to be limited to telling us that we ought to act according to principles which make for the general good, or, negatively, that we ought not to do things which are socially injurious like lying, stealing and killing. We may say that bad actions are selfish actions, as when a man advances the interest of his children by fraudulent means, even though the motive was altruistic in a limited sense, since he did not show the concern for the good of society which he should have shown. The moral sense cannot, of itself, apart from intelligence, supply definite rules of conduct; it merely demands that our action should not be contrary to a supposed will to universal good; in other words, we must not permit our desire for our own good and for the good of those who are dear to us to become operative in cases where it would be going contrary to a will to universal good. In short, the moral sense cannot tell us what is useful and what is injurious; it also cannot inform us concerning the motives of other people or of ourselves; these are both functions of intelligence. It does, however, condemn us when our desire for our own good or for the good of those whom we favor leads us into actions contrary to rules which tend to the common good. Here the action is bad and the motive from which it springs is also bad in so far as it shows a lack of concern for the general good.

Hutcheson did not in fact assign to the moral sense the function of telling us what is useful and what is injurious. It is nevertheless clearly a utilitarian faculty, which unfailingly tells us that we should act in a manner conducive to the general good. According to Hutcheson, it is easy to account for the "vast diversity of moral principles in various nations and ages." [3] This diversity, he tells us, is a good argument against innate ideas, but is not contrary to the thought that we have an indeterminate moral sense which is rendered specific by the findings of intelligence. There are four principal reasons which explain why men differ in the moral rules which they accept. These are (1 and 2): different opinions of natural good and of the most effectual means to advance it. This heading is two-fold and covers differences of temperament as well as differences of opinion. Hutcheson illustrates the first by comparing those who, being of courageous disposition, prefer liberty with those who prefer peace and security. The second part may be illustrated by any case where men differ with regard to the consequences for good and evil of any proposed law or constitution. (3) The third ground of diversity is the variety of systems by which men, from foolish opinions, confine their benevolence. The principle of the greater good leads us to favor those who are more useful to the whole of mankind over those who are useless or pernicious. If people form an opinion that some sect of men are bent on the destruction of the more valuable part of the human race or are mere useless burdens on the earth, they will be led by benevolence itself to neglect the interests of these pernicious or useless persons. Here

Hutcheson touches on the fact that men are divided into nations, parties, sects and races and that they naturally think not of the universal good of mankind but of the good of these smaller groups. This he regards as an arbitrary confinement of benevolence based on "foolish opinions." Whatever may be its cause, this limitation of sympathy produces an inescapable relativity of moral valuations, since what is for the good of one group, is contrary to what is for the good of another. This fact produces a familiar perspectivism according to which the same action may be good or bad depending on *whose* good we have in mind. This raises the question of a higher and more authoritative moral sense, whose pronouncements might correct the conflicting and partisan judgments which are actually passed. Had Hutcheson confined himself to a descriptive and explanatory treatment of ethics he could only have recorded this *de facto* relativity. But he too was seeking for an authoritative principle which he found in the idea of *the* moral sense, which was by definition directed on the good of humanity. (4) The fourth ground of diversity is "false opinions of the will and laws of the deity." The deity is believed to have a right to dispose of his creatures as he pleases and gratitude to him must prompt us to obey his will, or, again, if God is not thought to deserve obedience on these grounds, we are led to obey him by the thought that we are thereby promoting the greatest good for the greatest number. Different interpretations of the divine will by leaders of different religions and sects will produce different opinions concerning the rightness and wrongness of various types of action, although all will agree in declaring that God is to be obeyed.

The moral sense is not free from ambiguity; the expression sometimes seems a mere popular phrase but at other times it is taken in a more specific manner. Hutcheson declares that the moral sense is natural and

86

independent of custom and education.[4] Against this skeptics cite the fact that there are practices which are approved by some nations, actions which are regarded with abhorrence by Christians, *e.g.,* incest. In Greece the marrying of half-sisters was permitted and among Persians the marrying of mothers. Hutcheson explains our aversion to incest on religious grounds. He considers the moral sense to be an indeterminate pre-disposition to be concerned for the common good; its detailed content can be explained in various ways and is variable from one society to the next. The moral sense does not issue a single set of commandments to all people, since we may happen to include larger or smaller groups in our benevolence and we may entertain varying opinions about what truly makes for the common good of whatever group we have in mind. He did not question that if we listen attentively to the moral sense we shall find that it always bids us act for the universal good of humanity. But this law gives definite guidance only when supplemented by certain postulates which are in part based on experience. We form the idea of a system of rights and duties which we believe tends to the public good and within this system we are permitted to be solicitous of our own good.

> "Our reason can indeed discover certain bounds, within which we may not only act from self-love, consistently with the good of the whole, but every mortal's acting thus within these bounds for his own good, is absolutely necessary for the good of the whole; and the want of such self-love would be universally pernicious." [5]

The moral sense commands us to act according to principles which tend toward the universal good, but the statement and justification of these principles must be a matter of reason and experience. The phrase *the moral sense* is a convenient one, since it suggests the thought of an indefinite and plastic faculty, in which feeling plays a large part and which can vary from individual to individual. It is open to criticism in so far as it suggests a faculty which is independent of custom and education and also a power of perception which apprehends something which exists prior to perception. There is no doubt that such qualities as right and wrong, morally good and morally bad, do appear to the unsophisticated to be realistic attributes of actions and people as they are in themselves; reflection tends to suggest, however, that moral values are properties which we ascribe to actions and agents because of our emotional response to them.

The proposition is formally laid down by Hutcheson that "every action, which we apprehend as either morally good or evil is supposed to flow from some affection toward rational agents." [6] Hutcheson was engaged in combatting the proposition that the motive of virtue is either fear of God or the hope of some supernatural reward. Hutcheson's argument consists of two parts; there is, first, a clarification of the idea of love, in which it is brought out that love is, in its very essence, disinterested, and, secondly, there is an appeal to experience to show that disinterested love actually does occur. Love, apart from the love between the sexes (which he regards as only a desire for pleasure and does not consider to be a virtue) is either what is called "love of esteem" or else "love of benevolence," that is, altruism. "Love of esteem" is a feeling of moral admiration towards a person without any impulse to benefit the person in question. "Love of benevolence" is an active tendency to confer good on some person or group of persons. The word *altruism* was not used by the 18th century moralists; it is, however, more precise than benevolence, which might refer to a willing of good in general including one's own good. In this essay we shall continue to speak of altruism. Benevolence may or may not be a consequence of the esteem we feel for a person; in any case, the two kinds of love are distinct. Love of esteem is essentially disinterested and cannot be obtained by a bribe; it is directed on people who are generous, kind, faithful and humane. Hutcheson's thought that esteem is essentially disinterested is a matter of definition. If in fact we do esteem people because we think that it will be to our advantage to do so (in the sense of knowing on which side our bread is buttered) Hutcheson would have to say that such esteem is not true esteem; that is, it does not correspond to his definition. A selfish man, according to Hutcheson's definition, does not actually esteem generous people; it is only a conventional pretense. We need not object to Hutcheson's statement as long as it is realized that he is not propounding an empirical proposition but merely clarifying the meaning of a word. The same type of reasoning is applied by Hutcheson to the love of benevolence. Disinterestedness belongs to its essence. The benevolent man, the altruist, seeks to benefit others; he may incidentally profit himself either materially, by receiving some reward, or spiritually, by the pleasure he receives from helping others, but as an altruist he is intent on the good which he plans to do to some person or persons other than himself. It is not necessary to Hutcheson's argument that he show an instance of altruism existing in absolute purity; it may actually always be mixed with egoism; nevertheless, altruism or what Hutcheson called benevolence is in its essence disinterested. The benevolent man is clearly distinct from the man who is merely beneficent. The latter is illustrated by the unknown inventors of the fundamental arts such as the use of fire in cooking or in the working of metals or by the countless millions who serve others not out of love but for the sake of reward. It is only pure benevolence which, in Hutcheson's eyes, constitutes essential virtue.

It is said that we serve mankind because of fear of God. But experience shows that there may be benevolence where there is no thought of the deity. Furthermore, such "benevolence scarce deserves the name, when we desire not, nor delight in the good of others, further than it serves our own ends." [7] Furthermore, we suppose that the deity is benevolent. If God does not love his creatures, why may we not suppose an evil God who delights in the misery of his creatures? The egoists maintain that we perform virtuous acts because of the pleasure which we derive from thinking of ourselves as virtuous. But this presupposes that we have some sense of the virtuousness of altruism before we could derive pleasure from thinking of ourselves as altruists. This implies that we have already admitted the possibility of altruism. It is true that in compassionate actions we do remove our sympathetic pain but only by altering the state of the object. "If our sole intention, in compassion or pity, was the removal of our pain, we should run away, shut our eyes, etc." [8] This we do only when some contrary passion, such as fear, is aroused or when reason tells us that we cannot relieve those who suffer. The conduct which is aroused by compassion is centered, not on ourselves, but on others.

These arguments remove, Hutcheson supposes, the false theory that virtue is merely prudence. The true spring of virtuous action, he tells us, must be some instinct which is antecedent to reason, which causes us to desire to benefit others. An honest farmer will tell you that he studies the preservation and happiness of his children and loves them without any design of good to himself. Our love for our children is not a result of a conjunction of interest, as in the case of business partners; it is the cause of a conjunction of interest rather than a result of it. Our children are parts of ourselves only in the sense that we love them disinterestedly, but not because they are literally parts of our bodies. We feel some slight degree of benevolence towards all virtuous persons, where there is no conflict of interest. We love our country disinterestedly because we have known many characters whom the moral sense leads us to approve and hence to love; this is strengthened by recollections of our younger days. Hutcheson shows that we have desires of varying degrees of strength, which seem to terminate in the welfare of others. We love our children, our friends and our country; this means that, to an extent, we find happiness in serving others. Hutcheson does not, like Kant, glorify duty for duty's sake; the motive of virtue remains material rather than formal.

We are told that an absence of concern for the public good is positively evil and hateful.[9] "Nor is the direct intention of public evil necessary to make an action evil, it is enough that it flows from self-love, with a plain neglect of the good of others, or an insensibility to their misery, which we either actually foresee or have a probable presumption of." [10] In comment on this the Kantian would say that it cannot be our duty to feel benevolence; it can only be our duty to act as if we did feel such a desire. Let us suppose that we discover that we really feel little concern for people whom we do not see and whom we are not likely ever to meet; we may even find that we feel little concern for those whom we do see; why should we act according to a non-existent desire? The Kantian is prepared, by means of his doctrine of transcendental freedom, to defend a law of duty which is independent of our empirical constitution; Hutcheson can uphold the theory of benevolence only by taking the term in a very broad sense, although there would be agreement between Hutcheson and Kant that in any case the motive of virtue must be disinterested.

Hutcheson comes closest to the classic doctrines of utilitarianism, as later stated by Bentham and Mill, when he lays down the doctrine that the moral sense tells us to consider both the number of persons and the quantity of happiness which can be produced. Virtue is proportional to the compound ratio of the quantity of good and the number of enjoyers. "In comparing the moral qualities of actions, in order to regulate our election among the various actions proposed we are led by our moral sense to judge thus:" and he proceeds to state that we must consider the quantity of happiness, the number of persons and the dignity of moral importance of the persons.[11] Just what Hutcheson meant by dignity or moral importance of persons is not clear. In point of fact, however, people do not commonly consider all human beings as on a level but feel much greater obligations towards their kinsmen and fellow-nationals and co-religionists than they do towards others; this was partly taken account of by Hutcheson later. The utilitarian method of reasoning enjoined upon us by the moral sense is not understood as superseding our traditional and legal obligations; it does seem, however, to impose on us the duty of attempting to reform society, as far as practicable, to bring it into accordance with the greatest happiness of the greatest number.

Why should we act according to the utilitarian law? Hutcheson did not explicitly repudiate the traditional view that we must obey the moral law, revealed to us by our moral sense, because it is God's law, and because he will punish us if we fail to obey it. A man who serves others from this motive, however, will not illustrate the highest type of virtue. Hutcheson seems to say, help others if you want to, as in that case you possess virtue, but, if you do not have a benevolent soul, you had better obey the law anyway in order to escape punishment. The basic tendency of Hutcheson's doctrine, like that of Shaftesbury, is to make the path of virtue more attractive by showing that it is in accordance with certain strong human instincts.

In 1728 Hutcheson published a short work entitled *On the Nature and Conduct of the Passions and Affections* in which he elaborates a classification of the "senses" and the desires, which deserves a moment's consideration. The senses are classified as follows: (1) The five traditional senses; (2) the internal sense, which gives us aesthetic pleasure and pain; (3) the "public sense," which is the tendency to be pleased with the happiness of others; (4) the moral sense by which we perceive virtue and vice in ourselves or in others; (5) a sense of honor which causes us to be pleased with the approbation of others, and (6) a sense of decency and dignity, which corresponds to the fact that some experiences seem to be more noble than others. Hutcheson thus elaborates what amounts to a doctrine of six "senses" or departments of experience. In distinction from the five traditional senses, the other "senses" are easily recognized as phases of affective life, which result in our ascribing value or disvalue to ourselves or to others. The chief justification for speaking of these regions of experience as *senses* would be that in each case certain "perceptions" or value-experiences are involved which cannot be reduced to the "perceptions" of the external senses. Each "sense" is a source of a distinct class of ideas.

Desires are also a distinct class of experiences "which arise in our mind, from the frame of our nature, upon the apprehension of good or evil in objects" [12] and are directed upon obtaining for ourselves or others an agreeable sensation or preventing an uneasy sensation. Hutcheson's theory of desire tends to be hedonistic in accordance with the teaching of Locke. Desire is directed on either (1) the pleasure of the external senses or (2) the pleasures of the imagination or internal sense or (3) pleasure arising from public happiness, or (4) desire of virtue and aversion to vice, and (5) desire of honor and aversion to shame. It is evident that Hutcheson here comes very close to a theory of egoistic hedonism, which would be quite contrary to the theory of disinterested benevolence. He proceeds to attempt to avoid this contradiction by laying down such propositions as "that no desire of any event is excited by any view of removing the uneasy sensation attending this desire itself."

> "The desire of the happiness of others which we account virtuous is not directly excited by prospects of any secular advantage, wealth, power, pleasure of the external senses, reward from the deity, or future pleasures of self-approbation." [13]

This is proved by the fact that desires must arise spontaneously and not as a result of our thinking that our having such a desire would be advantageous. "There are in men desires of the happiness of others, when they do not conceive this happiness as a means of obtaining any sort of happiness to themselves." [14] It is true that we *may* desire the happiness of others as a means to our own, but such "egoistic altruism" is quite distinct from the genuine article. We should not confuse a true benevolence with a desire for the pleasure of the public sense. Should the deity give us a choice between truly relieving the suffering of a person in distress and obliterating all thought in our minds concerning this person, we would choose the former; or, again, should the deity assure us that we were to be annihilated but that, by our choice, at our exit, we could make our children or our country happy, we would choose to make them happy, although we could neither gain nor lose by such a choice. Or, if we failed to choose in this manner, we would assuredly not be good men. We may sum up Hutcheson's theory of desire by saying that all desire is concerned with pleasantness or unpleasantness, which may be either our own or that of others. Our desire may, therefore, be either egoistic or altruistic. Egoism and altruism, although distinct in essence, may either co-operate in producing a given action or else conflict and cancel each other. As we have seen, Hutcheson tends to identify altruism, i.e., disinterested benevolence, with an inner virtue, or true moral goodness, which is distinct from an external conformity, which might be produced by egoism.

In his *Illustrations of the Moral Sense* of 1728, Hutcheson comes to grips with rationalism very decisively. The traditional description of virtuous action has always been "reasonableness," "conformity to reason." In what sense can we be reasonable or act in conformity with reason? There is a difference between approbation and election, but in both cases there can be, even according to Hutcheson, a rational ground. In the case of approbation, an action may be approved because it falls under some principle accepted by the moral sense, but the moral sense is itself a matter of feeling. In the case of election, that is, of choice, there may also be a "rational ground" in the sense of choosing a means to gain some end; one may pursue wealth in order to indulge a taste for luxury. But the ultimate reason for choice must always be some affection, such as self-love, self-hatred, benevolence or malice. The traditional dualism of reason and emotion is false, since in all action there is an emotional element. The *appetitus rationalis* is the disposition of the soul to pursue what is presented as good; the *appetitus sensitivus* covers the particular desires. The ultimate ends must be desired for their own sakes, rather than merely as a means. No reason can be given why we desire our own happiness. The proposition is true that "there is an instinct or desire fixed in man's nature, determining him to pursue his happiness" but this truth merely describes man's nature and does not determine it.

We may form an idea of an infinite good or greatest possible aggregate of happiness, but, in truth, each particular pleasure is desired for its own sake. In the same way, in the benevolent affections, the happiness of any one person is an ultimate end. The concept of a sum of happiness, either private or public, may exercise a regulative function and thus enable us to gratify either our self-love or our benevolence to the greatest possible extent, but it would be an error to suppose that the totality of pleasures is the primary object of desire. Man is not ruled by reason or by rational concepts. The fact that the happiness of two is greater than the happiness of one does not guarantee that any given individual will give preference to the greater good. He will do so only in so far as he possesses the public affections. Without these affections the truth that "a hundred felicities is a greater sum than one" will no more cause a man to strive to produce a hundred felicities than the truth that "a hundred stones are greater than one" will cause a man to pile them together. The grounds of choice are, therefore, to be found in our desires rather than in any concepts as such; in a similar fashion, the ultimate basis of approval and disapproval must be found in principles which appeal to our moral sense but for which no further reason can be given. We approve of pursuing the public good, but this is not because pursuing the public good is "conformable to truth." No further justification can be given to our approval of the pursuit of the public good, just as no justification can be given for our liking some particular fruit.

If moral judgment is a function of a moral sense, it might appear that relativism would have the last word and that morals would be a matter of taste. Hutcheson dogmatically declares that the moral sense of every man is constituted in the same manner. In the sphere of external perception, reason can criticize the senses and distinguish between appearance and reality; it does so, however, by relying on certain sensuous data as authentic. In the moral sphere, reason can inform us that a sense approving benevolence is more to the public good than one glorifying hatred; still, Hutcheson would insist, this argument does not establish reason as superior to the moral sense, since it is only the latter which tells us that the public good is to be pursued. It is clear, however, that moral sense, in proclaiming such a comprehensive principle, is very close to the reason of the rationalists. The moral sense, as found in everyday life, has been shaped, to a very great extent, by law, custom and education, and differs greatly from one individual to the next. Hutcheson tends to retreat to the thought that at any rate virtue is disinterested benevolence. It would, however, be extravagant to demand that we be influenced only by pure benevolence; we are in fact pleasantly surprised when we discover a man who is slightly above the average in such goodness of heart.

In Hutcheson's *System of Moral Philosophy* we find a further elaboration of the ideas which came later to be called utilitarian. Pleasures are considered not only with regard to their intenseness and duration but also with regard to their dignity or nobility. There are, in short, higher and lower pleasures. Without a recognition of such qualitative distinctions "the meanest brute or insect may be as happy as the wisest hero, patriot or friend can be." [15]

"We are conscious, in our state of mature years, that the happiness of our friends, our families or our country are incomparably nobler objects of our pursuit, and administer proportionately a nobler pleasure than the toys which once abundantly entertained us when we had experienced nothing better." [16]

It is, of course, the moral sense which perceives the superior nobility of certain satisfactions over others. We are all familiar with the distinctions between the

97

elevated, the trivial and the base. One may understand such qualities either naively as objective features of experiences or else as objectifications of the emotional response of the spectator. The vaguely conceived moral sense of Hutcheson had the advantage of permitting either interpretation.

Just as Shaftesbury was answered, from the standpoint of theological orthodoxy, by the Rev. John Brown, so Hutcheson was sharply criticised by John Clarke, a schoolmaster of Hull.[17] The attack centers on the doctrine of disinterested benevolence and Clarke urges that this is contrary to the traditional belief in divine rewards and punishments. For, if we accept Hutcheson literally, the man who is guided by hope or fear concerning a future life would not be virtuous.

> "For to induce men by rewards and punishments to act without any views of interest, is, I take it, just as feasible as to give a man a hundred pounds to do a piece of work for nothing."[18]

The arguments of Clarke are familiar. Self-love, he declares, is the dominant tendency of human nature. He does not, however, mean to assert the dominance of self-love in a sense which would exclude benevolence.

> "For the love of benevolence is . . . a desire or inclination to do good to others. Now the object or cause of desire is pleasure alone and the means of obtaining it."[19]

If we desire to do good to others, it is in order to obtain the delight or satisfaction which attends acts of benevolence. Clarke takes his stand on a dogmatic egoistic hedonism, which had, for him, the force of an *a priori* insight. All things other than pleasure and pain are perfectly indifferent to the mind; to assert the contrary is a visible contradiction; it is the same as to affirm that the mind may be troubled by what gives it no uneasiness at all.

> "And where the mind is perfectly at ease without a thing, there it is absolutely free from all desire of it, or inclination for it, because desire of, or inclination for a thing, is nothing but an uneasiness for the want of it." [19] "No man can desire, or be under any concern for, the happiness of others, but where it makes a part of his own, either by the pleasure and satisfaction it naturally and immediately gives him, or the hopes of future benefit and advantage to arise from it." [20]

The benevolent man is therefore merely a man who happens to find his happiness in the happiness of others. Such a character is indeed pleasant to behold and we take satisfaction when we see such benevolent beings made happy. But although the benevolent man is truly benevolent and amiable, he is also under the sway of an inescapable egoism. We are so constituted that in some cases we take pleasure in making others happy but our action springs from our desire for our own happiness. When the mind is persuaded of the being of a God, who will reward our kind acts and punish our excessively selfish ones, we are given an additional motive for performing actions benefitting others. The actions ordinarily ascribed to parental affection and to love of our friends are likewise founded on self-love; we are animated by a desire either for the pleasure which accompanies such acts or else by desire for applause or by fear of divine punishment and hope of divine reward.

Clarke grants that a man is entitled to be called benevolent when he serves others with a view to the pleasure of serving them. Such a man acts upon as disinterested a principle as is possible to human nature. We take pleasure in displaying gratitude and the desire to serve a benefactor arises spontaneously just as does a desire for some particular sensuous pleasure. We choose to perform the act of gratitude for the sake of the pleasure it will give us. Let us attempt to resolve the contradiction between Hutcheson and Clarke. The word *desire* has different senses. In one sense it refers to a readiness for, or potentiality of, a certain specific pleasure, *e.g.*, hunger or thirst. Thus we are said to be hungry when our condition is such that our uneasiness would be allayed by eating and a pleasant feeling ensue. This might be called the physiological meaning of the word *desire*. There is also a more psychological meaning; it may refer to a conscious attitude in which we anticipate a pleasure of which we have previously had experience. If, having this attitude, we choose to do the thing which we think will produce this anticipated pleasure, we are said to act for the sake of this pleasure; such an action is called egoistic, or, in the 18th century phrase, it springs from self-love. Hutcheson maintained, however, that in certain circumstances, we would choose to do the generous deed even though we anticipated no pleasure for ourselves. Whether or not such is the case, each of us must answer for himself. If we take pleasure in serving others, we must have a "readiness" for such a pleasure and such a readiness is what we mean by benevolence as a desire. If we act for the sake of this pleasure our action is egoistic. But if we act for the happiness of others, without regard to our own happiness, we are disinterestedly benevolent in Hutcheson's sense.

Let us try to sum up with regard to Hutcheson. We have seen that the moral sense alone cannot tell us specifically what we should do. It merely determines us to approve of benevolence. No clear distinction was drawn by Hutcheson between benevolence and beneficence. At most the moral sense can be conceived to issue some such imperative as "Act according to principles which make for the common good." But just what we are to do depends upon (1) what our intelligence informs us to be truly for the common good and (2) what area we bring within the scope of the common good, such as family, city, nation, religion, etc. This is a basic variable in man's moral consciousness, which can be rendered definite only by an arbitrary definition of some sort. There are few people who are strictly humanitarian in their feelings and there are none who include the pleasure of non-human creatures in the common good in a truly impartial manner. The moral sense is merely a name for the moral consciousness in general and in fact it is rendered definite by law, custom, education and experience. With regard to disinterested benevolence, it is safe to say that most later ethicists have been in agreement with Hutcheson, at least to the extent of granting that it is a considerable force in human life. However, it may well be contended that duty is a more proper motive for virtuous action than benevolence, although both are disinterested. We may do our duty, in the sense of telling the truth and paying our debts, without feeling benevolence. The feeling of kindness, or active altruism, arises from imagination and instinct, but is quite different from the feeling that we *ought* to do so and so. On the other hand, the view of John Clarke and other orthodox thinkers that the primary foundation of morals is the hope of heaven and the fear of hell can hardly be accepted literally today. Belief in such concepts is admittedly a matter of faith, which may itself be an expression of an underlying ethical attitude. If such doctrines are taken literally and supposed to be matters of knowledge rather than faith, then indeed morals is reduced to prudence and there is no further point to the idea of disinterestedness.

101

CHAPTER VII

BUTLER

The ethical theory of Bishop Joseph Butler, as propounded in his Sermons of 1726 and the *Dissertation upon Virtue* of 1736 may be regarded as occupying an intermediate position between those of Samuel Clarke and Francis Hutcheson. The latter's *Inquiry into the Original of our Ideas of Beauty and Virtue* (later called *An Inquiry concerning Moral Good and Evil*) had been published in the preceding year and may have been in Butler's mind. Butler's doctrine is similar to ethical rationalism, save that attention is no longer fixed on the self-evident fitness of things, as apprehended by a quasi-mathematical reason, but rather on human nature and conscience. In the *Dissertation* Butler remarks that the moral faculty may be called conscience, moral reason, moral sense or divine reason and may be considered "as a sentiment of the understanding or perception of the heart; or which seems the truth, as including both." [1] Conscience is a somewhat mysterious faculty clearly involving the emotions, and yet, as Butler insists, claiming a natural right to rule. It is this emphasis upon the authoritativeness of conscience which makes him more akin to the ethical rationalists than to Shaftesbury, Hutcheson, Hume or Adam Smith. Butler was in no sense a naturalist, although he taught, as did the Stoics, that we should *follow nature.* By nature, however, he meant human nature. The latter involves many tendencies, and, in one sense, we cannot avoid following nature, since, whatever we do, we shall be following one of our tendencies. The ethical maxim *follow nature* does not mean that we should always follow our stronger impulse, but rather that we should follow the higher part of our nature. Butler, like Plato, ascribed to human nature a certain hierarchical structure; some phases of it are higher than others and have a natural right to rule; the sovereign faculty is conscience, but self-love, guided by wisdom or prudence, is superior to particular selfish desires and has a natural right to control them. Like Shaftesbury and Hutcheson, Butler emphasized the existence of disinterested benevolence or what we today call altruism.

The guiding conception of Butler, as of Shaftesbury, was the doctrine of teleology. The idea of a "system, economy or constitution" of anything is the idea of a whole made up of parts, and in this idea of a whole, the relations of the parts are as important as the parts themselves. We are told that every work of nature or art is a system which can be understood only if we consider its purpose. Thus one cannot understand a watch until he understands the functions of each part in fulfilling the end of a watch, which is to tell time. It is the same with regard to the "inward frame of man"; we do not understand man's nature when we merely list his appetites, passions and affections, together with the principle of reflection; we grasp it as a whole or constitution only when we take into account the inherent right to rule which belongs to the latter. A machine or an organism may be out of order and when the disorder is increased the machine or organism ceases to exist. We differ from machines in that we are agents and are, at least partly, responsible for any disorder in our constitution. Vice is contrary to human nature, since it goes against its very constitution, although it may be

103

in agreement with some part of our psychic structure. Poverty and death are not as contrary to human nature as vice, says Butler, paraphrasing the Stoics. The doctrine of teleology is in accordance with theism, but, in so far as it is taken as authenticating conscience, does not avoid the difficulty that it must be conscience which confers upon itself a right to rule. We are told that we should obey conscience because the latter has the function, in the economy of our nature, of regulating conduct. But it is conscience which tells us that we should do that which is in accordance with nature and thus permit each faculty to perform its proper function. Conscience thus has the role of authenticating itself. Butler could just as well have said that conscience has an inherent right to rule, since it apprehends right and wrong.

Conscience is flanked by two subordinate principles, self-love and benevolence. Butler has a great deal to say about both of these phases of human nature. With regard to self-love he recognizes its proper sphere and the fact that it demands an ultimate reconciliation with conscience; with regard to benevolence, he follows Shaftesbury and Hutcheson in insisting that it is not to be regarded as disguised egoism. Self-love is the desire for one's own greatest good or happiness; it may be present along with other desires, such as the desire for food or for fame or with benevolence itself. In short, an action may spring from a mixed or complex motive but self-love is still distinct in its essence from benevolence or hunger. "Everything is what it is and not another thing." [2] Had we no benevolence or altruism, we would take no satisfaction in generous actions; the occurrence of the satisfaction is a consequence but not the essential motive of a kind action. There may be present, along with benevolence, a desire for this satisfaction, but this would be an egoistic part-motive which would not exclude the co-presence of

104

a genuinely altruistic part-motive in the action. There are such desires as "desire of esteem from others, love of society as distinct from affection to the good of it, indignation against successful vice;" these tend to the public good and naturally lead us to regulate our behavior in such ways as will be of service to our fellow-men. The desire for the approval and love of others is a desire which, when gratified, leads to the good of ourselves; it may be regarded as egoistic and yet it may tend to make us socially useful. Our particular appetites and affections are distinct from both self-love and benevolence and yet may tend either to private or public good in their incidental consequences.

Does benevolence have a right to regulate our conduct? Self-love, says Butler, has a natural right to regulate our particular desires, since we necessarily seek for our own greatest happiness. The theory that benevolence is inherently regulatory would imply that we have a desire to produce the greatest possible amount of good for others and that our affections toward others are to be regulated by this desire to produce a maximum of good. However the existence of such generalized benevolence is doubtful; it is not a necessary part of human nature. Benevolence may be regulatory in certain cases, however. I may have a desire for the general good of some person, say, a child, and this sort of general benevolence may regulate my kindness in helping this individual gratify particular desires which may not tend to his general good. I can have a desire for the good of my country which causes me to restrain my impulse to assist certain persons. I may have a desire for the good of humanity, but I can desire the good of my country more strongly than I desire the good of humanity. Conscience would have the function of telling me that I ought to prefer the good of the one to the other in spite of the relative strength of my desires. It

105

appears, therefore, that there are only two powers of human nature which are essentially regulatory, in Butler's ethical theory, namely, conscience and self-love, although no one has insisted more strongly than Butler on the existence of disinterested benevolence. It is the function of conscience to tell us to what extent we should follow self-love and to what extent benevolence. It may, in fact, tell us that we *ought* to try to benefit those toward whom we feel no benevolence.

Butler's chief doctrine is the inherent authority of conscience. He accepts the "ancient precept," *Reverence thyself*. Shaftesbury had shown that virtue is generally the interest of such a creature as man placed in such a world as that in which we find ourselves. But suppose that there is an exceptional case in which happiness lies in one direction and virtue in another. Shaftesbury, Butler felt, provided no remedy since he did not properly recognize an authoritative conscience. In such a case, since "one's own happiness is a manifest obligation" we would feel it our duty to act viciously. On the other hand, we can never have more than a probable opinion concerning the advantages of wickedness. When we take into account the possibility of a future life, we may be sure that we shall not be acting unwisely when we do what we *know* is right. Butler held that the authority of conscience is such that it cannot be shaken by the greatest possible degree of skepticism. It carries with it an assurance with regard to the future, namely, that we cannot ultimately lose if we follow its commands.

We have seen that in Butler there is a strong emphasis upon self-love. It has a natural right to rule over our passions in all cases where conscience is not involved, where, in short, we have no duties either to God or to our fellow-men. An action is contrary to human nature if it goes against either self-love or conscience; it may be against any of our other tendencies without being truly contrary to human nature.

> "Conscience and self-love, if we understand our true happiness, always lead us in the same way. Duty and interest are perfectly co-incident; for the most part in this world, but entirely and in every instance if we take in the future and the whole." [3] "Let it be allowed, though virtue and moral rectitude does indeed consist in affection to and pursuit of what is right and good as such; yet, when we sit down in a cool hour, we can neither justify to ourselves this or any other pursuit, till we are convinced that it will be for our happiness, or at least not contrary to it." [4]

To Butler, ultimate self-sacrifice is an absurdity. If there is an apparent conflict between duty and self-interest nevertheless "all shall be set right at the final distribution of things." [5] Butler's statements are appropriately vague. They would naturally be understood to imply the existence of a future life. One who follows this line of reasoning will be disposed to proceed to faith in a redeemer, belief in whom may enable us to escape in part the punishment which would otherwise be due to our sins. We suppose that by repentance and penance our misdeeds will be forgiven. An unbeliever, however, may feel that he can bring about a reconciliation of self-love and conscience, without admitting a future life, by insisting that if we do what we know to be wrong we shall suffer, in this life, such agony of conscience that our action will be unwise as well as wicked.

Butler holds that there are real indications that we were made for society and to do good to our fellow-creatures; these consist in the various forms of benevolence which are normal parts of human nature, such as compassion, paternal and filial affection, friend-

107

ship, etc. It would be captious to point out that the presence of desires does not always indicate that we should gratify them and that we cannot directly discover what the Creator had in mind in giving us certain desires. The distinction of benevolence from any form of self-love can, however, be clearly made out. There are desires for the good of others, and, although satisfaction results from gratifying these desires, still this is an accidental consequence of the action rather than its essential motive. Butler emphasizes the fact that self-love is, in its essence, distinct from the particular passions. Self-love cannot be identical with either hunger or desire for the esteem of others, although it can lead us to take steps leading to avoiding the pain of hunger or to gaining the pleasure of being esteemed. There may be creatures with self-love who feel neither hunger nor desire for the esteem of others. "One man rushes upon certain ruin for the gratification of a present desire; nobody will call the principle of this action self-love." [6] Hunger is a "private appetite" since it tends primarily to individual good; love of esteem is a "public passion" since it tends to the social good. We must distinguish between the objects of particular desires, which belong to their very essence, and the consequences which happen to follow according to the laws of nature. Hunger is therefore distinct from self-love, although it is contributory to self-good, just as the love of being esteemed is distinct from benevolence, although tending to the social good.

Butler assumes that there are such things as desires and that they may be known by reflection, in Locke's sense of the word. We know what we desire in hunger and in ambition, for example. However, let us carry this analysis a step further. In hunger do we desire food or the experience of eating food? And do we not anticipate that this experience will be pleasant or at least less unpleasant than the experience called hunger? We would not desire this experience apart from its pleasantness or non-painfulness. The difference, therefore, between the particular passions and self-love is merely that between a desire for this particular kind of pleasure and a desire for a maximum of pleasure in general for ourselves. Butler does not assert that either a particular passion or self-love is always dominant; he does, however, assert that self-love has a natural right to regulate the particular passions, except in so far as conscience demands that we subordinate ourselves to the claims of others. The particular passions are by no means derived from self-love; they are rather impulses which originate independently but which can and should be regulated by prudence and conscience. Self-love is a higher-order regulatory principle, but it cannot directly produce either natural appetites or affections; it must find them already existent.

Shaftesbury had established the existence of benevolence; Butler adds a "principle of reflection in men" by which they approve and disapprove of their own actions and those of others. The question may well be asked whether Butler advanced any theory of conscience at all. He does not stress the thought that conscience is a God-given faculty; this would have proved too much, since ambition, greed, lust and revenge are also, in some sense, God-given. When he calls attention to the fact that we do continually approve and disapprove of our actions and those of others he cites an undeniable fact of life. In so far as we can discover a theory of conscience in Butler it would seem to be somewhat as follows. In part, we approve and disapprove according to the standards which society has impressed upon us by way of education and custom. But there is a deeper and more authoritative level of conscience which grasps the unchanging "law of nature," the everlasting principles of natural justice. It is quite true that Butler does not emphasize the thought of an "eternal and immutable" law of nature after the manner of Cudworth

109

and Clarke. But the doctrine is implied when he tells us that we must separate the true dictates of conscience from the false teachings of custom. He assumes that conscience is something belonging to human nature as such and that we are able to distinguish the more authentic commands of conscience from those due to custom and personal peculiarities; in practice this can only mean that Butler recognizes the superior authority of our reflective moods when we try to see things as *any one* would see them, rather than in the light of our personal wishes.

Butler does not furnish us with any rule to serve as a universal criterion of right action. The idea of following nature is given three possible interpretations, two of which are rejected as "licentious talk." The first is that we may follow any of our impulses; this is meaningless, since, whatever we do, we shall be following nature. In this sense it is impossible not to follow nature. The second interpretation of the phrase is that we are to follow our strongest desire; the licentious are to pursue pleasure, the ambitious power and the virtuous should seek to do what is right. Here again the principle gives no guidance, especially if we assume that we always do act according to our strongest desire. But if we do not make this assumption and regard the principle of following our strongest desire as a genuine imperative, then the thought that we should follow pleasure or power rather than righteousness is ethically unacceptable. The principle of following nature, therefore, can only mean that we are to follow conscience and do what we think is right. It must be granted that this interpretation only serves to show up the emptiness and meaninglessness of the idea of following nature. We know that society is rarely content to leave us merely with our own consciences as our guide; it has established an elaborate system of laws and customs; these are supposed to be absorbed by our consciences

110

and to be used in guiding all our decisions. The principle of "doing what you think is right" may be taken to imply an attitude of non-interference on our part, which would be quite impracticable, since, whatever people do, they can claim that they are doing what they think right. There is, however, another possible interpretation. We cannot be sure that people are acting according to their own consciences even when they say that they are. Their minds may be divided and in their hearts they may know that they are doing wrong. In coercing them, therefore, we are merely giving their better natures a chance to be dominant. In short it is very difficult to find out what it is that conscience decrees either for ourselves or for others. In practice, we permit people to follow their individual consciences only in so far as they are not thereby led into conflict with the laws and customs established and permitted by the supreme political authority.

Inquiries have been made by men of leisure, says Butler, after some general rule to guide our conduct and these inquiries have been of great service. But if "any plain honest man" asks himself about the rightness of an action he is about to engage in Butler does not doubt that the question will be answered agreeably to truth and virtue "by almost any fair man in almost any circumstance." [7] The difficulties of this position are obvious when we think of the civil wars, revolution, religious struggles, economic and social conflicts, etc., which have taken place in the past and are still taking place. To find illustration of Butler's doctrine of a "plain honest man" we must consider an established society with a definite code of morals and an absence of intense partiality.

"For a man to judge that to be the equitable, the moderate, the right part for him to act, which he

111

would see to be hard, unjust and oppressive in another; this is plain vice and can only proceed from great unfairness of mind." [8]

This is a clear statement of the principle of impartiality, which demands that we use an imaginative transposition of persons as a test of our objectivity. It merely demands that we judge ourselves by the same standards that we apply to others; it does not tell us what, in detail, these standards are to be.

Butler was engaged in preaching sermons; this purpose calls for a tone of edification different from that demanded by a pure theoretical analysis of morals. We are to love our neighbor as ourselves. We have already seen that Butler recognizes benevolence as an irreducible and wide-spread principle of human nature; he also emphasizes the fact that benevolence and self-love are not necessarily in conflict. With regard to material possessions mutual exclusiveness is the rule; what one has, another has not; but with regard to happiness we are so constituted that we often add to our happiness by adding to the happiness of another. We may, on the other hand, be so excessively concerned with our own happiness that we gain less of it than we would have gained had we been more generous. The love of self does not exclude benevolence, even though in essence the two desires are absolutely distinct. Benevolence is truly disinterested. There have been persons in all ages, says Butler,

"who have professed that they found satisfaction in the exercise of charity, in the love of their neighbor, in endeavoring to promote the happiness of all they had to do with, and in the pursuit of what is just and right and good, as the general bent of their mind, and the end of their life. . . . Persons of this character would add, if they might be heard, that they consider themselves as acting in the view of an infinite Being, who is in a much

112

higher sense, the object of reverence and love than all the world besides." [9]

If we study this passage, as well as certain others, we see that Butler regarded the motive of virtue as being altruism only in a limited sense; the dominant motive should be the pursuit of what is fitting and in accordance with the will of God. We may agree that man does have certain benevolent tendencies and that when he gratifies these tendencies he experiences happiness. This fact does not of itself make benevolence the proper guide of life. A sense of fitness sometimes bids us cultivate a feeling of kindness and at other times suppress our generous tendencies. There can be an over-indulgence in commiseration from the point of view of the common good, to say nothing of our own happiness.

The scriptural teaching of loving thy neighbor as thyself is open to various criticisms. It may be said to be impossible to cause ourselves, by an act of free choice, to wish for the happiness of the man next door as ardently as we wish for our own. At most the scriptural injunction bids us act *as if* we loved our neighbor as much as ourselves. But this is really impracticable. We may understand the principle to mean that we are to act according to a set of rules which tend to the common good and these rules include sometimes insisting on our rights even when it would add to the cosmic sum of happiness were we to relinquish them to our neighbor. These same rules include giving to charity, engaging in public service and sacrificing ourselves for our country in time of war. In short the doctrine of loving our neighbor as ourselves does not literally mean what it says; it calls for an elaborate interpretation, as Butler was well aware. Benevolence is the sum of virtue only in connection with reason, which leads us to consider the distant consequences of actions and the fact that the care of some persons, rather than others, is committed to our charge by the social system under which we live. Reason and benevolence together oblige us to consider these special relations and circumstances.

Butler was convinced that we are not to make the greatest happiness the sole and direct guide of our lives. Conscience places us under certain particular obligations. Many things are approved and disapproved by mankind without explicit regard to the universal happiness. "Fidelity, honor, strict justice, are themselves approved in the highest degree, abstracted from consideration of their tendency" to promote the common good.[10] Men of "great and distinguished merit" have expressed themselves in a manner to suggest that the "whole of virtue" consists in

> "singly aiming, according to the best of their judgment, at promoting the happiness of mankind in the present state, and the whole of vice, in doing what they foresee, or might foresee, is likely to produce an overbalance of unhappiness in it; than which mistakes none can be conceived more terrible. For it is certain that some of the most shocking instances of injustice, adultery, murder, perjury and even of persecution may . . . not have the appearance of being likely to produce an overbalance of misery in the present state. . . . The happiness of the world is the concern of him who is the lord and proprietor of it; nor do we know what we are about when we endeavor to promote the good of mankind in any ways but those which he has directed, that is, in all ways not contrary to veracity and justice." [11]

With this passage may be compared Butler's description of virtue:

> "It is that which all ages and countries have made profession of in public; it is that which every

114

man you meet puts on a show of; it is that which
the primary and fundamental laws of all civil constitutions over the face of the earth make it their
business and endeavor to enforce upon the practice
of mankind; namely, justice, veracity and regard
to the common good." [12]

Butler's view is that the Creator aims at the universal
happiness of mankind but that he has given men consciences to command them to consider "justice and
veracity" and their particular obligations to their
parents and children and their countries even when
these obligations seem to go against the universal
happiness. We may feel that we owe a debt to a certain man which is more binding on us than our obligation to promote the general good. Or again the
demands of veracity may go counter to the production of a maximum of happiness. These reflections
tend to show that conscience cannot be tied down
to any one principle, not even the greatest happiness
principle. Butler's teaching is that man, by virtue of
conscience, is a law unto himself. The theory of the
supremacy of conscience was not intended to have
any direct political application; men differ concerning what is just and what is truly for the common
good and conscience can be appealed to by both radical and conservative.

One may say that Butler does not offer any explanation of conscience; he merely describes it as a
necessary phase of human nature. It is clearly connected with the idea of God, in that it seems to speak
to us with an absolute authority and is sufficient to
assure us of the existence of an ethical world-order
which guarantees that we shall not ultimately lose
if we follow its decrees. It is by definition the power
which apprehends right and wrong; it has the re-
markable feature of conferring on itself the right to
regulate all our actions. Butler would have been the
first to admit that human life cannot proceed on the

115

basis of conscience alone; there must be positive laws enforced by temporal punishments. On the other hand, if we wholly deny the existence of conscience, with its claim to a supra-legal authority, we have no basis for a criticism of existing laws and institutions but must passively accept all alike. It is possible to deny in theory the existence of any such faculty (as something superior to law and custom) but we know that in practical life and politics we must use ethical ideas and therefore we must postulate a faculty for apprehending these ideas; naturalistic explanations tend to undermine its authority, although they never destroy it. For Butler conscience was in essence supernatural and therefore beyond the reach of any naturalistic explanation.

CHAPTER VIII

BALGUY AND PRICE

Balguy and Price belong to the rationalistic tradition of the 18th century and continue along the lines of Cudworth and Clarke. John Balguy, a clergyman, wrote on *The Foundation of Moral Goodness* and defended ethical rationalism against the doctrines of Hutcheson. Virtue, says Balguy, consists in acting according to the self-evident fitness of things. This constitutes the *honestum* or rightness of actions and characters. There is also the *pulchrum* or moral beauty of actions and characters; this involves a feeling of pleasure on the part of the spectator. Since pleasure is a feeling, it falls outside the scope of the strict rationalism which Balguy propounds in this treatise. In an interesting note, included in a later edition of the work, Balguy declares that he has since been convinced

"that all beauty, whether moral or natural, is to be reckoned as a species of absolute truth, as resulting from, or consisting in, the necessary relations and unchangeable congruities of ideas; and, by consequence, that in order to the perception of

117

beauty, no other power need be supposed than what is merely intellectual." [1]

But, since pleasure remains a feeling, one must speak of an "intellectual pleasure" to be ascribed to a "rational soul" which is curiously blended with our "instinctive" or "animal" souls. It will be best to leave this complication aside, for the present, and to consider merely the rightness of actions, which Balguy holds to be an objective feature, capable of being intellectually cognized.

Balguy takes the position that only a rational perception of the fitness of a certain action in a given set of circumstances is consistent with the authority which is proper to the moral judgment and that Hutcheson, because of an excessive devotion to the ideas of Shaftesbury, had grievously erred in making virtue identical with instinctive benevolence in ourselves or others.

Let us first state the objections which Balguy brings to bear against Hutcheson. (1) God, at least, cannot be ruled by instincts but must have rationally perceived that the happiness of his creatures was more worthy to be produced than their misery. (2) According to Hutcheson, we cannot act for the good of others without "natural affection," which means an implanted propensity, not essential to the rational nature and which may, therefore, very well be missing. Balguy holds that, as rational creatures, we can perceive that we *ought* to serve others and that we can freely choose to serve others because of this perception. In so far as our actions are determined by instinctive desires, they are less free and less virtuous.

"To represent a rational agent as incapable of performing or approving actions morally good, without presupposing certain instincts, seems to me inverting the frame of our nature and transferring

118

the supremacy from the highest principle to the lowest." [2]

(3) Hutcheson must ascribe some degree of virtue to brutes, which show "affection to their respective kinds and a strong degree of love and affection toward their off-spring." [3] Balguy, on the contrary, holds that the brutes are ignorant of "the reasons and relations of things" and incapable of an idea of moral good. (4) Hutcheson should have concluded that the stronger the affection, the greater the virtue. Actually, Hutcheson had said that there is a greater virtue in the agent who produces a greater good from a weaker attachment. Hutcheson and Balguy agree in holding that an act of kindness to a dear friend is less meritorious than doing the same for a stranger, but each explains the fact differently. Hutcheson had said that benevolence which flows from the nearer attachments of nature is less virtuous because it can extend to only small numbers of people. Balguy replies by asking whether, if men acquired the same affection for the whole species that they now have for their friends, they would become thereby more virtuous; his reply is that they would thereby become less virtuous, since they would be less free. "To be determined to the doing of a good action merely by the reason and right of the thing is genuine goodness; this is the purest and most perfect virtue of which any agent is capable." [4] We may admire the wisdom of the Creator who did not rely on the frail reason of men but rather gave them strong instincts which tend to racial survival, but it is still true that virtue, in the quintessential sense, is greater when we are not influenced by natural instinct. Rulers of a state, who are not connected with their subjects by consanguinity, and who nevertheless rule well, are more virtuous than rulers who have a natural affection for their subjects because of racial similarity.

119

(5) If virtue and approbation are merely instinctive, we must think less highly of them; furthermore, Hutcheson's definition of virtue as that which gains approbation from an observer is incorrect, since virtue is rather that which *deserves* or is *worthy of* approbation. The absolute fitness of virtue, Balguy holds, renders it suitable to be chosen by every rational being. Reason is superior to every interest, even the public interest.

> "It would be improper and absurd to say that we hearken to reason for the sake of our fellow creatures; but it is very just and proper to say that we oblige and serve our fellow-creatures because reason enjoins it." [5]

Although moral good promotes pleasure, it is itself, like pleasure, an absolute good. Virtue is therefore good in itself; it is not merely esteemed for its consequences; its lovely form is not merely a cornucopia.[6]

Balguy's treatise is an admirable statement of the formalism involved in the doctrine of the eternal fitness of things. It is an elaboration of two propositions: (1) that we can *see* or perceive intellectually that a certain course of action is right or wrong and (2) that we can freely choose to do our duty no matter what instinctive desires we may have or not have. Both of these propositions are implied in our usual attitude toward morals; neither is compatible with the implied emotivism of Hutcheson's moral sense theory. We can point out that although Balguy may have succeeded in stating clearly enough the philosophical presuppositions of our usual ethical language, his doctrine has no definite practical application. It is easily understood as a sanctification of the existing social order. On the other hand, one might understand it as authorizing revolution, namely, if "reason" told us that it was our duty to change

120

the form of government existing in our part of the world. It cuts short all speculation on the origin of the system of rights and duties and commits us to an acceptance of theism and rewards and punishments after death. It is quite incompatible with naturalism but, with certain supplementary assumptions, can easily be used by teachers of revealed religion.

Richard Price's *Review of the Principal Questions in Morals* (1758) [7] was published a generation later. In the sequence of publication, it belongs after Hume, but its doctrine is similar to that of Clarke and Balguy. Hastings Rashdall described the *Review* as "the best work on ethics until quite recent times." (*Theory of Good and Evil*, Second Edition, Vol. I, page 81). Rashdall's words are probably meant to express the fact that he agreed with Price on certain fundamentals, but there is no doubt that Price's treatise possesses considerable merit, although its doctrines are quite along the lines of Cudworth, Clarke and Balguy. The virtue of the *Review* is its lucidity and its elaboration of the philosophical implications of the doctrine of a rational perception of moral truths. The essential teaching of Richard Price is that right and wrong and moral values in general are perceived by intuitive reason and are, like the truths of arithmetic and geometry, eternal and immutable. To promote happiness is everlastingly right and to produce undeserved misery, where no greater good is likely to result, is everlastingly wrong. Happiness-production is, however, not our only duty; we have also justice to consider. Price did not proclaim any new practical truth; his view of the content of morals was, in substance, the same as that of Locke, Clarke and Butler. On the theoretical side, Price revives some of the arguments which Plato used against Protagoras, turning them against Hume; he holds that Hutcheson was wrong in ascribing ethical judgment to an implanted sense, since, like the multiplication-table, it expresses something which is intrinsically necessary and which, therefore, could not be otherwise.

A discussion of Price's intuitionism outside the domain of ethics would involve consideration of such topics as analytic and synthetic judgments, tautologies, the nature of logical and mathematical truths and in fact the problem of truth in general. If we were to follow Price we should be committed to the view that mathematics either contains self-evident truths or is entirely self-evident or would be, if our minds were capable of a greater span of attention, and, furthermore, that such truths as the law of universal causation and Newton's three laws of motion are all intuitively certain. Even if we make these rather extreme concessions to intuitive rationalism we shall not have proved that ethical "truths" are self-evident in the same sense. The following is a somewhat curious argument given by Price in support of the view that rightness is an intrinsic or objective quality of some actions. He accepts the view that secondary qualities are not qualities of things in a naively realistic sense and concludes that the notion of a colored body is just as absurd as that of a round square. In comment we may say that, since people see colored bodies around them all the time, it would take a person unusually gifted in the power of abstract thought to see that it was absurd that bodies should be colored in the literal sense of the word. One is, in fact, tempted to agree with Berkeley that it is absurd and unthinkable that bodies should exist devoid of all secondary qualities. Price, however, consistently upholds the dualistic realism of Locke and maintains that it is inconceivable that bodies should literally possess color as a quality. The application to ethical theory made by Price is that there is no such incompatibility between actions and rightness as there is, according to his supposition, between body and color. The answer can be made that when we examine an action physically and psychologically by means of sense-perception and introspection, we can never discover either rightness or wrongness to be a feature of an action. It is rather evident that emotions are involved in ethical judgments and not in the external way (suggested by Price) in which the joy of Pythagoras in discovering his theorem was connected with the theorem itself.

According to Price, the idea of right is not of empirical origin but, like a number of other important ideas, belongs to the mind as part of its innate equipment. It is interesting to note how Price, making his own the teachings of Plato and his English disciple, Cudworth, works out an elaborate critique of Locke, which contains many of the ideas set forth later by Leibniz and Kant. The understanding, Price holds, is itself a source of ideas not found in either sense or reflection (in the Lockean sense); among such ideas we find essence, number, identity, substance, solidity, duration, space, power, causation, possibility, existence, etc. Why then may not the ideas of right and wrong be equally innate? A being who had only sense could never understand such words as possibility, necessity, existence or non-existence, substance, attribute, essence, etc. Such a being would likewise lack the ideas of right and wrong. Price, to be sure, did not wish to deny Locke's discovery that such basic categories are not found in the minds of infants, idiots and savages. The mind, as it develops, uses the categories in organizing its experience; at a later time it may become aware of them in a process of philosophical reflection and at the same time discover that these basic concepts could never have been extracted from the sensory material.

The argument of Price involves three steps or stages; he must first show that right and wrong can be perceived by reason; secondly, that there are such things as "rational feelings" which are involved in approval and disapproval; and, thirdly, that there are "rational desires and aversions" directed on what is intrinsically good or evil. The first step is perhaps the most plausible of the three. According to Price, our ideas of right and wrong are simple ideas and must be ascribed to some power of immediate perception. This can only mean that the terms right and wrong are essentially indefinable. Any attempt to define them results merely in giving synonyms. Furthermore, some actions must be approved without our being able to give a reason for our approval, just as certain ends must ultimately be chosen for their own sakes. The thesis of Price is that the power which approves is the understanding, just as it is the understanding which sees that certain ends are intrinsically desirable.

In defense of this thesis Price advances a series of arguments. (1) It implies no absurdity. Many of our ideas are derived from the mind itself; this may be the source of our moral ideas. (2) Let each of us consider his own experiences. When we attend to moral judgment we know that we apprehend truth rather than receive an impression from sense. Every being must desire happiness for himself. In the same way, every mind must perceive something amiss in a creature bringing ruin on himself and others. "Is there nothing truly wrong in the absolute and eternal misery of an innocent being?" [8] (3) If right and wrong denote effects of sensation, it must imply an absurdity to think them applicable to actions. But there is no incompatibility between actions and rightness and wrongness. (4) On the supposition that right and wrong are merely sensations, there would be no possibility of mistaking right and wrong, since all sensation is true sensation. (5) If no actions are right or wrong, then all must be indifferent. But how absurd to regard all actions as equally indifferent! (6) If all actions are in themselves indifferent, this would be perceived by the Deity, who would therefore have no reason for pursuing universal happiness as an end; he should rather be indifferent to what we humans call good and evil.

Let us try to imagine what the reply of an ethical naturalist would be. He might point out that the term *right* may be indefinable in one sense and yet definable in some other sense of the word *definition*. Thus the names of colors are technically indefinable, and yet this causes no difficulty since we can easily point to them. In the same way, we can discover the experience of rightness and wrongness in our experience; when we do so we find that they are connected with the emotions. With regard to the necessity for self-evident truths, we find that the idea of a postulate is a useful one; in the case of a postulate, we agree to regard a certain proposition as self-evident without deciding whether it is really self-evident or not. Price tells us that we are to consult our own experience. Here it seems that we can adopt different attitudes. When our attitude is strictly scientific we neither praise nor blame and moral judgment is out of place. On the other hand, we can choose to look at matters ethically; this means bringing in our feelings. We accept certain postulates and give human beings certain rights and duties. Moral truth has a different sort of objectivity from that found in perception and natural science. Thus "conduciveness to certain ends" is a property which is either present or not present; on the other hand, rightness and wrongness are not sensuously verifiable.

There is always an element of arbitrariness in "taking a stand" and declaring an action right or wrong. Price makes the point that if ethical judgment is a matter of feeling, there would be no such thing as error with regard to right and wrong. Naturalism replies that the ideas of right and wrong are commonly used without our having in our minds a perfectly determinate meaning. We *can* be in error with regard to the usefulness of an action and also with regard to its legality or usualness. It is rare that we judge of right and wrong without thinking vaguely also of one or more of these attributes. But even if we are thinking of a "pure" rightness or wrongness, we have the option of taking our own judgment as truth and regarding those who disagree with us as in error. It is a matter of the assertion of our own personality against the personality of others; no verification or argumentative defense of our position is possible but we can still freely choose to regard our feeling as expressing truth and the feelings of others as expressing error. The only possible objection to this procedure would itself be ethical and would be merely an expression of feeling. Price makes the point that if right and wrong are not truly attributes of actions, then all actions are indifferent. If we suppose that right is equivalent to not-wrong, then the law of excluded middle tells us that when actions are viewed from an ethical point of view they cannot be indifferent but must be either right or wrong, although it may be the case that we do not know in which class a given action falls. On the other hand, we need not look at actions from an ethical point of view; from the standpoint of sense-perception and science all actions are equally indifferent, however much they may differ in effectiveness in accomplishing their ends. On the other hand, we can easily judge men's actions from the standpoint of certain ethical postulates. The reason why we adopt a given set of postulates, naturalism tells us, is emotional. Mention may be made of Price's argument that it was unthinkable that the Deity should be indifferent to what we call good and evil. This was because Price's God was conceived as the enforcer of the decrees of conscience. Spinoza, who approached the problem of God from a naturalistic point of view, found the idea of an indifferent God acceptable. We may agree with Price that *if* there is an objective law and God is good, then God must know and obey this eternal rational law. From the standpoint of naturalism, the existence of an ethical deity is an ill-founded hypothesis.

The first step in ethical rationalism is the postulation of a rational perception of right and wrong. Price agreed with Cudworth that morality is eternal and immutable.[9] This does not necessarily mean that what is right in one age is also right in every other age. Let us suppose that intuitive reason tells us that we should obey God. It may then be the case that God wills that men behave differently in different ages. We are always obeying God as long as we do his will but it is conceivable that he should issue different commands at different times. Or let us suppose that reason commands us to promote the universal happiness; it might well be that this would lead to different modes of conduct in different circumstances. Price would have accepted Butler's dictum that virtue is "justice, veracity and regard for the common good;" this would leave a certain amount of free play in determining the details of conduct. Ultimately, Price must tell us to do what we think is right. Nevertheless, the theory of right and wrong is the most easily understood part of Price's system. In order to explain moral beauty and deformity he must postulate "rational feelings" and to explain good and evil he must postulate "rational desires." How are rational feelings and rational desires different from non-rational feelings and non-rational desires?

In speaking of the beauty and deformity of actions, Price does not mean to refer to qualities of actions distinct from rightness and wrongness. He notes that in common language the epithets *beautiful* and *amiable* are confined to actions and characters that please us greatly. But rightness, he holds, always involves some degree of pleasure in the spectator.

"I cannot perceive an action to be right, without *approving* it; or *approve* it, without being conscious of some degree of satisfaction and complacency." [10]

The beauty of actions is based on their tendency, as right, to produce pleasure in the spectator. The moral sense theory had put all emphasis upon this pleasure in the spectator and had defined moral values in general as the power in actions and characters to produce this pleasure. According to Price, the ethical qualities are, in general, indefinable in their essence, but they do, nevertheless, have the power of producing pleasure and unpleasantness in the spectator; the question is whether they produce this pleasure by some inscrutable law of nature going back to the will of God or by a self-evident fitness to produce pleasure in a rational soul. In the case of the sensations produced by external objects, there is no rational connection between the stimulus and the sensation; we can only say, that such is the divine decree. But in the case of the moral predicates, the external quality has a rationally intelligible fitness to produce pleasure in a rational soul. A happy and orderly universe is intrinsically a pleasanter object of contemplation than an unhappy or disorderly one. The moral virtues necessarily tend to produce pleasure in the spectator just as their opposites necessarily tend to produce unpleasantness. The rational feelings, however, are mixed with the instinctive; our Maker has provided remedies for our imperfections and "established a due balance in our frame by annexing to our intellectual perceptions sensations and instincts which give them greater force." [11]

The idea of a rational contemplative pleasure was further developed by a sketch of aesthetics with reference to Hutcheson's *Inquiry into the Original of our Ideas of Beauty and Virtue* (1725). Beauty, said Hutcheson, is based on uniformity amidst variety.

128

Price denies that aesthetic pleasure is due to an implanted sense. Orderly and harmonious forms are more readily comprehended by our minds than their opposites. Beauty, therefore, may have a basis other than mere instinct; it may rest on a certain constitution which has an essential tendency to produce pleasure in a rational being. Furthermore we find that there is a scale of perfection in which all beings can be graded according to their intrinsic excellence or perfection; an intelligent being is more *noble* and *perfect* than a clod of earth; and God is the most perfect and excellent being of all. Perfection is an objective quality which has a necessary connection with pleasure in a rational spectator, although, in any given case, it may fail to produce its appropriate effect because of an interference with pleasures and pains due to our instinctive constitution, or, as we may say, with the laws of psycho-physical correlation which God has established. All rational beings would take pleasure in the contemplation of virtue and perfection were it not for the fact that our souls have a mixed or dualistic constitution; in part we are rational beings and in part we are creatures of instinct and habit; we are capable of pleasantness and unpleasantness, Price holds, as rational souls. Such was Price's theory of *rational feelings;* it was part of a system of rational psychology, very unlike the empirical psychology of Hume and Adam Smith; one could hardly hope to find support for it in the writings of modern psychologists. It is, however, thoroughly in line with the teachings of Plato and Aristotle and strongly suggests Kant's *Critique of Judgment.* It involves the supposition of a rational soul, which is more than a mere cognitive faculty, since it has feelings, and, as we shall see shortly, desires as well; the rational soul is weak, however, and is being perpetually drawn aside from its essential laws by the instinctive feelings and desires with which the infinitely wise author of nature has also endowed it.

Desire may spring merely from instinct or again it may arise from the rational nature. A rational being must necessarily desire his own happiness. "The desire of happiness for ourselves certainly arises not from instinct. The full and adequate account of it is, *the nature of happiness.*" [12] Hedonism is an *a priori* truth; it is self-evident that a rational being must seek his own greatest pleasure. This necessary desire for happiness for ourselves is merely the outstanding instance of something rationally desired for its own sake. The rational soul also desires virtue, the happiness of others and even fame and knowledge. God must be able to perceive that happiness is better than misery and to prefer to create the former rather than the latter, yet God can have no instincts. But "in men, the sentiments and tendencies of our intelligent nature are to a great extent mingled with the effects of arbitrary constitution." [13] Our rational benevolence is in itself too weak; we have been given by our Maker certain instincts, such as parental affection, hunger and compassion, which make it easier to do what reason ordains. We have *affections* and *passions;* the former are desires which belong to us as rational souls, such as self-love, benevolence and love of truth; the passions are tendencies or instincts which belong to our positive or empirical constitution.[14] Our affections and appetites are all disinterested with the exception of self-love.

> "Though the seat of them be *self* and the effect of them the gratification of *self,* their direct tendency is always to some particular object different from private pleasure, beyond which they carry not their view." [15]

They often draw us away from our true interest; men are carried by them into actions and pursuits which they acknowledge to be ruinous to them.[16] Some of the passions and appetites were given to us with a view to our preservation as individuals; others have reference to the happiness of the species. If reason were stronger we could accomplish all our essential purposes without the aid of these implanted tendencies.

Price's moral psychology may be condensed into the statements that there is an intuitive apprehension of duty and that there are rational feelings and desires as well as instinctive. The theory of a rational perception of duty offers least difficulty since we assimilate it to the apprehension of facts, that is, of certain "states of affairs" describable by saying that such and such is the case. We therefore tend to accept the view that we can apprehend certain ought-propositions in the same way; we think that we simply *perceive* that one ought to keep his word and the like. But rational feelings and rational desires seem rather difficult to conceive. Price would have us divide our feelings and desires into two classes, namely, into those which belong to us as rational souls and those which belong to us as animals. How can we draw any such distinction?

The following is suggested as an explanation of rational feelings and rational desires which would be open to an ethical theorist who accepted a rational perception of right and wrong but found difficulty in the other parts of Price's theory. We judge by intuitive reason that a certain act is right; the pleasure of a spectator in considering that act may also be regarded as right and *as in that* sense rational. The word *right* cannot be defined in a strict sense, but such words as *fitting* and *proper* are synonyms. The feeling of approval may be called fitting and also rational, using the word *rational* here as a synonym for fitting. This is certainly not what Price meant, since he speaks in terms of the theory that we have two blended souls. "Rational desire" can be explained along similar lines. My own happiness, when others are not affected, is a thing which it is proper for me to seek to produce; my desire for it may, therefore, be termed rational. To desire the happiness of the universe is rational, since reason tells me that the happiness of the world is a thing which it is intrinsically fitting for me to seek to produce. In a word, reason tells me that universal happiness is desirable, that is, intrinsically good. On the other hand, reason does not tell me that the possession of money is intrinsically desirable; if however I do nevertheless desire it, I may put the desire in a lower category and call it a merely instinctive desire. We may regard the desire for one's own happiness as rational; the desire for fame may be put in the class of non-rational desires. In this way we are spared the necessity of elaborating a dubious dualistic psychology, according to which feelings and desires would in part belong to us as rational souls and in part as animal souls. Intuition would be cut down to an irreducible minimum, namely, the perception that something ought to be done. The statement that happiness is intrinsically good would mean that we ought to try to produce happiness; the statement that our feelings, when we approve of a just act, are rational would mean that justice is a thing which is intrinsically desirable. The thought that something ought or ought not to be done, we may say, is involved in the ethical attitude as such. The only proof of the existence of moral truths is the practical necessity we are under, as beings having to make decisions, of having authoritative practical propositions to guide us. But Price was not prepared to carry simplification to such an extreme; he preferred to conceive the soul as complex; it had, as Plato and Aristotle and Butler had taught, an hierarchical structure; it was in part rational and in part merely animal and the rational soul had a natural right to rule.

The rationalists used a variety of expressions to

describe right actions, such as "acting according to the nature of things; treating things as they are; conformity to truth; agreement and disagreement, congruity and incongruity between actions and relations." [17] These expressions, Price says, have little use and presuppose the idea of rightness. "Treating an object as being what *it is*, is treating it as it is right such an object should be treated." [18] Price refers to Wollaston's *Religion of Nature* as a work which obtained a "great and just reputation" but which had defined moral good and evil as signifying or denying truth.[19] But veracity is only one of several self-evident obligations. The evils of ingratitude and of cruelty are different from the evil of denying truth and the person who fails to worship God does not literally deny his existence. Wollaston had merely stressed a manner of speaking; if we did not already know that ingratitude was wrong, it would not occur to us to regard it as a form of falsehood. When we say that virtue is acting according to truth or according to the nature of things we have not defined rightness, neither have we given any reason why we should practice virtue; we have merely given synonyms for the idea of rightness.

It will not be necessary for us to follow the details of what Price has to say concerning the subject-matter of virtue, i.e., what in general we are to do; his views were in agreement with those of Butler. He endorses Butler's contention that benevolence is not the whole of virtue; we have our special obligations; there is, along with other duties, a duty of veracity. The value of veracity is deduced by Price from the fact that the rational soul attaches an immediate value to knowledge of truth. The duty of veracity includes

"impartiality and honesty of mind in our inquiries after truth, as well as a sacred regard for it in all

133

that we may say; fair and ingenuous dealing; such an openness and simplicity of temper as exclude guile and prevarication, and all the contemptible arts of craft, equivocation and hypocrisy,"

etc.[20] Beneficence is the study of the good of others. We have, Price declares, a clear intuitive perception of this duty; it cannot "be consistently supposed that our own good should make an action fit to be performed but that of others not." [21]

"We are surrounded with fellow-men, beings of the same nature, in the same circumstances, and having the same wants with ourselves; to whom we are therefore in a peculiar manner linked and related, and whose happiness and misery depend very much on our behavior to them." [22]

Here the *similarity* of other men to ourselves is made the basis of special duties to other humans; this implies that we have little obligation to cows, fish or insects. The same consideration may lead us to restrict our obligations, at least in part, to our own flesh and blood; this can be understood in a variety of ways.

"The different moral qualifications of different persons; their different degrees of nearness to us in various respects; and numberless circumstances in their situations, and characters, have a like effect, and give just reason, in innumerable instances, for a preference for some of them to others." [23]

We see then that the duty of beneficence does not involve a definite rule of conduct; we are really thrown back on our feelings no matter how much we may talk of intuitive reason.

Price insists that property-rights cannot be wholly derived from the public good; this would imply that

134

where two isolated men were involved, and where the article belonged to A by prescriptive right, and yet would do more good to B, were B to take it from A, then there would be no moral reason why B should not take it from A. If the public good were the only test of property it would be right to make a few miserable for the sake of the happiness of many.

> "Nothing is more evident than that, in order to the happiness of the world, and the being of society, possessions should be stable, and property sacred, and not liable, except on very extraordinary occasions, to be violated." [24]

Price's theory then is that occupation, prescription, etc., create a *prima facie* obligation, which may, nevertheless, be set aside on occasion by the over-ruling demands of the public good. The public good, says Price, is the leading consideration in all our inquiries concerning right and is so important

> "that it may set aside every obligation which would otherwise arise from the common rules of justice, from promises, private interest, friendship, gratitude, and all particular attachments and connections." [25]

We see that none of the principles on which the intuitionist lays emphasis is strictly exceptionless.

Although he believed that there were self-evident axioms of morality, Price was willing to admit that there are great difficulties in determining what is right in detail. Our "natural sentiments may be altered by custom, education and example."

> "Notions the most stupid may, through the influence (of custom, education and example) come to be rooted in the mind beyond the possibility of

135

being eradicated, antipathies given to objects naturally the most agreeable, and sensation itself perverted." [26]

The following passage indicates that Price was aware that the problems of life are not removed by the doctrine of self-evident moral truths.

"But, if we will recollect the observations which have been made concerning the interference between the principles of morality, and the impossibility of a complete and scientific deduction of what we ought to do and avoid in particular circumstances, we shall own, that the subject itself is often involved in real darkness, and attended with insurmountable difficulties, which, therefore, must be a further ground of much greater and more unavoidable disagreements." [27]

This frank and revealing statement shows that even Price cannot deny that there is an element of arbitrariness in ethical judgment; the concrete application of the eternal and immutable moral law is not made known to us by pure reason and we have no assurance that agreement will ever be reached concerning all questions of right and wrong.

Abstract or absolute rightness or wrongness is a quality of the action considered apart from the agent's opinion that he ought or ought not to do a certain thing; practical rightness or wrongness takes into account the agent's opinion that he ought or ought not to perform the action in question. This distinction might perhaps be more easily understood were we to say that an action can be objectively right and yet subjectively wrong, or again it may be subjectively right and objectively wrong. "A magistrate who would adjudge an estate to a person, whose right it appears to be, upon a great overbalance of evidence, would certainly do right in one sense; though, should the opposite claimant, after all, prove to be the true claimant, do wrong in another sense." [28] Price thus acknowledges that conscience is not infallible; if the existence of objective right is an inescapable postulate, there must be a difference between an enlightened and an erroneous conscience.

> "It is happy for us, that our title to the character of virtuous beings depends not upon the justice of our opinions, or the constant objective rectitude of all we do; but upon the conformity of our actions to the sincere convictions of our own minds." [29]

It is clear enough that we may be in error concerning some matter of fact and such error or ignorance is commonly held not to involve blame on our part. On the assumption of the existence of an objective right and wrong, we may also be in error through regarding one obligation to be more sacred than another, when in fact the opposite is the case in the mind of an ethically omniscient being. One man may regard his obligation to his family as more binding than his obligation to his country, while another may rate the obligations in the reverse order. Granted that one of these judgments is erroneous, there seems no way in which the error could be corrected, unless we are to fall back on "what most people think." Sometimes we say that the judgments of those who differ from us on questions of right and wrong are "immature" or "undeveloped" implying that they do not really see the false to be true but rather that they fail to see that the true is true; or, again, one may say that the differing ethical judgments of others are corrupt and biased, and that, if they would only make an effort to think clearly, they would agree with us. But however we may understand ethical differences, still, says Price, practical rightness is in its way real and absolute.

> "It is truly and absolutely right, that a man should do what the reason of his mind, though unhappily misinformed, requires of him; or what, according to his best judgment, he is persuaded to be the will of God. If he neglects this, he becomes necessarily and justly the object of his own dislike and forfeits all pretensions to integrity." [30]

This passage strongly suggests that we must above all seek the approval of our own minds. Organized society, however, is never content merely to let people do what they think right but seeks to make them think and act in certain ways.

Price teaches that an agent can be called virtuous only if "he acts from a consciousness of rectitude, and with a regard to it as his rule and end." [31] The action may be right in itself if it conforms to objective rightness, without regard to its motive; and yet it can be regarded as virtuous, as far as the agent is concerned, only if it was done because it was right. We only *do*, in a strict sense, what we intend to do. It is evident that Price here ignores the distinction between intention and motive and that he is concerned chiefly with the latter. He maintains that the perception of right is sufficient to excite us to action.

> "Excitement belongs to the very ideas of moral right and wrong, and is essentially inseparable from them." [32]

This statement means that the perception of right and wrong stirs our feelings and impulses to action as rational souls, since, as we have seen, Price insists upon the existence of both rational feelings and rational desires. The righteous man does what is right because it is right. Instinctive benevolence is not a

138

principle of virtue; rational benevolence, on the other hand, coincides with rectitude. The action of a mother risking her life to save that of her child has less moral value in so far as it is derived from natural instinct rather than from reflection on the reasonableness and fitness of her action. Price, therefore, agrees with Balguy, that virtue is less in proportion to the extent to which action is derived from instinct.

The doctrine that rectitude for its own sake is the highest motive of conduct is likely to be understood to mean that we should only act from this motive. It is generally recognized that this is an impossible ideal. Men are usually animated by such instinctive desires as hunger, lust, ambition, revenge and sympathy for the sufferings of others. Human nature, according to Price, has a dualistic constitution which involves instincts as well as rational desires, and he recognizes that instincts and passions are also necessary.

"But in man it is in fact impossible so far to improve this faculty (reason) as that the greatest evils should not arise from taking away our instincts and passions. They were very wisely and kindly given us to answer the purposes of our present state; to be the sources of many pleasures to us; to be our sole guides until reason becomes capable of taking the direction of us, and, after this, to enforce its dictates, and aid us in the execution of them; to give vigor and spirit to our pursuits; and be, as it were, sail and wind to the vessel of life." [33]

We are not to try to eradicate our passions; this would be wicked and pernicious; we are merely to see that they are always subordinated to reason. We must distinguish between an external rightness of actions, in which motive is irrelevant, and a pure inward virtue, in which without any thought of reward or punishment, we do what we think is right solely for the sake of its rectitude. Our duty is primarily to do what is right; if it happens that we are motivated by a pure love of righteousness without any thought of reward or punishment, we then illustrate moral goodness. On the other hand, if our passions lead us to act contrary to what we believe to be right, we then exemplify moral badness.

CHAPTER IX

H U M E

David Hume's *Treatise of Human Nature* (1739-40) is the classic statement of one type of naturalism, although it is a sort of naturalism quite unlike the materialism and evolutionism which came into vogue in the 19th century. Hume's naturalism is set in a frame-work of associationistic psychology. We are here concerned only with ethical theory and may ignore, for the most part, Book I, which deals with the general theoretical foundation of Hume's system, as well as Book II, which covers the psychology of what Hume called the passions, namely, love, hate, pride and humility. Hume as an ethicist is a naturalist in the sense that he seeks to explain man's moral consciousness without reference to such ideas as God and a future life. He is also a naturalist in a more technical sense, in that, without denying the validity of man's moral insights, he nevertheless seeks to define ethical predicates in empirical terms and to deduce moral truths from psychological statements. Hume's ethical system may be called approbationism and is developed by means of a consideration of the psychology of approval and disapproval. It involves at least three basic ethical categories. First, there is intrinsic as opposed to instrumental good and evil; secondly, there is virtue and its opposite; and, lastly, there is the great question, What ought we to do? Good and evil, in general, were not a problem for Hume; they were defined, without more ado, simply as pleasure and pain. He was rather concerned, in part, with virtue, that is, with admirable character-traits, and, for the rest, with right and wrong and especially with the nature of justice.

The ethical theory of Hume was part of an all-inclusive analysis of the meaning of existence and of man's experience. We know only phenomena, which are capable of being analysed into actual and possible sense-data or impressions. This involves a conception of man as primarily a psychological being, a stream of consciousness, obeying certain psychological laws. Hume therefore denies free-will in the sense of an absolute spontaneity, although he does not deny moral responsibility as presupposed in everyday life and in law. The denial of free-will is closely connected with Hume's theory of causation in general. Although Hume demonstrates convincingly the lack of a "proof" in any usual sense for the law of universal causation, he nevertheless made the basis of all his thinking the proposition that there is a causal order, which covers all of nature, including man, such that the same kind of cause, operating in the same kind of circumstances, is always followed by the same kind of effect. The denial of free-will is a mere application of the fundamental "axiom" or "postulate" which came later to be called the "uniformity of nature," which seems to be the basic presupposition of all empirical thinking. The "will" is governed by pleasure and pain. What is will? It is, we may say, the faculty of choice. Willing is *doing*, moving our hand or summoning up some idea; it is choosing or deciding or doing something. When Hume speaks of willing as an impression he calls attention to the conscious side of what, for dualistic realism, is a psycho-physical process. The denial of free-will is the assertion that willing or doing always has a cause in a sense similar to that in which events of physical nature have causes. The subsumption of human choice under the principle of universal causation is supported, by Hume, by observations of human life. History shows that human nature is always much the same. Men fall into different classes which play different parts in society. Their characters are differentiated according to the "necessary and uniform principles of human nature." [1] The irregularities and unpredictability of human conduct do not show causelessness in nature; there may be obscure and irregular causes at work in either case. The actions of madmen are unpredictable but madmen are commonly believed to have less liberty than sane persons. Unpredictable actions may be due to unusual characters in unusual circumstances rather than to some departure from the universal law of causation. However, Hume's law of causation is a general formula which may cover a number of different kinds of processes. The motion of a billiard ball under impact of the cue is one thing and human choice is another, even though the latter is under the sway of motives, just as the former is under the sway of physical forces. Hume does not deny that we choose; he merely asserts that choice is necessitated by motives. These motives, however, such as ambition, lust, greed, benevolence, hatred, etc., are not events; they are also not directly observable, but are merely certain underlying forces, of an obscure nature, which are supposed to explain human choice. In the same way, a force, like gravity, is not observable; it comes into play or is released under certain conditions, as when a cord is cut and a weight falls to the ground. The statement that a person always acts according to the kind of person that he is (or according to his character or his strongest motives) does not imply that a person does not *choose*. If we identify free-will and choice, then we cannot deny free-will. Determination by motives, that is, by one's character, in and through a

143

process of conscious choice, may be called freedom, since it is something totally different from mechanical causation. When motives are involved, there is a thought of the future; we are determined either by a thought of a good to be gained or an evil to be avoided. The process of choice can be influenced by punishment and reward, praise and blame. Hume's denial of free-will is not to be understood as implying a fatalistic denial of moral obligation. If the future is fore-known it can only be in the infinite and incomprehensible mind of God.

We have already noticed that the subject of good and evil as such is not regarded by Hume as requiring any extended treatment; good is identified with pleasure and evil with pain. This refers to intrinsic good; instrumental good is easily defined in causal terms. Hume's hedonism is a matter of definition. He is within his rights in arbitrarily defining one of the meanings of good and evil in hedonistic terms. There is no reason to think that he wished to offer hedonism as a synthetic judgment *a priori*. A rival definition of good may be found in Hobbes and Spinoza, namely, that the good is the desired. Thus, if a man desires death, then death is good for him, although it involves neither pleasure nor pain. Hume, in choosing to define the intrinsic good as pleasure, does not mean to assert that pleasure is the sole object of desire. He recognized the existence of anhedonic desires, *i.e.* desires for something other than pleasure.

> "Besides good and evil, or, in other words, pleasure and pain, the direct passions frequently arise from a natural impulse or instinct, which is perfectly unaccountable. Of this kind is the desire of punishment to our enemies, and of happiness to our friends; hunger, thirst, and a few other bodily appetites. These passions, properly speaking, produce good and evil and proceed not from them, like the other affections." [2]

144

With this passage may be compared a statement with regard to the calm passions.

"These passions are of two kinds; either certain instincts originally implanted in our natures, such as benevolence and resentment, the love of life, and kindness to children; or the general appetite to good and aversion to evil, considered merely as such." [3]

Hume's position is, then, that our actions are determined by our desires and that these desires go back to certain instincts. We have an original or unacquired desire for pleasure and aversion to pain and we have also certain equally original desires for things other than pleasure as such. We may feel "a violent passion of resentment" which makes us desire the evil and punishment of another; we may even desire pain for ourselves, as when a person feels anger or malice toward himself.[4]

Moral distinctions, says Hume, are not derived from reason. To show that morals are not matters of reason, Hume cites the fact that moral distinctions do influence action and refers to a proposition supposed to have been previously established by him to the effect that "Reason is, and ought only to be, the slave of the passions, and can never pretend to any other office than to serve and obey them." [5] The logical ground of this thesis is Hume's thoroughgoing hedonism:

"It is from the prospect of pain or pleasure that the aversion or propensity arises toward any object; and these emotions extend themselves to the causes and effects of that object, as they are pointed out to us by reason and experience." [6]

If a man acts for his own greater good in a cool detached way he is acting from a calm passion; the calm passions are commonly mistaken by philosophers for pure reason. Some men are more disposed to act from the calm passions, and others from the violent passions; the former are said to be more rational than the latter. Reason is a purely cognitive faculty and, therefore, cannot by itself determine our conduct.

Hume does indeed recognize two senses in which an emotion can be called unreasonable. It may be founded on a false supposition of the existence or non-existence of certain objects or events. It is scarcely necessary to seek illustrations of how hope and fear, joy and sorrow might be based on such false suppositions. The second case in which Hume would permit us to use the label *unreasonable* is when, in choosing a means or method for accomplishing some result, we are deceived with regard to the underlying causal relations involved; we choose the wrong means to gain our end. But, declares Hume, "It is not contrary to reason to prefer the destruction of the whole world to the scratching of my finger. It is not contrary to reason to choose my total ruin to prevent the least uneasiness of an Indian, or person wholly unknown to me." [7] The rationalists had said that virtue is conformity to reason; they held that there are eternal fitnesses and unfitnesses of things, which are the same to every rational being who considers them. To them it would have been self-evident that the destruction of the whole world was a greater evil than scratching David Hume's finger, and, similarly, it was self-evident that reason ordained that we should not accept total ruin to prevent a slight uneasiness to some unknown person. Hume's position was that these things seem contrary to reason because they are really contrary to certain calm passions which we possess; when we consider matters in a detached mood we feel a calm desire for the good of the world as a whole and also for our own good. Hume's position rests on the assumption that reason is a purely cognitive faculty; however, it may be that ethical reason apprehends a peculiar sort of truth, namely, a kind containing the idea of *ought*, that is, the idea of the *fitting* or the *proper* and this kind of truth might possess a dynamic quality which other truths do not possess. According to Kant, virtuous action does not spring from desire but rather from respect for the moral law. If we insist that this is mere subterfuge and that all action must spring from desire, we are led to postulate a desire distinct from all others, namely, a desire to do what is right. No doubt, the existence of such a desire is problematic but it is in accordance with common forms of speech to say that a man did so and so because he wanted to do what was right. Butler, we recall, said that virtue consists of "affection to and pursuit of what is right and good as such." [8] If we admit, contrary to Hume, that intuitive reason tells us what we ought to do and also that we have a desire to do what is right, then we should have to grant that reason, though not dynamic of itself, nevertheless can guide our conduct in so far as it appeals to this peculiar desire.

Hume's argument was that moral distinctions cannot be derived from reason, since they are supposed to influence conduct, and reason, being purely cognitive, can only influence conduct by presenting possible ends or goals to our desires and suggesting means of reaching those ends. In saying that reason *ought* to be only the slave of the passions, Hume was himself proclaiming a dubious normative proposition. He did not mean it in any very startling sense, since he acknowledged that what is called strength of mind is found in those in whom the calm passions predominate. The man called rational is animated by a calm desire either for his own good or the universal good. Had Hume, like Hegel, declared that great things in the world are only accomplished by violent passion, he would have belonged to the romantic

147

mood characteristic of the 19th and 20th centuries; in fact, however Hume's skepticism was of a thoroughly classical temper. It is likewise true that the moderate irrationalism of Hume is not closely akin to the teachings of the psycho-analysts; the latter tend to make man a slave of his sub-conscious and emphasize a process called rationalization, according to which we are perpetually deceiving ourselves with regard to our motives. Hume's irrationalism consisted merely in the doctrine that all men's actions are expressions of desires, which are either hedonic or non-hedonic, and concern either ourselves or others. In general we desire pleasure for ourselves and others, but we may desire other things and may even be inspired by malice toward ourselves. In asserting the impotence of reason, Hume meant merely that bare knowledge of things and persons and their relations cannot, by itself, cause us to act. He did not deny that desire involves an idea of what is desired and that successful action involves knowledge of causal relations. What he seeks to establish is that moral distinctions are matters of an emotional response rather than of a rational perception in any strict sense.

Hume shows clearly enough that error as to fact is innocent and cannot be a source of immorality. Can it be that it is an error of right which is the cause of immorality? The notion of an error of right presupposes a "real right and wrong." The supposition of a real or objective right and wrong, to be apprehended by reason, is precisely what Hume seeks to overthrow. An error of right can only mean that some person is misinformed concerning what is legal or customary in a given society. In order to prove that rightness does not consist in relations which can be apprehended by reason, Hume points to the fact that certain relations between humans can be paralleled in the plant and animal kingdoms without any ethical problem being involved. The young sapling destroys the parent tree but we do not speak of ingratitude or parricide; and, in the animal world, relations may take place, which, in the human, would be incestuous and criminal. The rationalist would reply that it is not the "physical relations" which count; we are to consider that human beings are not plants or animals and that reason reveals certain unique "moral relations," involving obligations which are meaningless when ascribed to beings lacking rationality. Hume correctly remarks that in writings on ethics there is often an unnoticed transition from propositions containing *is* and *is not* to propositions containing *ought* and *ought not*. He also states correctly that it is inconceivable "how this new relation can be a deduction from others, which are altogether different from it." [9] Nevertheless, Hume has not refuted the doctrine of the intuitionists that intuitive reason, on the occasion of apprehending certain facts, perceives a rightness or wrongness to belong to a certain kind of action in a certain type of situation. An objective rightness, to be apprehended by an intuitive reason, is still a possibility, in spite of Hume's arguments, and, furthermore, it seems impossible to construct a system of ethics in which some types of action are not perceived to be right and others to be wrong.

Moral distinctions, not being discoverable by reason, are "derived," Hume says, from a moral sense. Hutcheson had thought of the moral sense as an emotional faculty, planted in us by God, leading us to approve what we think makes for the universal happiness; Hume was prepared to explain the so-called moral sense in terms of hedonistic and associationistic psychology, but for both the moral sense involved an affective response. The moral sense does not apprehend anything objectively pre-existent but is merely a response to our own actions or those of others with pleasure or dissatisfaction. We cannot discover the goodness or badness of actions by empirical examination in the usual sense. The values, positive or negative, lie in ourselves rather than in the object.

> "So that when you pronounce any action or character to be vicious, you mean nothing, but that from the constitution of your nature you have a feeling or sentiment of blame from the contemplation of it." [10]

Modern critics have pointed out that this is *not* what we mean when we say that an action is vicious, since what we literally mean is that an action has a certain property. We are not talking about ourselves or our feelings. A reply which an advocate of Hume's theory might make would be that there is a difference between what we verbally or formally mean and what we *really* mean.

> "Vice and virtue," says Hume, "may be compared to sounds, colors, heat and cold, which, according to modern philosophy, are not qualities in objects, but perceptions in the mind; and this discovery in morals, like the other in physics, is to be regarded as a considerable advancement of the speculative sciences; though, like that too, it has little or no influence in practice." [11]

In short, virtue and vice are like the secondary qualities. We normally speak as if cold and heat were intrinsic qualities of snow and fire respectively, and yet a person even slightly trained in science does not hesitate to say that what he *really means* is merely that snow gives him a sensation of cold and fire of heat. In the snow and the fire, such a person is likely to say, there is merely a *power* of producing these sensations. Hume's position that ethical qualities are purely "subjective" is highly plausible, since everyone knows how variable and partisan such valuations are. On the other hand, it should be remembered that, although Hume insisted that virtue and vice were merely "perceptions in the mind," yet he did not deny the *reality* of moral distinctions for the individual, since "nothing can be more real, or concern us more, than our sentiments of pleasure and uneasiness." [12] If we act contrary to our own standards, we shall be punished by the condemnation of our own minds; if we act contrary to the standards of society, we shall be punished by society.

When we regard an action as morally good, Hume would say, we mean that it causes us pleasure when we consider it from a certain point of view. This "meaning of meaning" is, as we have already noticed, not the formal or "logical" meaning, since, taken that way, moral goodness is a quality of the action. But we may also use the word *mean* in a more psychological sense, according to which what a word *means* is what it *expresses*, namely, pleasure or uneasiness, just as a frown expresses anger or a smile joy. In this psychological sense, the ethical judgment is an emotional expression and may be said to mean what it expresses. Approval is an expression of pleasure and disapproval an expression of displeasure. There are, however, many different kinds of pleasantness and unpleasantness; wine and music are pleasant in different ways and yet to neither of them do we ascribe moral goodness; even within the sphere of human actions there are those which please us by conferring some special benefit on us and yet which do not please us in such a way that we attribute moral goodness to them.

> "It is only when a character is considered in general, without reference to our particular interest, that it causes such a feeling or sentiment as denominates it morally good or evil." [13]

151

Moral praise and blame logically presupposes considerable power of discrimination; we must consider a character in general and distinguish between the pleasure which we receive as private people and that which we receive as universal well-wishers. The point of view is all-important; a character can appear in different lights when regarded with reference to the good or evil it tends to produce for self, for family, for country or for humanity. The strictly ethical point of view is the humanitarian, which would demand that even patriotism be limited by consideration of the universal good. It is evident that, for Hume, reason or rationality is an essential element of the moral judgment, since there is presupposed an attitude of impartiality; on the other hand, feeling and desire are also necessary, since by itself the impartial point of view would leave us cold and inactive did we not participate by sympathy in the feelings of others.

Hume's ethical theory is based on a distinction between the many natural virtues and the one "artificial" virtue, justice. The topic of justice covers the sphere of man's so-called natural rights, the general theory of government, international relations, and the rules regarding sex. Hume did not accept the theory of certain self-evident or intuitively discerned natural rights; rather he thought it possible to provide a psychological explanation for what had traditionally been regarded as natural rights. In a broad sense, natural rights can be brought under the headings of property and promises. Hume had little to say concerning the rights of life and liberty; his discussions of "property and promises," on the other hand, were very searching. In essence, property is anything of which we cannot rightly be deprived and may be taken to include life and liberty.

In order to show that justice is an artificial virtue, Hume considers the fact that we often seem to have no natural motive to pay our debts, since we cannot connect the payment with self-interest and have no love for our creditor. The only motive which would cover all cases is a love of justice for its own sake and an "abhorrence of villainy," but this is a motive which is inconceivable in man in his natural state. We may understand Hume to be saying, as most sociologists and psychologists would say today, that the tendency to do what is right in such circumstances is due to training or conditioning; it is a matter of habit-formation, or perhaps one can say that it is a matter of individual acceptance of certain social standards which have been impressed upon us during the process of education. But if ideals of justice have been communicated to us in this manner, we may nevertheless reflect that the individual must have had, from the beginning, a readiness to accept the conventions which society imposes on him or at least the majority must have had such a susceptibility. The actual argument of Hume is based on the dubious premise "that all virtuous actions derive their merit only from virtuous motives and are considered merely as signs of those motives." [14] But actions are often regarded as right even though they spring from a selfish motive; thus if I pay my debt out of a desire to maintain my credit, I have still done the right thing. Rightness may be taken to mean conformity of an action to certain rules, without regard for a man's reason for doing the thing. Hume appears to be overemphasizing the importance of motive in judging the value of actions. His reasoning was founded on such a case as blaming a father for neglecting a child because this shows a lack of natural affection. The person who finds himself wanting in some natural affection may hate himself on this account and perform the action from a sense of duty in order to acquire the virtuous motive or at least to disguise from himself his lack of it.[15] Here Hume appeals to the usual or the normal as a standard to be called "the natural." What is natural in this sense, however, is

153

merely the customary or conventional in some group and differs from one society to the next. One must postulate a will to conformity which supplies a motive for following the rules of justice, whatever they may be, in the absence of any other motive.

The conclusion which Hume drew from the lack of a "natural" motive for observing the laws of equity was that the sense of justice and injustice is not derived from nature, but arises from education and human convention. Hume's attitude is that of a naturalistic sociologist who seeks an explanation of morality in terms of human nature. Like the Sophists and Epicurus he believed that justice, from top to bottom, including man's so-called natural rights, was a result of artifice or contrivance; it was an invention by which man, by means of intelligence, remedies what is lacking in his instincts and emotions. We have already noticed that this presupposes a certain educability on the part of man. We may also say that nature has provided most men with a sense of honor which leads them to respect the fundamental conventions which are the basis of their lives and of their hopes for future security. This corresponds to Kant's respect for the moral law or the intuitionist's desire to do what is right. The system of natural rights may be an invention of intelligence, but the will to conform to laws which seem to be for the good of the society in which we live, may not be wholly a product of training, but in part something inherent in man's nature.

Hume's account of the origin of justice, that is, of what are called man's natural rights, and especially those concerned with property, may be stated briefly as follows: the idea of property, the thought that a given object or piece of land belongs to an individual or a group in such a way that it would be wrong to deprive them of it is a fiction or invention or convention which would inevitably occur to an

154

intelligent being in such a world as that in which man finds himself. This *belonging*—in the sense that a watch belongs to a man—is a relation between a person and a thing which cannot be discovered by the senses and is likewise neither self-evident nor capable of being deduced from any self-evident relation. It is something established by a given society and is observed by all loyal members of that society.

> "Our property is nothing but those goods, whose constant possession is established by the laws of society, that is, by the laws of justice." [16]

It is evident that Hume does not use the word *justice* in the sense of a fair or equitable distribution of good and evil as this might be made in abstraction from tradition; the original distribution may be based on force or chance rather than merit; still justice, according to Hume's basic conception, is the maintenance of the original distribution save in so far as it is modified by a voluntary surrender either for other goods or services or out of sheer good-will. In short, justice, for Hume, was by definition the *status quo* and he does not suggest any other idea of justice which might serve as a basis for criticism of the existing distribution.

The idea of rights and possessions antedates recorded history; Hume was therefore not in a position to describe its actual origin in the dim regions of prehistory. But, looking at the nature of man, we see that he can only live with the aid of his fellows. In society, says Hume, his weakness is replaced by strength, his stupidity and inefficiency by skill and his hazardous life by one of relative security. Men, in their uncultivated state, may fail to perceive the advantages of society but the natural appetite between the sexes unites them "until a new tie takes place in their concern for their common offspring." The family is, therefore, the most elemental form of society. But man also has anti-social tendencies, especially selfishness. How selfish is man? Hume ventures the opinion that

> "though it is rare to meet with one who loves any single person better than himself, yet it is as rare to meet with one in whom all the kind affections taken together, do not overbalance all the selfish." [17]

There is a degree of altruism within the family which goes along with family-egoism in the relations of families to each other. This family-egoism tends to unfit men for larger societies. Justice was invented to remedy this situation. It is especially concerned with the laws of property, which is a matter of goods, which, in turn, are either those of mind, of body or of fortune. Hume passes over the goods of the mind and those of the body all too lightly; we may indeed be deprived of the goods of the mind by intellectual tyranny and of those of the body by slavery. He chooses to devote all his attention to external possessions which others are able to take from us, while, at the same time, there is not a sufficient quantity of them to satisfy everyone's desires. It is because of the instability of the possession of these goods as well as their scarcity that they tend to produce social disorders.

Man's limited benevolence, his love for his family and his friends, could not produce social peace did he not establish a convention entered into by all members of society to "leave everyone in the peaceful enjoyment of what he may acquire by his fortune and industry." What is a convention? It is not a promise in an explicit sense, since Hume is shortly to undertake to explain how promises themselves rest on a prior convention.

"It is only a general sense of common interest; which sense all members of the society express to one another. . . . I observe that it will be for my interest to leave another in possession of his goods, provided he will do the same with regard to me." "Two men who pull the oars of a boat, do it by an agreement or convention, although they have never given promises to each other."[18]

Languages are likewise established by conventions without any promise; in the same way gold and silver are common measures of exchange. The difference between promise and convention may, perhaps, be explained as follows. A convention is an implicit promise; it is something which would be promised were language available in which to promise. Language is itself the fundamental convention; rights and duties, property, promises, and, we may add, marriage, royalty, nobility, serfdom, slavery, etc., can all be traced back to this wonderful invention. Both Hobbes and Locke had founded government on a hypothetical promise; Hume makes it clear that back of the idea of a promise there is the fundamental convention of language itself which includes the ideas of both property and promises. Natural rights are basic conventions going back to prelinguistic understandings or agreements.

Justice is, therefore, says Hume, not founded, as the rationalists supposed, on the discovery of the immutable relations of ideas, since property would not exist in a world where the institution was useless. It is based on man's selfishness and limited generosity and the scarcity of external goods in comparison with man's desires. If we remember the poetic fiction of the golden age we find, by substituting in imagination either unlimited generosity for man's selfishness or a superabundance of external goods for the present scarcity, that in such conditions property would be unnecessary and there would be no mine and thine. Justice, in this sense, exists because most individuals perceive that it is, as a system, essential to their own existence and happiness.

> "Without justice, society must immediately dissolve, and every one fall into that savage and solitary condition, which is infinitely worse than the worst situation that can possibly be supposed in society." [19]

Everyone is aware of the interest he has in maintaining the institutions of society and tends to make known his resolution to act according to these institutions on condition that others do likewise. When society becomes large and complex men may lose sight of their interest in maintaining justice and follow a lesser and more pressing desire; but we never fail to feel the danger involved in the injustice of others. We participate sympathetically in the resentment which their victims feel toward those who injure them.

Hume tends to make us aware of the positive or historical element in what we consider to be right; he does not wholly refute the notion that there are certain higher principles of reason which ought to regulate our conduct. It is true that reason can discover no self-evident relation between an individual and his possessions. A watch belongs to a given man, or a farm to a family or a territory to a nation because the "world" or "society" recognizes these claims; after a time, the owners may lose them even by sheer conquest and no longer be regarded as their rightful owners. When we seek to adjudicate such claims we necessarily consider history. But a rationalist may say that it is still possible to believe that ethical reason issues such universal principles as "Every human being is to be regarded as an end in himself" or "One should act according to principles which

158

make for the common good" or "All should be given equal *consideration* even if there is some reason based on the common good why some persons should receive unequal *treatment.*" It is still possible to maintain that reason tells us that we should act in such a way as to gain the approval of an impartial and benevolent spectator who seeks the maximum good of all human beings. Hume's conception of justice may be called conventional in a specific sense; an opposing "rational" conception would be based on a combination of the principle of impartiality with the thought of the common good.

Justice, understood as the system or institution of property, is based, Hume says, on utility both to the individual and to society. Nevertheless, a direct application of utility in the distribution of goods, a giving to each what would be most useful for him to have, is impracticable. The relation of fitness, in the sense in which it might be useful for a given man to have, let us say, a farm, might be common to a number of individuals; furthermore, this matter of fitness is subject to so many conflicting arguments and men are so "partial and passionate" in judging such matters that such a rule would be incompatible with the peace of society. The details of distribution, where they cannot be determined by usefulness, are handed over to the process known as *the association of ideas,* which plays such a great part in Hume's philosophy in general. When a man has possessed a thing for a length of time a connection or association is established in people's minds between that thing and that person and the individual is regarded as the rightful owner of the thing. In some passages Hume follows in the Hobbesian and Lockean tradition of a social contract. If we seek to reconstruct in imagination the process by which the convention of property was established and imagine that what actually took place by slow stages was accomplished in a short time, we see that a group of men, in order to establish peace as

159

quickly as possible, would agree among themselves that "everyone continue to enjoy what he is at present master of." [20] In comment upon this we may point out that it presupposes a condition of approximate equality among the original contractors; if a few possessed very large holdings and the majority nothing at all, it is likely that some redistribution would have to take place before the social contract could be set up. The fact seems to be that Hume was in process of passing beyond the social contract theory; the setting up of social institutions by a formal act of promising was too fanciful an idea to be worked out in detail. When men start to reflect they find themselves in a society in which rights and privileges are already recognized. Nevertheless, the Humean theory that property is primarily a matter of the association of ideas, that is, of custom, seems to contain a large measure of truth. The four principles by which "justice" assigns property, *occupation, prescription, accession* and *succession,* are all easily understood as matters of a connection established in people's imaginations. Occupation is merely the easy method of letting each person keep what he has; prescription considers the length of time that the owner has had the thing; accession gives us "the fruits of our gardens, the offspring of our cattle and the work of our slaves," [21] while the rules of succession are the principles of inheritance. Even our alleged right to the product of our labor is founded on the fact that when we have produced a thing, we have established a strong association between ourselves and that thing. Although Hume's personal attitude seems to have been conservative and his purpose in the *Treatise* primarily one of psychological and sociological explanation, we can easily see that there is nothing in Hume's theory of property which would wholly exclude expropriation for the common good by a socialistic state.

Hume's discussion of the duty of promise-keeping

is highly significant with reference both to rationalism and to the social contract theory. With reference to the former, promise-keeping has always been a shining example of a self-evident duty. The social contract theory, on the other hand, may be regarded as an attempt to reduce all our duties to this one obligation; it is *as if* we had promised to obey the law, to respect our fellow-citizen's property, etc. The *as if* statements are all true and yet it may be questioned whether we have gained anything by the introduction of the notion of an imaginary promise. The essential doctrine of Hume is that the convention of language, by which the word *promise* has a meaning, precedes and is the basis of any particular act of promising and the conventions of language cannot rest on any prior act of promising. To promise consists essentially in saying *I promise* in a tone of voice which excludes the possibility that I am joking. Hume points out that *to promise* is not *to resolve* to do something, neither is it *to desire* to do a thing. I am morally bound by my promise even though I promised falsely in the sense that I had no intention of doing the thing when I promised.

> "When a man says he promises anything, he in effect expresses a resolution of performing it; and along with that, by making use of this form of words, subjects himself to never being trusted again in case of failure." [22]

Hume's analysis, while no doubt substantially correct, specifies too heavy a penalty; some promises are more important than others; the promise-breaker may merely impair his credit and people, having short memories, and needing his co-operation, may trust him again notwithstanding.

The usefulness of promises is connected with co-operation, especially in cases where the mutual services cannot be performed at the same time; it is also connected with buying and selling property at a distance or in dealing with goods which are considered merely in general, as, for example, "ten bushels of corn or five hogsheads of wine." Even at an early stage of social life, people perceive the value of being able to bind themselves by means of promises. They learn that they can satisfy their passions better "in an oblique and artificial manner than by their headlong or impetuous motion." [23] And since they perceive the general usefulness of promises, they view the promise-breaker with uneasiness and resentment and honor those who faithfully fulfil their obligations. Property and promises may both be regarded as fundamental inventions of the human mind; the old question as to the origin of the ideas is irrelevant and meaningless; we only know that we have them. No one who understands the words *I promise* can fail to know that violation of promises involves some degree of moral turpitude unless there is a good reason why the promise should not be kept. Common sense tells us that a promise is not binding if it involves doing something wrong, such as committing a crime; keeping such a promise would be violating our previous implicit promise to obey the laws. Furthermore, a promise may have been extorted from us by violence or threat of violence; it would be contrary to the common good were such promises to be regarded as binding. The *prima facie* wrongfulness of violating property and promises is an obvious implication of the conventional meanings of the words, although these same conventional meanings also permit exceptions.

Man's instincts and emotions were not sufficient to establish a happy and fruitful life; his intelligence had to intervene with two great fictions; on the one hand we fancy that a thing can *belong* to a person even though our senses can never discover this alleged "belonging." The other is the fiction that promising is some sort of inner mental act which magically

162

creates a new obligation; in fact, the "act" of promising consists merely in saying "I promise," so that a person, in uttering this magic phrase, cannot possibly be telling a lie, even though he may be planning to pay no attention to his promise; he promises merely by saying that he does. It is conceivable that the institutions of property and promises might be honored apart from any government; the state may be regarded as set up to protect people in their "natural rights." Hume is, therefore, not committed to the view that our basic rights are conferred upon us by the state. They are rather conferred on us by our minds which inform us of the value of property and promises to ourselves and to people in general. The chief difference between Hume's account of natural rights and that of Locke and Thomas Jefferson was that Hume proposed a naturalistic and psychological explanation of the fact that these rights are generally recognized, while Locke and Jefferson regarded natural rights as conferred on men by God. Locke and Jefferson dealt in political ideology which tends to be stated in theological terms.

Hume's theory of government is outside the main interest of this study and can be treated briefly. Government can be regarded as a mechanism by which egoism restrains egoism; in some fashion there arises a set of rulers or magistrates, kings or chiefs, who have an interest in the maintenance of order and no particular interest in promoting the selfish schemes of any of their subjects. Governments, Hume says, do not necessarily or usually arise from a promise on the part of individuals to obey a common ruler; they may arise from force or conquest and yet have a rightful claim to the obedience of the citizens, since even bad government is preferable to anarchy.

"The right of the stronger, in public affairs, is to be received as legitimate and authorized by morality, when not opposed by any other title." [24]

The long succession of Roman emperors was always a matter of superior military power.

"The election of the senate was a mere form, which always followed the choice of the legions. It was by the sword, therefore, that every emperor acquired, as well as defended, his right." [25]

We must either grant that for centuries the world had no legitimate government or else that *might* can indeed establish a government which has a rightful claim to obedience. It is really for everyone's interest to respect the natural rights of his fellows, but men are passionate and short-sighted; they are drawn to the nearer good and neglect the remote. To remedy this fault of human nature, governments are necessary, which are originally monarchical in character but which may become republican when people suffer tyrannical and unjust treatment from their kings. The obligation to obey the laws established by our rulers is not founded on the legitimacy of the right to rule of these kings or magistrates, since few governments can endure a close scrutiny of their origins, but rather on the general usefulness of conformity to the social order; if it is obvious that this usefulness is illusory then we have a right to rebel and to attempt to set up a new government. In short, it would seem that we have generally a *prima facie* obligation to obey the laws of the state in which we live; this obligation, however, is not absolute; there may be circumstances in which it would be our duty to disobey the laws and to attempt to overthrow the established order.

The principles of international law, says Hume, do not supersede the laws of nature, that is, the fundamental principles of justice which are "the stability of possession, its transference by consent and the performance of promises." [26] The same laws apply to the relations of states but with less force

164

than to the relations of individuals. It is generally accepted in practice, although not openly avowed, that

> "there is a system of morals calculated for princes much more free than that which ought to govern private persons." [27]

Justice, the strict recognition of the rights of other nations and adherence to treaties, although desirable, is not as necessary or indispensable in the case of the relations of states as in the relations of individuals to each other. The human race can continue to exist even under unjust international relations; for this reason we give

> "a greater indulgence to a prince or minister who deceived another, than to a private gentleman who breaks his word of honor." [28]

Similar reasoning is applied by Hume to the double standard of morals with reference to the two sexes; since the evil consequences of a lack of chastity are greater and more obvious in the case of the female, she is subject to stricter regulation. In short, these two instances of double standards afford evidence in support of the view that moral principles are founded on considerations of utility. These arguments suggest that Hume's theory of ethics countenances moral laxity of various sorts; it may be accused of founding *what ought to be done* on *what is done*. The fact is that, strictly interpreted, Hume's naturalistic ethics is silent concerning *what ought to be done* and merely offers a sociological theory concerning moral judgments as they actually occur.

Sympathy is the basic principle used by Hume in explanation of the aesthetic and moral judgment. We tend to adopt in imagination the feelings and wishes of those whom we observe or consider. It is sympathy which explains our love of fame; our self-esteem is enhanced when we think of others admiring us. Sympathy also explains our unadmirable tendency to esteem the rich and powerful; we put ourselves in their favored situations and enjoy in imagination their luxuries and grandeur. We sympathize both with individuals and with whole societies, and, in so far as we do, we wish for their good and view with resentment actions which tend to injure them. Sympathy is the basis of the so-called moral sense. Justice is a virtue because it has a tendency to the good of mankind; the same is true of loyalty to our leaders, the principles of international law and the rules of modesty and good manners. All these, Hume thinks, are mere contrivances for the good of society. Bernard de Mandeville, as we have seen, had previously regarded all moral principles as the effects of artifice and education used by politicians to control the passions of men and to turn them toward the public good by the motives of shame and honor. Against this view, Hume cites the fact that there are many virtues which tend primarily to the good of the individual; he also urges that education could not teach us the fundamental meanings of the ethical predicates. He speaks of the moral sense as the faculty by which we apprehend the meanings of certain phrases such as just and unjust, morally good and morally bad. His psychological account, in terms of sympathy, may be taken as telling us how the moral sense operates, much as an account of the structure and functioning of the eye tells us how we see and yet does not disprove the existence of a unique faculty of the mind, namely, vision, the sense of color and shape, by which we apprehend qualities indefinable in terms of the other senses.

The difference between the natural virtues and the artificial virtue of justice is that the latter has to do with the following of rules which tend as "a general scheme or system" to the public good, although the individual action may be injurious to society.

> "Judges take from a poor man to give to a rich; they bestow on the dissolute the labor of the industrious; and put into the hands of the vicious the means of harming both themselves and others." [28]

The natural virtues, such as kindness, courtesy, courage or frugality tend more directly either to the good of others or of oneself; they do not depend on the maintenance of a system, although it is true enough that even such actions may fail accidentally of their purpose and produce evil rather than good.

In both cases, sympathy is the basis of approval and disapproval. But sympathy is a highly variable factor; we naturally sympathize more with those close to us in space and time or in blood and temperament than with those who are remote or markedly different. From this it seems to follow that the goodness or badness of actions or characters would be as variable as visual size and shape and would lack all objectivity. This difficulty is guarded against by Hume by the observation that we do not merely express our actual feelings when we praise or blame; we rather ascribe moral virtues according to what we think would be our feelings were we closely associated with the persons we are judging.

> "It is therefore from the influence of characters and qualities upon those who have an intercourse with any person, that we blame or praise him." [29]

We thus prevent the contradictions which would arise from our perpetual change of relationship with people; we "arrive at a more stable judgment of things." This substitution of potential feelings for actual feel-

167

ings gives rise to our habit of regarding the ethical judgment as a matter of reason. Reason is in fact

> "nothing but a general calm determination of the passions, founded on some distant view or reflection." [30]

Reason in ethical discourse is not something wholly dissociated from the dynamic places of human nature.

The ethical judgment, in Hume's account, is not a simple emotional expression; it is ambiguous, being in part an expression of a pleasure or displeasure which we actually feel and in part an expression of an opinion concerning what we would feel under certain other conditions. In so far as it is an emotional expression it cannot be either true or false; but in so far as it is an expression of opinion it can be in agreement with facts or contrary to them, and, therefore, true or false. Hume was well aware that ethical judgment demands and presupposes an "objective point of view," a certain disregarding of our immediate feelings and desires. We substitute the hypothetical emotional response of the impartial spectator for our more vivid feelings and this is to be considered the voice of reason. Even this maneuver does not reveal anything objective in the sense of naive realism; the ethical judgment is always, strictly speaking, subjective. But, using the idea of a hypothetical spectator, we have gained what may be called a sufficient degree of objectivity for practical purposes, since it enables us to escape from the conflicts and instability of our actual feelings. An intuitionist would say that a more exact analysis of such terms as right and wrong, morally good and morally evil, reveals that they are not capable of being defined empirically at all. Right does not mean that which *is* approved by those in close contact with the agent or by an impartial bystander or by God;

it means that which ought to be approved by every judge, human or divine; it is that in which every one ought to take pleasure whether he does or not. Hume, however, does not proclaim a doctrine of indefinable ethical predicates; he rather leaves them, as we have seen, in a state of ambiguity, partly as emotional expressions and partly as opinions concerning potential emotional responses of an enlightened, impartial and benevolent spectator. If we stress the second interpretation then Hume is a cognitivist who defines the ethical predicates in terms of the feelings of an imaginary onlooker, surprisingly similar to the traditional idea of God.

Human nature, says Hume, is characterized by extensive sympathy and limited generosity; it is on the former that our moral judgments depend. We are pleased by what benefits others and pained by what injures them, although in fact we are unwilling to do anything to help them. In part we are universal benevolent spectators and in part narrow egoists. Aesthetic judgment is also founded on sympathy; a building which seems inconvenient and likely to fall down is judged to be ugly.

> "The imagination adheres to the *general* view of things, and distinguishes the feelings which they produce from those which arise from our particular and momentary situation." [31]

In ethical judgment we respond with pleasure or uneasiness to character-traits and actions and thus assign the ethical predicates, which seemingly designate objective features but which are in reality merely expressions of our feelings, actual or potential. The explanation of the ethical judgment in terms of sympathy covers, as we have seen, both the artificial virtue, justice, and the natural virtues. The latter can be divided into four groups; they are either self-regarding or other-regarding and again each class can

169

be further divided by asking whether the actions involved are immediately agreeable or disagreeable, or only beneficial or injurious in their consequences. Among the self-regarding virtues are listed prudence, temperance, frugality, assiduity, enterprise and dexterity.[32] Hume's ethical theory is formulated in terms of virtue rather than duty; in this his procedure resembles that of Aristotle rather than that of Kant. The self-regarding virtues are traits of temperament or character and have nothing to do with the problem of motivation, in a sense in which the motive might confer moral goodness; their motive would commonly be self-love. Nevertheless, the facts that these traits are admired and that their ascription to a given person constitutes praise is readily explained by Hume's theory of sympathy; we adopt in imagination the wishes and feelings of the person whom we are considering and therefore regard these traits with pleasure. This theory of the self-regarding virtues contrasts with that of Hutcheson, who, as we saw, identified virtue with benevolence. No doubt Hutcheson would have granted that the traits in question were qualities tending to the happiness of the individual and also contributing to his usefulness to society; they nevertheless, do not show *moral goodness,* which involves an element of benevolence.

A character is said to be good in a special sense, which reveals such traits as generosity, humanity, compassion, gratitude, friendship, fidelity, disinterestedness and liberality. In this case our emotions of approval and disapproval are primarily determined by sympathy with those who have intercourse with the person in question or are affected by his actions. There is also an element of sympathy with the agent himself; love is immediately agreeable and hatred immediately disagreeable; we may approve or disapprove without thinking of the probable consequences of the actions of such a person. A man may, from

friendship, sacrifice a considerable interest of his own
for a small concern of his friend; such an action may
have little effect on society as a whole and actually
result in a smaller amount of good in the world than
would otherwise have been the case; still the action
may be approved out of sympathy with the agent; we
share in imagination the pleasurable feelings of
friendship. Benevolence, declares Hume, echoing
Hutcheson, is the supreme virtue; even its weak-
nesses are amiable. We consider a man in all his relations in society, and love or hate him according to the
effects he produces on those who have dealings with
him.

> "And it is a most certain rule, that if there is no
> relation in life in which I would not wish to stand
> to a particular person, his character must so far
> be allowed to be entirely perfect. This is the ulti-
> mate test of merit and virtue." [33]

Hume here purposes a criterion of moral perfection
based on imaginative experimentation. A possible criticism would be that a guilty man, brought before a
judge, might wish that the judge would not be morally
perfect, but rather lenient in this one instance. Hume
would probably have answered that this guilty man,
as a citizen, would wish the judge to fulfil his function
without undue sympathy. The test of virtue can only
be in what we wish when we regard characters in
detachment from our own private interests. The doctrine that benevolence is the supreme virtue is open
to the criticism that it involves taking benevolence in
an unusually extended sense. Thus a man who acts
according to rules tending to the common good and
fulfils all his obligations to others may be considered
virtuous even though he does not feel love for his
fellow men. On the other hand, a man who sins
against justice is still condemned even though his

171

motive is benevolence toward certain particular persons.

The natural abilities are distinguished from the moral virtues by the fact that they are, to a great extent, not under control of the will. Voluntary actions can be controlled by rewards and punishments and by praise and blame, while natural abilities are not capable of being changed by these means. The ancient philosophers, perhaps because they were not so much under the sway of the notion of a divine legislator enforcing his laws by supernatural sanctions, considered as virtues certain traits which are not strictly under control of the will. They made prudence or wisdom a cardinal virtue and considered courage and magnanimity to be virtues although neither wisdom, courage nor high-mindedness can be directly produced by any individual choosing to have them. The ancient virtues are merely certain admired character-traits; they are admired because they are useful either to the individual or to others. Whether they are innate or acquired as a result of effort on the part of the individual is irrelevant to their usefulness. The virtues in the Aristotelian sense are not sharply distinguished from the natural abilities; neither involves choice in the sense in which choice can be controlled by reward and punishment. Hume's theory of approval based on sympathy covers both, since both are regarded with pleasure by the disinterested spectator because of their usefulness.

In the preceding pages we have commented upon the *Treatise* in so far as it bears on ethical theory. We may now give much briefer consideration to the *Enquiry concerning Morals*, which Hume regarded as the best of all his works. It is, like the other *Enquiries*, a re-writing of the *Treatise* in a more popular vein and contains a good many citations of Greek and Roman authors. There is no reason why the *Enquiry* should be commented upon in detail here,

172

although there are several statements of doctrine to which it is desirable to call attention. In the first Section the following passage occurs:

> "The end of all moral speculations is to teach us our duty; and by proper representations of the deformity of vice and the beauty of virtue, beget correspondent habits and engage us to avoid the one and embrace the other." [34]

This raises an important question concerning the primary purpose of moral philosophy; is it directed on the discovery of truth or is its purpose one of edification? At the commencement of the discussion of morals in the *Treatise* Hume had said:

> "Morality is a subject that interests us above all others; we fancy the peace of society to be at stake in every decision concerning it; and it is evident that this concern must make our speculations concerning it to be more real and solid than where the subject is in great measure indifferent to us." [35]

It would appear from this passage that Hume's attitude toward morals was primarily theoretical. We merely *fancy* that the peace of society is at stake and our speculations merely *appear* more real and solid because of the seeming practicality of our subject-matter. The preaching of morals, according to this view, belongs more to the clergyman and the political leader than to the philosopher. The passage from the *Enquiry* just cited, on the other hand, admits the existence of duty; the function of the philosopher appears to be rhetorical; his task is merely to portray the beauty of virtue in such eloquent terms that we shall be induced to practice it. We may say that the *Treatise*, in comparison with the *Enquiry*,

173

remains more consistently theoretical in attitude; perhaps the more edifying tone of the *Enquiry* is part of its striving for greater popular appeal. The question is fundamental: should philosophical ethics be a matter of psychological and sociological description and analysis or should the philosopher proclaim a normative truth for all to follow? If we grant that philosophy should, in some sense, be normative then it would be desirable for the philosopher to discover some *reason* why we should do our duty rather than seek to dazzle us with the beauty of self-sacrifice and heroism.

The guiding thread of the *Enquiry concerning Morals* as well as of the Third Book of the *Treatise of Human Nature* is the relation of reason and sentiment; Hume is throughout convinced that morals is a matter not of reason but of sentiment. In the opening section of the *Enquiry* he says that it is probable that the final sentence which pronounces characters and actions amiable or odious, praiseworthy or blamable, depends on some internal sense of feeling, which nature has made universal in the whole species.[36] But, although nature has given all human beings a faculty of moral judgment, she has by no means given them a faculty which judges uniformly. What they have from nature, is merely a general tendency to approve, that is, to regard with pleasure, what seems to make for the good either of the individual or of society; what in detail will make for the good of the one or the other will be a matter of intelligence and information or misinformation; people will necessarily differ with regard to what they approve or disapprove. In the first Appendix entitled *Concerning Moral Sentiment*, Hume formulates his hypothesis as follows:

"It maintains that morality is determined by sentiment. It defines virtue to be whatever mental ac-

174

tion or quality gives to a spectator the pleasing sentiment of approbation and vice the contrary." [37]

This definition, taken literally, implies ego-centric relativism; against this one can cite the fact that such words as *right* and *praiseworthy* mean rather what *ought* to give a spectator a pleasing sentiment of approbation. The words imply qualities having an objective status. Hume attempts to provide for this by his analogy with visual perception where, in judging size, we substitute for the actual sense-datum, what we think *would* be seen by a standard observer at a standard distance; we substitute for our own feelings the hedonic responses of those who are in intimate contact with the person being judged. It is possible to say that for Hume the ethical judgment does have a cognitive content, namely, that it is a judgment concerning what would be the feelings of a certain hypothetical spectator and as such would be either true or false. But such a cool opinion does not seem to be a complete account of a moral judgment, since the latter involves feeling and has a dynamic quality; it is better to say that ethical judgment is ambiguous in nature; there is always at least a pretense of objectivity but at the same time it is an expression of actual feelings. It expresses, or pretends to express, the feeling which we have when we look at the action in a certain frame of mind, namely, as a detached spectator. Against Hume, the intuitionist argues that the ethical predicates all contain the idea of *oughtness* (ought to be, ought to be done, ought to be promoted, ought to be praised, etc.), and that this element of meaning can never be reduced to empirical terms, even though the use of the ethical predicates is always occasioned by our feelings.

We have already considered Hume's conventional theory of justice. In the *Enquiry* he states more

175

clearly than elsewhere that justice is a working arrangement based on power. He considers the hypothetical case of certain non-human but rational creatures intermingled with men, it being supposed that these non-human rationals were possessed of such inferior strength that they were incapable of resistance. We would be bound by the laws of humanity to give gentle usage to these creatures but we would not feel any restraint of justice with regard to them.

> "The great superiority of civilized Europeans above barbarous Indians tempted us to imagine ourselves on the same footing with regard to them (as in the hypothetical case) and made us throw off all restraints of justice, and even of humanity, in our treatment of them. In many nations the female sex are reduced to like slavery, and are rendered incapable of all property, in opposition to their lordly masters." [38]

The question of inequality, that is, differential treatment based on race and sex, is one with which we are sufficiently familiar. Hume explains inequality in terms of his general theory of justice; the difference of power would render equal treatment useless to the stronger; a system of inequality is therefore set up and *is*, in such a world, justice. To those who accept the ideals of democracy, Hume's "justice" seems to be rather a system of injustice. It is possible to defend inequality by taking one's stand on certain rather dubious postulates, namely, to the effect that inequality is really for the good of all considered impartially. Everything depends on the truth of these postulates rather than on ethical theory as such. Hume, however, explains inequality in terms of a disproportion of power. Hume's naturalistic ethics, basing itself on *what is*, that is, on actual relations of power, is conservative in its implications and lacks the fervor of revolutionary equalitarianism. And yet the idea of equality makes a profound appeal to our emotions and makes democracy seem more desirable than some variant of the caste system. This emotional appeal is, however, easily explained in accordance with the fundamental principle of Hume's moral psychology, namely, sympathy.

CHAPTER X

ADAM SMITH

Edward Westermarck states that Adam Smith's *Theory of Moral Sentiments* is the most important contribution to moral psychology made by any British thinker. In contrast with Westermarck's opinion is that of Leslie Stephen, who declares that in reading Adam Smith on morals we do not have an impression of a thinker grappling with a serious problem but rather of an ambitious professor who has found an excellent opportunity for displaying his command of language.[1] H. W. Schneider points out that Adam Smith was originally a student of rhetoric and *belles-lettres* and that the *Theory of Moral Sentiments* was "not only a work in moral philosophy but a literary work in which he exhibited his rhetorical skill. To its rhetorical quality this work owed its immediate popularity and its later unpopularity."[2] The style of Hume is remarkably condensed; that of Adam Smith is more diffuse.

Westermarck, as we have seen, praises Adam Smith's treatise as a contribution to moral psychology. The question may well be asked whether moral psychology is the whole of moral philosophy; many have thought that the moral philosopher has the function of telling us, in some authoritative way, what we

178

ought to do, and of giving us reasons *why* we ought to do it. The basic outlook of Adam Smith's *Theory of Moral Sentiments* is similar to that of Hume; it is, however, less naturalistic in tone and is disposed piously to admire the wisdom of God who gave man his moral sentiments with a view to accomplishing the greatest amount of good. Adam Smith was the successor of Hutcheson in the chair of Moral Philosophy in the University of Glasgow; following the example of Hume, he replaces the theory of a specific moral sense with an elaborate account of the moral sentiments based on sympathy. It is possible to interpret Adam Smith as making no ethical statements at all, that is, solely as a moral psychologist engaged in analysing and explaining our acts of approval and disapproval. On the other hand, he had in mind no clear distinction between meta-ethics and ethics and speaks as one who shares the moral consciousness which he analyses.

In opposition to the moral sense theory of Hutcheson, Adam Smith points out that the moral sense itself should be beyond either praise or blame. In general no sense judges itself, since we do not see the sense of sight nor hear the sense of hearing. Yet if a man applauds what we condemn, we condemn his applause; his enthusiasm for what we think to be wicked strikes us as itself vicious. Furthermore, we do not approve and disapprove by a "peculiar sentiment," since the feeling of approval is different when we approve of a kind action and of an heroic one, just as the feeling of disapproval is different when we disapprove of cruelty and of cowardice. Adam Smith's doctrine is that approval is a matter of sympathy; we approve when we sympathize and disapprove when there is a lack of sympathy. It is in short a question of consonance and dissonance; if you think and act as I think that I would feel and act were I in your situation, I have a pleasant feeling of consonance; but if you feel and act in ways contrary to what I think I would feel and do, then I have an unpleasant feeling of dissonance and this constitutes disapproval.

It will be well for us to retrace our steps for a moment and to consider the ingenious way in which Hume introduces and illustrates sympathy in the *Treatise of Human Nature*. The subject is brought in in connection with the curious topic of our esteem for the rich and powerful.

> "Upon the whole," says Hume, "nothing remains which can give us an esteem for power and riches, and a contempt for meanness and poverty, except the principle of sympathy, by which we enter into the sentiments of the rich and poor and partake of their pleasure and uneasiness." [3]

We observe the operation of sympathy through the whole animal kingdom.

> "Whatever passions we may be activated by, pride, ambition, curiosity, revenge or lust, the soul or animating principle of them all is sympathy; nor would they have any force, were we to abstract entirely from the thoughts and sentiments of others." [4]

Hume tells us that the minds of all men are similar and that just as the motion of the strings is communicated from one string to another, so the affections readily pass from one person to another.[5] In so far as we are concerned for the good of society, it is because of sympathy. The word *sympathy* is used by Hume and Adam Smith to signify not merely commiseration but rather a passing of any sort of feeling or desire from a person observed to the observer. For Adam Smith it denotes "our fellow-feeling with any passion whatever." [6]

> "The mob, when they are gazing at a dancer on the slack-rope, naturally writhe and twist and balance their own bodies, as they see him do, and as they feel that they themselves must do in his situation." [7]

Sympathy, says Adam Smith,

> "does not arise so much from the view of the passion as from that of the situation which excites it." [8] "We sympathize even with the dead, and, overlooking what is of real importance in their situation, that awful futurity which awaits them, we are chiefly affected by those circumstances which strike our senses, but can have no influence on their happiness." [9]

The fear of death is really based on an illusion of the imagination but it puts a great restraint on the injustice of mankind, and while it thus afflicts the individual tends to protect society.[10] We have quoted enough to indicate what Hume and Adam Smith had in mind. According to the theory of the ethical judgment which the two have in common, sympathy, emotional contagion, is the basic explanation of the moral sentiments by which we praise or blame the actions either of others or of ourselves.

The ethical theory of Adam Smith gives a central position to *propriety* of sentiment and action. He refers to the systems of Plato, Aristotle and the Stoics as making propriety the essence of virtue; he then describes the doctrines of Samuel Clarke, Wollaston and Shaftesbury as "more or less inaccurate descriptions of the same fundamental idea." [11] In making the *proper* or the *fitting* the fundamental topic of ethics

181

Adam Smith was thus following classical models. He undertook to offer an account of the "precise or distinct measure by which the fitness or propriety of affection can be ascertained or judged of." [12] This

"precise and distinct measure can be found nowhere but in the sympathetic feelings of the impartial and well-informed spectator." [13]

Unfortunately, Adam Smith's "precise and distinct measure" turns out to be extremely vague and elusive. We may grant that the idea of a spectator is always involved but who is this spectator? Is it ourselves or our neighbors? Adam Smith frequently speaks of the "great inmate, the man within the breast" and we have just quoted the characteristic phrase "the impartial and well-informed spectator." Who is wholly impartial? What is the definition of "well-informed"? Men differ in their opinions concerning what the judgment of an "impartial and well-informed" spectator would be. There is, moreover, a fundamental ambiguity in Adam Smith. Did he mean that the test of propriety is the *feelings* of an individual or did he mean that it is a matter of *opinion* concerning how an "impartial and well-informed" spectator *would* feel? This latter standard is, in its way, cognitive rather than emotive.

With regard to that which is fitting and proper, it is clear that the consonance of the feelings of others with our own feelings does not touch the fundamental meaning of the word. The fitting or proper is not merely that which *is* approved by such and such persons but rather that which *ought* to be approved by every one who considers the case. Adam Smith himself acknowledges that we can and do appeal from actual spectators to an ideal spectator. The all-wise Author of nature has taught men to respect the sentiments of his brethren. Man has been rendered the immediate judge, but an appeal can be made from the sentence pronounced by this first judge to the tribunal of one's own conscience, *i.e.,* the man within the breast. The jurisdiction of our neighbors is founded on our desire for actual praise and our aversion to actual blame. The jurisdiction of the man within is founded on a desire for praise-worthiness and an aversion to blameworthiness.[14] Adam Smith thus comes very close to admitting that praiseworthiness and blameworthiness are in-definable terms. He goes on to point out that the accusations of others shake the confidence of the man within and destroy our tranquillity of mind. The demi-god within the breast, he tells us, is like the demi-gods of the poets, partly of mortal extrac-tion. In such cases a man must appeal to a still higher tribunal, that of the all-seeing judge of the world, whose eye can never be deceived and whose judgments can never be perverted.[15] Thus Adam Smith is led from an actual spectator in this world to a transcendent perfect spectator, God, whose approval and disapproval are, by definition, in accord-ance with the praiseworthiness and blameworthi-ness which really belong to the actions and affections in question. In comment we may say that the idea of God may be eliminated by supposing that certain actions and affections are in themselves fitting apart from any spectator. But it may still be true that we can come to an understanding of the fitting only by way of a consideration of the emotions.

From the standpoint of a strict sentimentalism, moral judgments are neither true nor false; they are merely emotional expressions. However, our emo-tions may be a corrupt guide. Our moral sentiments, says Adam Smith, elaborating on a thought expressed by Hume, are liable to corruption by our tendency to admire the rich and great and to neglect and de-spise persons of mean condition. Only a few are "real and steady admirers of wisdom and virtue. The great mob of mankind are admirers and worshipers of wealth and greatness." [16]

When Adam Smith speaks of corruption of the moral sentiments, he thereby claims an ability to distinguish between authentic and unauthentic moral judgments. When we judge people in a worldly way we no longer have our attention focussed on their characters and deeds in a strict sense. But our tendency to admire the rich and powerful contributes to the stability of society and gives us occasion to admire the wisdom of the creator, as do all our other impulses, however bad they may be from a moral point of view.

"Fortune has . . . great influence over the moral sentiments of mankind, and, according as she is either favorable or adverse, can render the same character the object either of general love and admiration or of universal hatred and contempt. This great disorder in our moral sentiments is by no means, however, without its utility; and we may on this, as well as on many other occasions, admire the wisdom of God even in the weakness and folly of men. Our admiration for success is founded upon the same principles with our respect for wealth and greatness, and is equally necessary for establishing the distinction of ranks and the order of society." [17]

We are thus told that our minds are commonly confused and that we grant moral admiration to those who do not truly deserve it, but that this confusion and corruption of our judgments is nevertheless a manifestation of the wisdom of God. In comment we may say that the doctrine of teleology, while tending to strengthen a belief in God, gives us no moral guidance whatever. Furthermore we see that Adam Smith is obliged to admit the unreliability of our actual feelings; he must ultimately take refuge in the hypothetical feelings of an ideal spectator.

An outstanding feature of Adam Smith's *Theory of Moral Sentiments* is his explanation of the law of *retaliation*. Our feeling that the wrong-doer should suffer is due to sympathy with the resentment of the sufferer. When we think of the anguish of the sufferers, we earnestly take part with them against their oppressors; we enter with eagerness into all their schemes of vengeance.[18] When resentment is excessive it becomes revenge, which is detestable. Nevertheless, resentment of wrong is a useful principle. The present inquiry, Adam Smith tells us, is concerned with fact; we are not concerned with what principles *should* be followed in punishing bad actions "but upon what principles so weak and imperfect a creature as man actually and in fact approves of it."[19] The Author of nature has endowed man with an instinctive approbation of retaliation, which is a process which tends to the preservation of the race. Resentment, either of the injured person or of the spectator, presupposes a notion of rights which have been violated. Hume had previously explained rights as conventional in character and they are not given any new explanation by Adam Smith, who several times refers to Hume in terms of admiration. We may regard Adam Smith as one who largely accepted Hume's naturalistic theory of morals but who added the thought that back of nature there is the wisdom of the creator. Hutcheson emphasized benevolence but Adam Smith brings out the fact that the desire to make wrong-doers suffer is an important and useful part of human nature. He did not accept what we have come to know as the deterrent theory of punishment.

"All men, even the most stupid and unthinking, abhor fraud, perfidy, and injustice, and delight to see them punished. But few men have reflected on the necessity of justice to the existence of society, how obvious soever that necessity may appear to be." [20]

He tells us that punishment is, as a matter of fact, inflicted not for the good of society but because people think it fitting that wicked persons should suffer.

"Nature teaches us to hope, and religion, we suppose, authorizes us to expect,"

that injustice will be punished in a life to come. Punishment after death does not serve to deter mankind who do not see it or know it.

"The justice of God, however, we think, still requires that he should hereafter avenge the injuries of the widow and the fatherless, who are here so often insulted with impunity. In every religion, and in every superstition that the world has ever beheld, accordingly, there has been a Tartarus as well as an Elysium, a place provided for the punishment of the wicked as well as one for the reward of the just." [21]

One can only wonder whether Adam Smith shared to any extent the beliefs mentioned or whether he was only explaining the laws of emotional thinking. Naturalism would assert that morals and religion in general are salutary illusions engendered by man's imagination and his will to racial and social survival. Adam Smith's suave way of expressing himself leaves open the possibility, as he no doubt intended that it should, that he too believed in heaven and hell in some literal sense.

If we regard Adam Smith as the successor of Shaftesbury and Hutcheson we see that he has greatly modified the doctrine that the essence of virtue is disinterested benevolence. Beneficence "is the ornament which embellishes, not the foundation which supports, the building. . . . Justice, on the contrary, is the main pillar which supports the whole edifice. . . . In order to enforce the observation of justice, therefore, nature has implanted in the human heart that consciousness of ill-desert, those terrors of merited punishment, which attend upon its violation, as the great safeguard of the association of mankind, to protect the weak, to curb the violent and to chastise the guilty." [22]

Here emphasis is placed upon the thought that human rights are maintained by resentment and the fear which it produces in those who are tempted to violate the rights of others. The social order is looked upon as evidence of the wisdom of nature. In place of benevolence, Adam Smith emphasizes self-respect. Why do we ever sacrifice our own interests? We are always in fact much more affected by what concerns ourselves than by what concerns others.

"It is not the soft power of humanity, it is not that feeble spark of benevolence which nature has lighted up in the human heart, that is thus capable of counter-acting the strongest impulses of self-love. . . . It is reason, principle, conscience, the inhabitant of the breast, the man within, the great judge and arbiter of our conduct. . . . It is from him that we learn the real littleness of ourselves. . . . It is not love of our neighbor. . . . which prompts us to practice those sublime virtues (of self-sacrifice). . . . It is the love of what is honorable and noble, of the grandeur and dignity and superiority of our own characters." [23]

The honest man feels the truth of the stoical maxim that for one man to deprive another unjustly of anything is more contrary to nature than poverty, pain or death. One should regard himself

> "as a citizen of the world, a member of the vast commonwealth of nature. . . . We should view ourselves not in the light in which our own selfish passions are apt to place us, but in the light in which any other citizen of the world would view us." [24]

The ideal which is set up by Adam Smith is that of a stoical and rational self-control. The man of virtue thus tends to identify himself with the man within the breast, the impartial spectator. We experience true self-approbation in proportion to the degree of self-command which we display.

The theory of conscience propounded by Adam Smith renders it identical with a *point of view*. When we look at others and ourselves with impartiality and feel satisfaction and dissatisfaction only as a detached spectator would feel them we have gained the standpoint of justice. This may be regarded as presupposed in the use of the ethical predicates; whether we are truly impartial or not, that is, whether we are or are not, truly speaking as citizens of the world, still impartiality is the logical presupposition of such words as *right, just, noble* and their opposites. But Adam Smith was aware that we live in a world of strife in which moral sentiments become instruments of partisan zeal. In war and in international negotiation, the laws of justice are little observed; truth and fairdealing are neglected. This is because in war and in international relations, we are commonly chiefly in contact with our fellow-countrymen, whose interests and passions are similar to our own; "the partial spectator is at hand, the impartial one at a great distance." [25] The animosity of religious sectarianism and political parties often leads to even more atrocious actions than the passions of hostile nations. Rebels and heretics are those unfortunate persons who happen to be of the weaker party. In time of civil and religious strife, there may be a few who observe a true impartiality but they are held in contempt by the zealots of both parties.

"Of all corrupters of moral sentiments, therefore, faction and fanaticism have always been by far the greatest." [26]

We see, then, that here again Adam Smith must distinguish between authentic and corrupt moral sentiment and that authentic moral judgment is precisely that in which selfishness is overcome and in which we praise and blame only as an impartial and benevolent spectator would do.

We are assisted in overcoming our natural bias by moral rules, which Adam Smith regards as inductive generalizations. The passions seem reasonable as long as we continue to feel them. It is, therefore, difficult for men to judge themselves and this fact counts against the theory of a moral sense as a peculiar faculty, since, if there were such a faculty, men would judge their own conduct with more accuracy than they judge that of other men. But nature has provided a remedy for man's tendency to self-deception; this is the habit of forming general rules by observing the conduct of others. Some of their actions shock our natural sentiments and we hear those around us expressing a similar detestation. We resolve never to be guilty of such actions. Thus the rules of morality are derived inductively from what our moral sentiments approve and disapprove. After the rules have been established, they come to be regarded as the ultimate foundations of right and wrong; but in truth the rules of conduct are derived by a process of generalization from particular instances. The recollection of these established rules often restrains us from acting in ways which would seem

189

appropriate if we listened only to the passions which animate us at the moment.

The theory of Adam Smith that the moral rules are inductive generalizations implies that the rules in question may have exceptions. It would follow that our moral sentiments have the power of setting aside any of the rules which we have set up, namely, in unusual circumstances. The rules have only a *prima facie* binding power. They challenge us to take thought and to ask ourselves whether we are prepared to make the exception itself a rule. A second point to be noted is that the rules of morality correspond to the customs and institutions of society. The rule that we are not to steal is a mere corollary of the institution, or, as Hume put it, the convention of property. The basic thought is that we have rights of various kinds; the moral rules follow, in many cases, from these rights and have exceptions only to the extent that we suppose that the rights themselves have exceptions. Adam Smith's doctrine of "inductive generalizations" overlooks the part played by the fundamental institutions of society. We can agree that laws, customs and institutions are all expressions of man's moral sentiments; it is also true that social institutions and customs greatly influence the moral sentiments. Adam Smith was right in maintaining, however, that the established rules of morality tend to correct man's egoistic bias.

A reverence for the general rules of morality, we are told, is enhanced by an opinion "first impressed by nature and afterwards confirmed by reasoning and philosophy" that the rules of morality are the commands of the Deity who will finally reward those who are obedient and punish those who are transgressors. Adam Smith was by no means an out and out naturalist; he may be described rather as a philosophical theist. But if we take him as a naturalist, then we may suppose him to be telling us that it is *nature,* that is, some instinct tending to the preservation of society, which conjures up the images of the gods and their commandments and the notion of supernatural sanctions. The whole complex of ideas may be regarded as a set of socially useful fictions. In support of naturalism, one may say that there are difficulties in the idea of divine commandments taken literally. A king issues decrees which he enforces by penalties; the will of an omnipotent being is necessarily fully realized. The naturalist argues that the Deity cannot be conceived in wholly unambiguous terms; God, as the supreme commander, cannot be fused into a single entity with God, the omnipotent being. Nevertheless, Adam Smith was justified in regarding the *belief* that moral laws are commands of the Deity as *natural,* that is, in accordance with the laws which govern man's emotional thinking. If now we follow the lead of this natural tendency we must suppose that

> "the happiness of mankind, as well as of all other rational creatures, was the original purpose intended by the Author of nature . . ." "If we act contrary to the teachings of our moral sentiments, we seem to obstruct the scheme which the Author of nature has established for the happiness and perfection of the world and to declare ourselves . . . in some measure, the enemies of God." [27]

In general virtue is rewarded even in this life, but to cover the exceptional cases in which "violence and artifice prevail over sincerity and justice" we must postulate a future life. Mankind are generally disposed to place great confidence in the honesty of religious people, since they are thought to have a keen sense of the "great Superior" who is finally to recompense them for their deeds.

Ought the sense of duty to be the sole principle of our conduct? Adam Smith draws no line between action for the sake of duty and action animated by concern for the will of God. Some theologians have taught that the pure love of God should take the place of every other motive. This doctrine is declared by Adam Smith to be no part of Christianity, since this religion, after telling us to love God, tells us also to love others as we love ourselves; it thus admits a permissible sphere of love for ourselves and other humans. The sense of duty, he thinks, should be the ruling motive but not the only one. There are relations in which we would prefer to be served from love of ourselves rather than from a sense of duty. It cannot be said that it is desirable that people should be animated only by a desire to fulfil the laws of morality. Adam Smith's views on the subject of duty as the sole motive of virtuous action may be compared with those proclaimed by Kant somewhat later. The latter takes the position that duty for duty's sake is the only truly virtuous motive, although altruistic actions may be amiable. The position of Adam Smith was that the quintessence of virtue is found when we act according to the decrees of the "man within the breast, the great inmate;" nevertheless, it is desirable that we should be animated by love and friendship in the intimate relationships of life, although love and friendship do not justify us in going against the laws of conscience.

The essential doctrine of Adam Smith in moral philosophy (and economics as well) is the theory of natural teleology, which is indistinguishable from philosophical theism. This is seen in his reflections on the disappointments of wealth and power to those who have achieved them. Our imagination normally paints the advantages of riches and power in glowing colors. This deception and illusion "rouses and keeps in motion the industry of mankind." [28] Evidently, God or nature thought industry better than idleness, presumably because more conducive to happiness. The following sentences show how the "wisdom of nature" proceeds in order "to advance the interest of society and afford means to the multiplication of the species." It is first laid down, in an anticipation of Malthus, that "the produce of the soil maintains at all times nearly that number of inhabitants which it is capable of maintaining." [29] And then Adam Smith proceeds to speak of the rich and the poor.

"The rich only select from the heap what is most precious and agreeable. They consume little more than the poor, and in spite of their natural selfishness and rapacity, though they mean only their own convenience . . . divide with the poor the produce of all their improvements. They are led by an invisible hand to make nearly the same distribution of the necessaries of life which would have been made had the earth been divided into equal proportions among all its inhabitants, and thus, without intending it, without knowing it advance the general good." [30]

Thus all is for the best in the best of all possible worlds. The invisible hand, of which Adam Smith speaks, is not to be thought of as supernatural intervention but rather as an immanent teleology, the mysterious "wisdom of nature" which brings it about that selfishness promotes the universal good in spite of itself. It is hard to see what ethical conclusions can be drawn from these considerations of natural teleology. If we are selfish, we are probably acting in accordance with a scheme which tends in the long run to the general good. If we are altruistic, we may be defeating, if that is possible, the divine plan. If we yield to our corrupt moral sentiments and admire the rich and powerful rather than those who are truly virtuous, we are still acting in accordance with the wisdom of nature. The fact seems to be that the point of view of natural teleology is irrelevant to that of ethics, since, whatever we do, the wisdom of nature will prevail in the end. The point may also be made that we are not obliged to look on nature and society from the point of view of purpose; chance variation and natural selection are often held to be a sufficient explanation. The doctrine of Adam Smith tends to acquiescence in the established order, however unjust and cruel it may seem to be, since it is an expression of the inscrutable wisdom of God.

Hutcheson had stated that the moral sense ordains the greatest happiness of the greatest number as the proper guide; Adam Smith points out that we often feel that we are morally bound to promote the greater good of the smaller number. Speaking of the antagonism which prevailed in the 18th century between the French and the British, he remarks that although France contains three times as many people as Britain, nevertheless the good British citizen will not prefer, on all occasions, the interest of France.

The "wisdom which contrived the system of human affections, as well as that of every other part of nature, seems to have judged that the interest of the great society of mankind would be best promoted by directing the principal attention of each individual to that particular portion of it, which was most within the sphere both of his abilities and his understanding." [31]

The doctrine of the wisdom of nature, in other words, lends sanction to sentiments which warrant a favoritism toward our own country. We may suppose that in favoring our own people, we are indirectly working for the good of the race; nevertheless our nationalistic loyalty is primary and our humanitarianism secondary. The same line of reasoning can be applied still further.

"Every independent state is divided into many orders and societies, each of which has its own powers, privileges and immunities. Each individual is naturally more attached to his own particular order or society than any other." [32]

We see how the doctrine of the wisdom of nature will tolerate a degree of selfishness in the struggles of these classes with each other. In short, the moral sentiments are not always directed on the good even of our own countries. We may believe, however, that it is for the good of the whole that each part of society defend its own interests. It is only a step from this to the position that cosmic teleology demands that each individual seek primarily his own good.

The virtue which Adam Smith finds most essential in the works of prudence as well as in those of beneficence and justice is a stoical self-command. It is by this quality that we subordinate our own feelings and actions to the decisions of the "the great inmate, the man within the breast, the impartial spectator." The perceptions of this being define propriety or rightness of feeling and action. Self-command is seen even in the courage of buccaneers and conquerors, whose actions are more in accordance with what seems necessary to a spectator than cowardice would have been, although in other respects the conduct of such persons departs greatly from the wishes of an impartial and benevolent spectator. Thus Adam Smith, starting with a theory of sentiment as the ultimate moral authority, nevertheless glorifies self-command in which we bring our feelings and actions into accordance with impersonal reason.

The "real man of virtue" feels "the full distress of the calamity which has befallen him" and "the whole baseness of the injustice which has been

195

done to him" but feels still more strongly what "the dignity of his own character requires" and governs himself "according to those restrained and corrected emotions which the great inmate, the great demi-god within the breast prescribes and approves of." [33]

Self-command, as a virtue, is far from insensibility, since in so far as we are insensible the merit of self-command is taken away.

We can agree that there is a "perception" or "judgment" of rightness or propriety of action and feeling. When we judge ourselves, the mind divides itself into two and one part speaks as an impartial spectator. No doubt in the beginning the ethical judge consists of actual bystanders, or else of our parents or friends, whose judgments are always echoing in our minds. But we are in turn perpetually judging others, and, by a natural transposition of persons, are led to judge ourselves by the same standards. We are supposed to be disinterested and unbiased in the same way that a judge or juryman is supposed to be disinterested. The question is, however, whether the standard is the actual feelings of particular individuals or the possible feelings of an ideal spectator; according to the first interpretation the moral judgment is an emotional expression and produces nothing which is true or false, while, according to the second, the moral judgment has a cognitive content since it is an opinion about how a perfectly enlightened judge would feel. But even if we accept the second interpretation and assert that the moral judgment is cognitive, it remains true that this type of judgment, in so far as it concerns justice, rather than happiness, is essentially unverifiable. Adam Smith's own point of view was a teleologically interpreted sociology of morals, in which he proceeds in part by a description of actual feelings and practices and in part by reference to the feelings of an imaginary ideal spectator. The ethical predicates have, therefore, an ambiguous character, being in part expressions of feeling and in part attributes definable with reference to the potential feelings of a perfect judge.

CHAPTER XI

BENTHAM

Bentham was neither a clergyman, like Butler, nor a literary free-lance, like Hume, nor a university professor, like Adam Smith; he was rather a legal reformer and his thinking had a distinctly practical aim. He gives, in his various writings, and especially in the *Introduction to the Principles of Morals and Legislation* (1780), a clear statement of the doctrine which has come to be known as utilitarianism. This doctrine he took primarily as a practical attitude resting on a set of definitions, which one can accept or reject as he chooses; this is combined with a thoroughgoing hedonistic psychology. He sought to discover an absolute and objective basis for morals and legislation in a definition of right, namely, right actions are those which are in accordance with the principle of utility. The principle of utility is the "greatest happiness or greatest felicity principle" which takes "the greatest happiness of all whose interest is in question, as being the right and proper, and the only right and proper and universally desirable end of human action; of every human action in every situation, and in particular in that of a functionary or set of functionaries exercising the powers of government."[1] In other words, right is defined as being a property which belongs, universally and exclusively, to actions which aim at the greatest happiness of all those whose interest is capable of being affected by the action in question. There is, in short, a class of actions to be called right, which are those which would be approved by a mind interested in the greatest happiness of the greatest number. This definition in terms of approval indicates Bentham's approach to the problem. We may conceive him to be defining an attitude, a point of view, the platform of a sect. He does not use the word *utilitarian*, which his disciple, John Stuart Mill, brought into prominence, but in substance he seems to be saying that this is the way in which members of a sect judge actions. They call those actions right which either do, or are thought likely to, produce the largest possible amount of happiness for those who can be affected by the performance or non-performance of the action.

According to Bentham, rightness must be defined in terms of utility; otherwise such words as *ought, right* and *wrong* have no meaning. He did not, like the intuitionists, recognize the necessity for indefinable ethical terms, neither did he, like Hume and Adam Smith, offer definitions in terms of the emotions. However, it may well be argued that Bentham has not succeeded in defining the word *right*. It may or may not be the case that all actions which make for the greatest happiness are right, but in any case the statement is a significant one. If right *means* "conducive to the greatest happiness" then the statement in question would read "Acts which tend to the greatest happiness are acts which tend to the greatest happiness." This is a barren tautology. Bentham held that the key ethical words, such as *ought, right* and *wrong*, are meaningless apart from utilitarian definitions. However, a person may prefer his own good to that of the community without feeling that he is thereby doing wrong; he may feel that he has a right to his possessions even though their distribution to the needy would clearly produce more happiness. A man may feel that it is his duty to favor his own nation against the larger mass of humanity. There is nothing meaningless or absurd about the assertion that such actions are right, even though contrary to Bentham's definition of the word *right*. In order to bring utilitarianism into agreement with common sense, it would be necessary to make the principle read "Act in accordance with *principles* which tend to the universal happiness, among which principles would be ideas of individual rights, etc." But this modified utilitarian imperative does not give any definite guidance; it virtually returns the problems of life to the individual conscience.

According to Bentham, the alternatives to utilitarianism are either asceticism (the diametrical opposite of the pleasure-principle) or else some appeal to the sentiments of individuals, which in turn results in an attitude which is either despotic or anarchic. Asceticism would be the pursuit of pain rather than pleasure, and no human being, no matter how stupid or perverse, is a consistent follower of asceticism. We agree with Bentham that no sane person chooses pain for its own sake; such a choice might well be regarded as contrary to the very meaning of the word *sane*. On the other hand, one can choose pain as an element in a life which appears to be pleasanter on the whole than a life without pain. It is commonly regarded as praiseworthy to choose a lesser good for oneself for the sake of a greater good for another. Bentham's conception of asceticism was a straw man easily destroyed, since no one chooses pain as an end in itself, although it is possible to be angry with oneself and to feel that one ought to suffer.

The principle of sympathy and antipathy was a more plausible rival to utilitarianism. No doubt Bentham had in mind the teachings of Hume and Adam Smith.

"By the principle of sympathy and antipathy, I mean that principle which approves or disapproves of certain actions, not on account of their tendings to augment the happiness, nor yet on account of their tendency to diminish the happiness of those whose interest is in question, but merely because a man finds himself disposed to approve or disapprove of them; holding up that approbation or disapprobation as a sufficient reason for itself and disclaiming the necessity of looking for any extrinsic ground." [2]

This, says Bentham, is no principle but rather the negation of all principle; it is either despotic or anarchic; it is despotic if we set up the approval or disapproval of ourselves or some arbitrarily chosen individual as the decisive test; it is anarchic if we permit the feelings of each individual to decide concerning right and wrong, and in particular concerning the right amount of punishment, which was the problem with which Bentham was primarily concerned. However, the fundamental question of ethical theory is precisely whether there is any way of escaping from the anarchy of conflicting judgments about right and wrong. It would seem that Bentham has merely set up his own judgment against that of others. The list of proposed bases for ethics which Bentham scornfully rejects is well worth pondering: moral sense, common sense, understanding, rule of right, fitness of things, laws of nature, truth, etc. Bentham's own grounding of ethics seems to be by way of arbitrary *definition*. This is what I mean by right, he seems to say: consider the consequences; if the consequences are good, then the action is right. The definition is a plausible one and many persons are disposed to go along with it. But since it defines the good solely in terms of the amount of happiness produced and ignores veracity and justice as intrinsically desirable ends it departs from ethical common sense.

Bentham was in general opposed to the doctrine of natural rights. In a note at the end of the *Introduction to the Principles of Morals and Legislation* reference is made to "the famous Declaration of Independence, published by Congress, July 5th, 1776" and the sentence is quoted which states that all men are created equal and endowed with certain inalienable rights. Bentham then asks,

> "Who can help lamenting that so rational a cause should be rested upon reasons, so much more fitted to beget objections than to remove them? But with men, who are unanimous and hearty about measures, nothing so weak but may pass in the character of a reason; nor is this the first instance in the world, where the conclusion supported the premises, instead of the premises the conclusion." [3]

In comment upon this, we may recall Hume's opinion that natural rights, such as life, liberty and property, make up a fundamental and very ancient convention. This convention is founded on the common good and its special clauses may be set aside on occasion by the greatest happiness (or better, the least misery) principle. Nevertheless, government cannot be directly founded on utility. The greatest happiness principle is compatible with all forms of authoritarianism or totalitarianism. It may entail the total neglect of the rights of minorities.

The traditional view is that the primary function of government is to maintain individuals in their natural rights. To establish a government solely on the principle of happiness without reference to justice would have been absurd and would have opened the door to every form of tyranny and abuse. Utilitarianism does not imply what we now call democratic ideas unless we add the postulate that the best way to gain the greatest happiness is by universal suffrage and a maintenance of individual rights. If we merely claim as our standard the greatest happiness of the greatest number, then there is no security of property; the state may take away whatever we possess as soon as it decides that it is in accordance with utility for it to do so. If we combine utilitarianism with the postulate that the greatest good can be achieved by the unquestioned rule of some church or party we see that a system would result very much at variance with ideals of individual liberty.

Hume had pointed out that justice does not directly consider utility. "Fitness," in the sense of giving each person what he can best make use of, is not a practicable guide; the rule of fitness, he says, involves so much controversy and men are so greedy that it is destructive of all social peace. Justice does not consider the fitness of objects to particular persons but is guided by certain general principles. In Bentham's *Theory of Legislation* (edited by Dumont) there is a story from Xenophon concerning the education of Cyrus, King of Persia. A big boy, having a small coat, took away from a little boy a coat which was too large for the little fellow but which fitted the big boy perfectly; he gave the small boy the small coat. Was this justice? The royal tutor pointed out to the prince that convenience had been considered but not justice, which does not permit anyone's property to be taken from him by force. Let us recall Bentham's definitions of right in terms of utility. If we are to uphold the view that the right action is always the action most productive of happiness, we must take account of indirect utility as well as direct; we must take account of the usefulness of certain principles to society as a whole and this usefulness or injuriousness may well outweigh the usefulness of a particular re-distribution of property. Bentham himself says that confiscation of property without compensation, even if it results in advantage to the state, is "a mere act of injustice, without the alleviations necessary to reconcile it with the principle of utility."[4] In re-distributing property it would not be in accordance with utilitarian justice to consider merely the good of the persons directly involved. Hume had pointed out that justice may demand that a judge take from a virtuous man what he needs in order to give to a profligate what he does not need. If judges neglect the rights involved in the system of private property they tend to tear down the whole fabric of society. Bentham was fully aware of these considerations. The fact seems to be that the judgment of utility is not less indeterminate, not less "either despotic or anarchic" than the judgment of conscience. One must weigh principles against the immediate good; each creates a *prima facie* obligation which can be set aside by some over-ruling higher obligation.

The greatest happiness principle of itself does not tell us how the sum of happiness is to be distributed. If the happiness is all given to half the population and the misery all to the other half we feel that this is a less desirable distribution than the same amount of happiness equally distributed. Furthermore, most people would feel that a distribution which gave the happiness to a set of unscrupulous and heartless egoists and the misery to conscientious and generous persons was less desirable than the contrary distribution, even though there was no effect of example on future actions to be considered. Ethical common sense tells us that justice is to be considered an end in itself no less than the universal happiness. Let us suppose that the happiness of a majority depends on the misery of a small minority. There will be some who will be more moved by the sufferings of the few than by the prosperity of the many. They feel that it would be better for the majority to forego some of their pleasure for the sake of a more equitable distribution even though the total happiness in the world is thereby diminished. One feels that we are not warranted in interfering with the welfare of even one innocent human being for the sake of the happiness of millions. This is because we naturally think in terms of a system of rights. Nevertheless, we realize on reflection that these rights are not absolute and that they may be set aside by the claims of the greater good. The point may be made that human justice is not infallible and that this implies that some innocent persons will suffer from unjust penalties; the justification of the whole system can only be the greater good, which itself involves justice as well as happiness. The fundamental demand of justice is that we approach the problem of the right distribution of happiness in an attitude of impartiality. We know that, as a matter of fact, our thinking is much influenced by imagination and sympathy. We more readily appreciate the claims of others when they are similar to ourselves and we can easily put ourselves in their place. This, however, does not affect the ideal demands of justice.

Bentham was primarily a student and critic of law; he might perhaps be dismissed as a legalist and reformer rather than a philosopher. He does, however, propose a definite and seemingly objective criterion of right which he offers as the only possible substitute for the ideas of previous philosophers who thought in terms of "the eternal fitness of things," the laws of nature, natural rights, natural justice, etc. If we assume that happiness is an objective quantity resulting from the algebraical sum of pleasure and pain then it is true, as a matter of fact, that any given action *either is or is not* the one action most conducive to adding most to the sum of the happiness in the world. But we cannot possibly know whether any past action was right in this sense, and, much less, with regard to actions whose consequences are in the future, can we know which is right. We would have to distinguish between actions objectively right and actions subjectively right; what actions are objectively right only God can know. The utilitarian law of duty would be: always do that action which you think most likely to have the best consequences. We have seen that "ethical common sense" demands that we include justice in our idea of what is good as well as universal happiness. The supreme rule, therefore, would be: always act in a manner likely to produce the greatest amount of good in the sense of happiness rightly distributed. This rule is acceptable but it is far from definite. People will always have different opinions about the probable consequences of their actions and they will also differ with regard to what they think just. There is also the difficulty of comparing pleasure and pain and again of comparing pleasure with justice. It is evident that Bentham's seemingly objective test of right and wrong was merely a matter of theory and was even theoretically unsound if we admit that justice is an end in itself as well as happiness.

It might be supposed that Bentham would have little to say concerning the problem of motives; he does, however, treat the subject at some length.

"On some occasions the word is employed to denote any of those really existent incidents from which the act in question is supposed to take its rise." [5]

Bentham cites the coming up of a lottery ticket. Let it be remarked that while such an event may be, in one sense, a cause of an action, it is more properly called an occasion; it is not what we commonly call a motive. Bentham's examples of motives such as avarice, indolence, benevolence, etc., are more to the point. Such motives are, Bentham says, fictitious entities, since we cannot think of an abstraction or universal functioning as a cause. "A motive is substantially nothing more than pleasure or pain, operating in a certain manner."[6] The pleasure or pain, however, is only in prospect and is not really existent at the time the motive operates. The internal event which stands nearest to the act is always an "expectation" of pleasure or pain; this is something in *esse* which engenders the act. This is what is commonly called desire and we may say that for all his technicalities Bentham has merely proclaimed the familiar doctrine that all motivation can be reduced to desire for pleasure and aversion to pain.

Bentham's hedonistic theory of action has often been criticized. Let us first state the usual arguments of the anti-hedonists. In the first place, we may be altruists and desire the pleasure of others. We may desire to keep a promise merely because we have promised. We may desire to see justice done in the sense of a right distribution of happiness. We desire continued existence; we desire that our future life be pleasant but we have a specific will to live. We desire to survive in our descendants and we desire the survival of the human race and of our branch of the human race in particular. We do not desire descendants in order that they may be happy, although we prefer that they should be happy if they are to exist. It is also true that the prospect of misery can cause the desire for continued existence, whether individual or racial, to be set aside and to be replaced by a will to die. We desire the good-will and esteem of others; we desire fame, wealth and power. There is in short a large group of "anhedonic desires" (to use the phrase of Frank Chapman Sharp) that is, desires for something other than one's own pleasure or freedom from pain. The evidence for the existence of such desires, the anti-hedonists say, is the same as that for hedonism itself, namely, reflection, self-examination. The hedonist replies that we would desire none of these things if we did not anticipate that their non-occurrence would involve unpleasantness for us. In the case of hunger, the hedonist is obviously right in maintaining that pleasure and the absence of pain are essential. In the case of altruism, desire for the common good, desire to see justice done, desire for posthumous fame, descendants and the like the argument of the hedonist is less convincing. The anti-hedonist seems to be irrefutable when he takes his stand on his reflective analysis of his own desires and finds that in fact his desires go beyond the limits of his own future hedonic states. The existence of disinterested benevolence may be regarded as having been established by Shaftesbury, Hutcheson, Butler and Hume. Bentham himself admits the existence of good-will or benevolence but thinks of it as a desire for the *pleasures* of good-will or benevolence.

But let us return to Bentham's theory of motives. He tells us that since pleasure is good and pain evil and the only possible motive desire for pleasure and aversion to pain, no motive is in itself bad. But motives may be characterized by their usual consequences; they may be listed as more or less useful in the production of public happiness. Motives are desires for different sorts of pleasures and aversions to different sorts of pains. There are desires corresponding to sensuous pleasures and aversions to sensuous pains; curiosity corresponds to the pleasures of knowledge, pecuniary interest corresponds to the pleasures of wealth. In a bad sense, this is called avarice, in a good sense, economy. For money you kill a man's enemy; your motive, says Bentham, is called lucre and is considered abominable. But your motive may be the same in ploughing a field for an employer. The motive may receive a different name in different circumstances and, by virtue of this name, may be considered good or evil, but it is still the same motive. The conclusion to be drawn is that the moral evaluation of motives is secondary and derivative; it depends on the rightness or wrongness of the action.

Motives are listed by Bentham under nine headings and are divided into good, bad and indifferent

according to the _usual_ consequences of actions spring-
ing from these motives with reference to the production of public happiness. Good: (1) Good-will or
benevolence, (2) Love of reputation, (3) Desire of
amity, (4) Religion. Bad: (5) Displeasure or desire
to cause pain. Indifferent: (6) Physical desire, (7)
Pecuniary desire, (8) Love of power, (9) Self-preservation, which is taken as fear of the pains of the senses,
love of ease and love of life. The nine groups of
motives can also be classified according to their
tendencies with regard to others; they may be divided into social, dissocial and self-regarding. The
social motives are generally good from a utilitarian
point of view; the dissocial, bad and the self-regarding, indifferent. Good-will or benevolence is, of all
motives, that which is most likely to lead to actions
in accordance with utilitarianism. Good-will is, of
course, in accordance with Bentham's hedonistic psychology, a desire for the pleasures of aiding others.
It does not always tend to the greatest happiness
since it may be extended to a single person or special
set of persons rather than to all humanity. "A partial
benevolence may govern the action, without entering
into any direct competition with the more extensive
benevolence which would forbid it." [7] In such
a case a man simply fails to think of the larger group;
his action is governed by benevolence and yet departs from the standard of universal happiness. With
regard to the various classes of motives, we may say
that Bentham does nothing more than express an
opinion concerning their social usefulness in general;
there is no reason why, in any given case, an action
from any one of the motives may not be good or bad
according to its consequences without regard to its
usual usefulness or injuriousness. The value of actions,
therefore, is for Bentham entirely a matter of whether
or not they are productive of human happiness and
not at all of the motive from which the action springs.

It is worthwhile to pause for a moment in order

to bring out the degree to which Bentham, in emphasizing consequences, has departed from what we must call ethical common sense. We are familiar with the distinction between the actual consequences of an action and its intended consequences. In general a man's intention is what he has in mind in performing a certain action; thus you may intend to kill A but accidentally kill B; this is entirely apart from the question *why* you sought to kill A, which is the problem of motive. The actual consequences of killing a man may be very beneficial. He may have been an unwitting carrier of a deadly disease and killing him may, therefore, cause the world to be spared a great deal of trouble. Still the killer did not know this and his action may have been animated by hatred; it was murder in a sense usually thought to deserve severe punishment. It must be considered morally bad even though the actual consequences were good. Or again, if I am a doctor, I may display heroism and self-sacrifice in saving a life which, without my suspecting it, turns out to be that of a villain who causes a great deal of suffering. Actions are classified by their intentions and intention seems to be what determines rightness or wrongness in a moral sense quite apart from motive. It is true that the word *intention* is frequently used in the sense of a "mere intention" in which no effort or an insufficient effort is made to accomplish the intended deed. This causes us to overlook the fact that every one of our acts has an intention, which is our idea of what we are trying to do. In addition to the definite end which we seek to achieve, there is an indefinite complex of consequences, good or bad, which may or may not be in our minds. We are often blamed either for our failure to anticipate the effects of our actions or for our lack of concern for the welfare of those who may be affected by our actions. In one sense to judge acts by their actual hedonic consequences is not to judge ethically at all. Such terms as right and wrong, morally good and morally bad, are terms of praise and blame and concern the agent and his state of mind. On the other hand, it may be our duty to consider the probable consequences of a proposed action as well as the rules which society has established for our guidance. In such a case our action is subjectively right if its probable consequences are good in the light of what knowledge we have even though the actual consequences turn out to be bad.

Actions are thus characterized by intention and always spring from some desire or motive. Back of motive, there is *disposition* which is, says Bentham,

> "a kind of fictitious entity, feigned for the convenience of discourse, in order to express what is supposed to be permanent in a man's frame of mind." [8]

It is a *likelihood* of being influenced by social or antisocial motives in certain classes of situation. In short, some men are better or worse than others, although not necessarily in such a way as to exclude a possibility of reformation. Disposition, according to Bentham, like everything else, is good or bad according to its effects in augmenting or diminishing the happiness of the community. An act may evidence a depraved disposition; thus a pre-meditated crime shows a worse disposition than one which expresses a sudden impulse; a man shows a bad disposition if, keeping his enemy in his power for a long time, he beats him at intervals and at his leisure.[9] An act of extraordinary depravity adds to the demand for punishment both according to common sense and according to Bentham. The latter upholds the maxim that the punishment must rise with the strength of the temptation; it is for this reason that a man of vicious disposition must be punished more severely.

Hutcheson had proposed rules by which moral goodness could be estimated. Bentham, as a legalist, was not concerned with the meritoriousness of actions but only with their depravity. His thought is summarized in the following four rules, which are here given a simplified statement. (1) On the supposition of a given gain for the individual, the badness of character shown in a crime is proportional to the amount of suffering caused by the crime. (2) If we suppose the amount of suffering caused by several crimes to be the same, then the depravity of character shown by the criminal is greater proportionally to the smallness of the gain which the criminal hoped to make. In other words, a depraved character needs slight excuse to inflict much agony on others; his action shows a high degree of insensitivity to the sufferings of others. (3) The stronger the temptation by which a man is overcome, the less evidence we have for inferring a depraved disposition. (4) Where revenge is the motive, the fact that an act is deliberate indicates a greater weakness of normal social concern than if it is impulsive; this is because deliberation gives the social desires time to assert themselves; if they fail to do so, we may infer that they are weak and that the character, in Bentham's language, is depraved. Depravity, in short, is merely a lack of normal concern for others, that is, of altruism. If altruism happens to be absent, the law steps in with a system of penalties which supply motives for acting in the manner in which a person would act who felt a proper sympathy for others. The question may be asked whether it is just to punish a man because he happens to be lacking in altruism. Are we responsible for our characters? Let us suppose that our disposition is partly inherited and partly due to our experiences and our past decisions. But we are not responsible for our disposition in so far as it is innate; we are likewise not responsible for the circumstances into which we happen to have been thrust. Our past decisions would seem to go back ultimately to our innate characters responding to given situations. Bentham held that in each case we choose what promises more pleasure and less pain for ourselves. Some dispositions are, however, (whether innate or acquired) especially injurious to society. When a man gives evidence of such a disposition he should be punished more severely since only heavy penalties are capable of preventing such an unsocial disposition from passing into action. The decision of the utilitarian legislator is guided solely by the thought of deterrence, but those who follow the theory of moral sentiments would reach the same practical conclusion, since they would regard those who lack all concern for others to be detestable and therefore deserving to suffer.

The general meaning of Bentham's theory of punishment is clear. The state is to establish a graduated series of penalties, taking care that the total social effect of establishing a punishment is not worse than the evil it seeks to prevent. The idea of a differentiated scale is essential, since, for example, it is more important to prevent murder than to prevent theft; it is, therefore, reasonable to punish the thief who kills his victim more severely than the man who merely steals. Bentham's theory of punishment is from the point of view of the legislator, who decides what laws should be established, rather than from the point of view of the judge who decides what application is to be made in an individual case. The legislator looks to the future, the judge to the past. The common idea of justice seems to be emotional in character and demands that the wicked should be made to suffer and the righteous be rewarded, even in cases where there can be no effect of example. It would seem that in such cases we have no recourse save to reward and punish according to our feelings. This would apply to the rewards and punishments after death postulated by theology, which are for the sake of simple justice rather than deterrence. According to Bentham, the punishment must rise with the strength of the temptation; thus, in a time of distress, crimes against property must be punished more severely than during times of plenty. This maxim is contrary to our moral feelings which judge that strength of temptation is an extenuating circumstance. However, in a period of social distress, a man who feels that the social order must be upheld will approve of the severe penalty even though he feels that those punished are not extremely wicked or perhaps not wicked at all; he will feel that there is a social necessity for the punishment. It would seem, therefore, that we sometimes reward and punish according to what seems to be justice and in other cases because of social necessity.

Bentham's theory of punishment, although it considers intention, motive and disposition, nevertheless does not regard offenders as wicked in a naive sense; we are all hedonists and the best is like the worst; Bentham merely classifies actions under various categories, which are to be punished in certain ways, in order to uphold the social order and so produce a maximum of happiness. Bentham's theory of punishment is "cold-blooded" since it judges actions only with regard to their consequences in the long run. Judges and law-enforcement officers cannot adopt so theoretical an attitude; for them the existing order is the proper definition of justice. They regard those who violate the existing order as wicked and as deserving to suffer. This is the vindictive theory of punishment. Punishment may be regarded as having several purposes; for one thing, it makes known the will of society. It also seeks to reform the criminal and those criminally inclined by making them share the feelings of abhorrence with which society views certain actions. Punishment exists as an institution and has several purposes of which deterrence is only one; it sometimes seeks to inflict deserved suffering on evil-doers as well as the reformation of the enemies of society.

Bentham does not give us an acceptable supreme law of conduct. There are, in terms of his system, two likely candidates for the position, namely, egoistic and universalistic hedonism. With reference to the former, there would seem to be no point in saying that we ought to pursue our happiness if in fact we always do pursue it. However, Bentham would say that although we always do seek our own pleasure, we sometimes fail to seek with sufficient effort our *greatest* pleasure, and thus fail to do what we *ought* to do. A rational man will seek his own greatest good and it is self-evident, we may suppose, that one ought to be rational. It is also evident that we are not willing that others should seek their own greatest good in *all* ways, namely, in ways which are contrary to what we regard as our rights. The notion of rights places a limitation on egoism. Seek thine own good, we say, but also respect the rights of your fellows.

We have already seen that universalistic hedonism neglects justice, that is, the right distribution of happiness. In addition the principle "Act so as to produce a maximum of happiness for all human beings" is open to the criticism that we sometimes feel that we are not obliged to sacrifice even small pleasures in order to add to the sum total of happiness in the world. We think that we have certain rights and that as long as we stay within our rights and do not violate the rights of others, we may do as we like. The idea of rights is deeply involved in all our thinking on the subject of morals. We are led to the thought that the one impeccable axiom of conduct is negative: Do not violate the rights of others. Against this one may object that the proposed law is circular since the very idea of a right belonging to others carries with it the thought that we should be doing wrong if we violated this right. This point may be granted and should in fact be insisted upon. "A right" is a fictitious entity; it is a curious invention of man in which a number of prohibitions are given a concrete existence. When we are obliged to defend any given right we are likely to argue along utilitarian lines, saying that it is for the common good that such and such rights should be recognized. The common good is always, to a certain extent, vague, since the scope of the community is left indeterminate and the good includes justice as well as the general happiness. The notion of rights is probably found in all societies, but different societies recognize different rights for their members and in fact different rights for different social classes.

The principle of respecting the rights of others may be regarded as a summary of the negative side of morality. But, after providing for himself, a man may have a surplus of energy and seek for a positive rule to guide him in the expenditure of this energy. The suggestion naturally occurs that he will find such a principle in the notion of producing the greatest happiness. According to the distinction between the negative and positive sides of morality, a man incurs no blame if he neglects this principle, but on the other hand he is praiseworthy if, after fulfilling all his obligations, he makes an effort to promote the universal happiness. But what is praise and what is praiseworthiness? The statement that a man is generous or public-spirited might simply record a fact, as when we say of a person that he is tall or short. But terms of praise express an emotional attitude on the part of the speaker, namely, an attitude of love or esteem. This frequently carries with it an impulse to favor, or to do something for, the person praised. The praised person is thought to illustrate moral goodness, which is something quite distinct from mere blamelessness. The various activities regarded as praiseworthy can all be brought in a general way under the heading of utilitarianism, but people do not normally start from the idea of promoting the greatest happiness of the greatest number. A man may be zealous for a school, or for an art museum or a music festival, and can be praised by those who share these interests; or again he may be a patriot or a party-worker or a union-worker and be praised by those who are enthusiastic for these same causes. In general a man is free to serve what public cause he wishes to serve or he may choose to serve none at all and lead an indolent life and still be free from blame as long as he does not violate the rights of others and fulfils his obligation to his country. It is true that there is an accepted saying to the effect that a man owes something to the community; this would remove public service from the realm of moral goodness and bring it into the sphere of duty. The sentiment is, however, a rather vague one and carries with it no definite penalty. In short a man lacking in public spirit is only slightly blamed in comparison with the man who violates the socially recognized rights of his fellows.

CHAPTER XII

KANT

Kant wrote several statements of his ethical doctrines, the chief of which are the *Foundations of the Metaphysics of Morals* (1786) and the *Critique of Practical Reason* (1788). These works have been expounded, criticized and commented upon many times. It is all too easy to fall under the sway of Kant's immense ability as an organizer and system-builder of philosophical thought. The fact is that the Kantian system tends to be a world apart, a private universe, in which it is easy to dwell in forgetfulness of the views of other philosophers and of the problems of ethical theory. One tends either to overlook the real difficulties of Kant's theories or else to exaggerate them to the point of finding nothing of value in Kant's ethical thought.

Kant's treatise on the metaphysics of morals deals with the most basic and abstract principles of morals. If we use the word *metaphysics* in the sense of the science of that which goes beyond the sensible world, then this work is metaphysical only to the extent that it touches on the freedom of the will; it does so merely to assure us that freedom is something which we cannot hope to understand. We must suppose that Kant, in speaking of a metaphysics of morals, was using the word in the sense of a science of first principles, and, in this case, of the first principles of morals. The first section of the work is described as "a transition from the common rational knowledge of morals to the philosophical." Kant thus assumes to start with that there is "common rational knowledge" of morals; naturalism would maintain that morals is merely founded on custom and emotion and is lacking any rational foundation. But let us listen to Kant and learn what we can. Kant commences with the statement that

> "Nothing in the world—indeed nothing even beyond the world—can possibly be conceived which can be called good without qualification except a good will." [1]

What did he mean? The term will is obscure, since it might mean, among other things, a faculty of choice, which might be capable of choosing either good or evil. But since Kant speaks of a "good will" he presumably means a persistent effort or striving in a certain direction. A man is good because of his will, his habit of choosing to act in certain ways; it might have been better if Kant had made it clear that goodness belongs to a personality rather than to a mere faculty, which obviously cannot exist by itself. Intelligence and courage, he goes on to tell us, are good in so far as they are useful, but they can be extremely bad and harmful if the will is not good. Power, riches, honor, health and even happiness may make for pride if there is no good will.

> "It need hardly be mentioned that the sight of a being adorned with no feature of a pure and good will yet enjoying uninterrupted prosperity, can never give pleasure to a rational impartial observer. Thus the good will seems to constitute the indispensable condition even of worthiness to be happy." [2]

219

With regard to the being "adorned with no feature of a pure and good will" it may be that Kant's roundabout phrase was designed to cover the case of a man who would have sacrificed himself to duty if an opportunity had arisen, but in whose life there was always a perfect co-incidence between the path of duty and that of self-interest. Or, in the case of an innocent child, it would seem that the rational impartial observer, if normally benevolent, would regard uninterrupted prosperity with satisfaction. The good will, it would seem, might be latent. Furthermore, may we not say that the "rational impartial observer" will wish wrong-doers to suffer but that he will likewise wish all innocent beings to be happy even though their "good will" goes no further than abstaining from wrong action. Did Kant mean that mere absence of evil will is itself good will?

Kant, as we have seen, commences with the statement that nothing is unconditionally good save good will but he has not told us the meaning of the word *good*. Obviously, he does not mean "instrumentally good" since a thing which is good only as a means may be used for a bad end and so would not be unconditionally good. Kant proceeds on the supposition that we already understand the meaning of the word *good*. He eventually discusses the concept of good in the *Critique of Practical Reason* and it will be instructive to examine what he has to say there. The concept of good, he tells us, may be derived from a practical law, namely, the moral law. A second idea of good would be that of something whose existence promises pleasure and thus determines the subject to produce it. In other words, the good is that which produces pleasure. This is the familiar hedonistic definition of good, found in Locke and his successors. This definition is, however, rejected by Kant on the ground that language distinguishes between the pleasant and the good and demands that good and evil be judged by reason rather than by individual feeling. However, language is an unreliable guide and there is nothing wrong with calling that good which produces pleasure, if we wish to. It is true that if only that is good which produces pleasure, then nothing is good in itself. If we say that pleasure is good, we have introduced an altogether different concept, namely, that of something which is intrinsically desirable. It is quite possible to adopt the position that reason tells us that pleasure and nothing else is intrinsically good, and, at the same time, admit that individuals differ greatly in what they find pleasant. Such a position, however, would not have been accepted by Kant, since his mind was fixed on moral good rather than natural.

Kant proceeds to distinguish two meanings of good, each of which has an opposite; on the one hand, there is what is traditionally called moral good and evil (*das Gute* and *das Böse*) and, on the other, what is called natural good and evil (*das Wohl* and *das Übel*). Thus a man may live well in the sense of fulfilling his obligations or he may live well in a hedonistic sense. Or again he may display wickedness or he may endure suffering. Kant declares that it is indubitably certain that

"we desire nothing, under the guidance of reason, except in so far as we hold it to be good or bad." [3]

He interprets this to mean that we desire nothing, under the guidance of reason, save in so far as it is morally good; we are averse to nothing save in so far as it is morally bad. This interpretation indicates an unusually restricted use of the word *reason*, since a man is usually held to desire his own greatest happiness under the guidance of reason. We must, in short, distinguish between ethical reason and prudential reason and there is a great departure from common usage when we take reason, as Kant does, in an exclusively ethical sense. It is unnatural to say that a

221

person who thinks of his own greater good is not acting under the guidance of reason.

Good and evil, in the Kantian sense, are properties of actions rather than of our affective experience in so far as pleasant or unpleasant. That which is good unconditionally, he thinks, can only be a manner of acting. This, says Kant, goes back to the "maxim of the will" and indicates that the acting person is a good or evil man. This is moral good and evil which is quite different from natural good and evil. Moral good and evil involve praise and blame and often reward and punishment. The morally good person is admirable; the morally bad person is despicable. We may admire either morally or non-morally; here we are speaking only of moral admiration. The good will is, therefore, morally admirable. It is far from being the case, however, that good-will, in the Kantian sense, is always admired. The man of duty may appear to us to be a narrow-minded fanatic. Still, Kant tells us that such a man is morally admirable. *Admirable* can only mean *ought to be admired* and *morally admirable* means that which is the right or proper object of moral admiration. Kant, therefore, whether he knows it or not, is stating a proposition, which, if true at all, can only be an intuition or immediate insight. He proclaims that for a man to do what he thinks to be right is intrinsically admirable. But if a man's belief is unorthodox his action may nevertheless be criminal in the eyes of the law. It follows that the moral goodness of which Kant speaks is something which may be important to God in passing final judgment on men but is not necessarily relevant to human justice. This transcendent reference gives the opening statements of the *Grundlegung* a mysterious impressiveness; nothing is unconditionally good, either within the world or beyond it, save the goodness of the will bent on doing what the individual thinks to be right. But we may ask, with reference to this intuitively discerned moral goodness, whether it is really good without qualifications even if it has bad consequences? Obviously, the action is only good from one point of view and there may be another sense in which it ought not to have been done and perhaps would not have been done had the person realized what social injury was to result.

Kant cites certain examples to show that pain is not always an evil. A Stoic, tormented by the gout, refuses to admit that his pain is evil; this, however, is merely a strict adherence to one sense of the word *evil*, namely, the moral sense; the Stoic experiences no evil in the sense that he need not reproach himself. Then there is the example of the surgical operation. One *feels* this to be an evil but it is regarded by reason as good; this example would be treated quite differently by a rationalistic hedonist. He would regard the pain as an entity distinct from the operation; the latter is good because of its consequences. The pain is itself evil, the hedonist would say, although the operation may be rationally worthy of being chosen because the operation plus the pain is supposed to involve less pain than life without the operation. Then there is the case of punishment. If a bully "who delights in annoying and vexing peace-loving folk" receives a beating, everyone approves of it; even the bully himself "because he sees the proportion between welfare and well-doing which reason inevitably holds before him, here put into practice." [4] Here the observer judges the deserved suffering of the bully to be good. This suggests that the Kantian Practical Reason is conceived in such a way as to include the retributive emotions. If the process were purely intellectual we would judge that the deserved suffering was good; in so far as we are pleased with it, it is clear that our emotions are involved. The suffering of the bully is not good in the same sense that an act of self-sacrifice is good; it is, however, felt to be fitting or appropriate. Hume would say that we are so constituted that we conceive of a system of rights which we think makes for the common good; we are concerned with the common good and the good of others because of sympathy; hence we are pleased with the suffering of the bully. The whole process is ascribed to Practical Reason by Kant.

Reason, we are told, was not given to us by nature for the sake of guiding us to happiness, but rather for the "far higher purpose" of revealing to us our duty. If we suppose that the function of reason is merely prudential then we are likely to fall into *misology,* in other words, into a cynical despair with regard to reason, since the use of intelligence to promote luxury does not produce happiness but rather increased anxiety and boredom. Kant dogmatically asserts that nature could have provided for the survival of the species by mere instinct. The assertion is dubious since man's intelligence is important in his efforts to survive; it is also true that without reason, man would not be man; the question is therefore meaningless. Had man not been provided with reason, the earth would have been populated merely by various species of animals who would survive by instinct and whatever sparks of intelligence they happen to possess. At any rate, Kant's position is that man is not merely an animal and is not wholly indifferent to what reason tells him, not as a mere instrument of the desire for happiness, but as an independent authority. Man is raised above animality only in so far as ethical reason gives him a sort of guidance which he can never gain from mere instinct. The higher purpose of reason, says Kant, is seen in that it considers what is in itself good and evil. Good and evil can only be defined after a moral law has been established; if we start with good and evil in the sense of happiness and misery, we reach a false system called heteronomy. Reason is then regarded merely as an instrument for the gaining of happiness;

the true system is called autonomy and regards the ethical faculty as laying down a law or set of laws prior to any conception of good or evil which might result from the law. This point is regarded as touching on "the method of all the deepest moral investigations." Most philosophers have erroneously commenced with the concept of the object of the will, namely, the good, rather than with the form of willing itself. For Kant the idea of rightness, that is, of duty, is primary.

Practical reason, we are told, lays down certain laws, ultimately, one law, the categorical imperative, and action for the sake of the law is morally good. We have not yet come to the proper place for examining this famous rule of conduct in detail. But let us dwell for a moment on the thought that Kant's Practical Reason is really, in spite of its name, an "emotive" faculty. It involves a sympathy with others in their striving for happiness and also in their desire to see wrong-doers punished. But Practical Reason necessarily has an impersonal point of view. This corresponds to the "form of universality" of which Kant speaks. All the ethical predicates, right and wrong, just, noble, morally good, etc., claim to express objective traits of actions and persons; they suppose that we are judging without reference to personal interest or any form of favoritism. It may be that we are not truly disinterested and that our judgment is a mere expression of selfish desire. But when we realize this we see that we are misusing ethical language and tend either to correct our language by ceasing to use ethical terms or else to mend our ways and to act in accordance with the demands of ethical impartiality. In short, in Practical Reason certain emotional demands are given a rational form. This implies that if a deed is noble or despicable or merely right or wrong or comes under any ethical predicate, then all deeds which are like it in certain relevant features come under the same predicates without regard to *who* the persons involved are. Thus what is right for anyone under a given set of circumstances must be right for anyone else under conditions which are essentially similar.

Kant would not have been willing to accept any form of naturalism; he frequently appeals to teleology which can hardly be understood without some form of theism. But he was also averse to any form of supernaturalism which went beyond the three postulates of practical reason which were matters of faith. One may question whether Kant's position is truly tenable; it often seems to rest on a careful balancing of denials and an adroit shifting from one side to the other. Let us follow, for the moment, the suggestions of naturalism. Man's intelligence conceives of a system of rights and duties according to which social life is possible and his emotions view with satisfaction the effort to conform to this system. The Kantian view-point is that of a man judging himself; if he can see that he has always acted according to the principles approved by his sympathetic emotions, he can regard himself with satisfaction; he finds himself morally admirable no matter how others may regard him and no matter what the consequences of his action may be. This is the manner in which a naturalist would understand the Kantian doctrine that the good will is good in itself. "Good in itself" signifies that it is morally admirable. In general we think that what we *do* admire is admirable, since, as has been said, all the passions justify themselves, that is, make the object appear to warrant the passion. The meaning of the word *admirable* contains the idea of *fitness* or *oughtness*. In Kant's language, it is by Practical Reason that we apprehend the intrinsic goodness of devotion to duty.

The system of rights and duties actually accepted in different societies differs from one group to another. Kant attempts to deduce all our duties from one principle, namely, the categorical imperative; he chose

226

examples of duties which are generally accepted. It may be urged that the concrete meaning to be found in various duties is derived from the laws and customs of society, which guide our emotions into certain channels, although it is certain that a "rational form" belongs to our rights and duties. By virtue of this rational form, duty appears as something objectively fitting. Since it seems to be objective, we feel that "all right-thinking persons" will agree with us and that what ought to be done by anyone is dictated, in an obvious manner, by the circumstances in which he finds himself. The categorical imperative, according to one of the many formulations which Kant gives of the principle, is that we should never act in such a way that we could not will that our maxim be a universal law. No other moralist emphasizes maxims as much as Kant, although several have brought out the importance of acting by right rules or principles. The Kantian principle is sometimes stated positively but its more obvious meaning is negative; this corresponds to the fact that the more basic part of morality is always a matter of forbidding certain types of action. May I give a promise which I do not expect to be able to keep? This would certainly be imprudent but the risk might be worth taking in an exceptional case. I ask myself whether I would be content that the principle of extricating oneself from any difficulty by a false promise should be followed by others as well as myself. This rule would render promises impossible and would therefore be incompatible with social life. Kant speaks as a rigorist who would condemn all deception; he does not consider the difficulties to which rigorism leads. Reason is, for Kant, a mysterious oracle, which is unconcerned with the welfare of society, and issues exceptionless rules, which, if not self-evident, are yet supported by short dialectical arguments showing that their denial is self-destructive. Since the "maxims" approved by reason have the same strict universality as the propositions of mathematics, Kant can preach rigorism; if men are not able to fulfil the exacting demands of rigorism, it only shows the "radical evil" of human nature and the necessity of religion.

Experience, says Kant, can never serve as a basis for ethics. We cannot cite a single case where we can be sure that the motive was duty for the sake of duty. Ethics cannot be founded on what is done in the world, since actual practice may be open to moral censure. In the same way, we cannot ground ethics on examples, since ethical ideals are the basis for the selection of the examples. Experience can never establish rules possessed of strict universality; Kant, therefore, can make it appear that an ethical empiricist will be an unreliable character ready to depart from the rules of morality whenever it is to his advantage to do so. The point to be noted, however, is that the real issue of ethical theory is not so much rationalism vs. empiricism as rationalism vs. the emotive theory. There is something artificial and unconvincing in Kant's glorification of reason, unless we recognize that practical reason is simply conscience and that conscience is a peculiar amalgam of feeling and rationality. Practical reason is indeed normative rather than descriptive; it tells us what ought to be done rather than what is done. But it may be said that it derives its practical hold over us from the fact that we are so constituted that we are always concerned to some extent with the common good and that we feel resentment towards those who violate laws which we think generally useful.

Kant, on the other hand, proclaims the necessity of a "completely isolated metaphysics of morals." The "pure conception of duty" has, he thinks, a powerful influence over the human heart; reason, conscious of its dignity, can gradually gain mastery over all our sensuous inclinations. His assertion that the decrees of pure reason make an appeal to the human heart and especially to "moderately young children" is an empirical assertion and admits the importance of emotion. In short, *a priori* practical reason is said to derive its power from the fact that it appeals to our feelings. But Kant regarded reason in a mystical way, as a voice from the transcendent regions. Moral laws, he says, hold for every rational being as such and are therefore not limited in their application to men, although their field of application beyond the human race remains a blank space. Hume had pointed out that justice, in his sense of the word, would have no application in conditions of great abundance of goods or of great good-will of men toward each other, and that, therefore "property"—to say nothing of "promises"—corresponds merely to the conditions of human life. Kant's alleged "metaphysics of morals" includes "developing our talents" and "not committing suicide"—two rules which presumably would not apply to supernatural rational beings. The fact is that Kant was concerned with the theoretical basis of human morality and that he seems throughout to be rather obviously thinking of the conditions of human life, especially as we cannot very well reason concerning angelic morality. We must watch his reasoning closely to see whether he succeeds in deducing the rules of morals merely from the concept of rational beings as such.

Practical reason, says Kant, lays down certain ethical principles. There is also a faculty of will or choice which is not always determined by the decrees of reason; it is influenced by certain incentives other than reason and is therefore subject to constraint. The laws of reason appear as imperatives which contain the idea of *ought* and are divided into hypothetical and categorical. The hypothetical imperatives tell us that we ought to do something on the supposition that we seek a certain end. We ought to be prudent if we seek happiness; Kant admits that we do necessarily seek our own happiness. Nevertheless he insists that the imperatives of prudence are only hypothetical, since they would have no validity were we not so constituted that we must seek our own happiness. The other class of hypothetical imperatives are more easily understood; they are the rules of skill, illustrated, let us say, by the principles of engineering. If we would accomplish a certain end, we must use such and such means. Imperatives of this sort scarcely deserve the name, since the *ought* which they impose is conditional on our prior choice of a specific goal.

Kant tells us that our concept of happiness is so indeterminate, that it can give rise to no definite rules of conduct. No one can "definitely and self-consistently state what it is he really wishes and wills." Even the most clear-sighted person cannot form a distinct idea of what it is he is seeking. The hedonistic philosophers, on the other hand, identify happiness with pleasure and draw a sharp line between pleasure and what produces pleasure. They say that pleasure has only two intrinsic attributes, intensity and duration. However, the indefiniteness, of which Kant complains, may be said to break out again when we try to establish a definite ratio between these two attributes. We are obliged to agree with Kant that something of vagueness always belongs to the idea of happiness and something of indefiniteness to the rules of prudence. But, unfortunately, the same imperfections belong to the concepts and principles of morality also.

A categorical imperative is one in which the will is left with no freedom to choose the opposite without being subject to blame. We are told to do this or that (to keep our word, for example) without being given any reason why we should do so. The rule is not, keep your promise if you would uphold the common good, but rather, keep your promise whether or not you happen to be interested in the common good. Promise-keeping has always been a most important example in the efforts of philosophers to establish rationalism. Kant saw that there can be only one unconditional imperative, since, if there were several, they might conflict in certain cases and could no longer be described as unconditional. But even Kant could not remain with only one ethical law but found it necessary to add two "alternative formulations" which are not literally identical with the first formulation. The three "formulations" were given concrete meaning by considering examples. Duties are either to self or to others and are either perfect or imperfect. The imperfect obligations leave the individual a range of permissible actions, but are equally binding. Thus everyone should, if he is able, give to charity, but he may choose among possible recipients of his charity.

The first formulation tells us that we are always to act in such a manner that we can will the maxim of our conduct to be a universal law. The example of a perfect duty to oneself discussed by Kant is the prohibition of suicide; the wrongness of false promise illustrates a perfect duty to others. Kant apparently felt that the wrongness of suicide in order to escape trouble could easily be proved by a short argument. The feelings of pleasure and pain have been given to us by nature to impel us to an improvement of life. But a system of nature whose law would be to destroy life because of the same feelings would be self-contradictory and could not exist. Therefore suicide is morally wrong. Kant has assumed without proof that feelings of pleasure and pain have been "given" to us for a purpose. One may argue that if only those people killed themselves who found themselves faced with a future containing more pain than pleasure only a few would take their own lives and neither human life nor nature would be destroyed. There is no reason why fear of pain should not cause death in unusual circumstances even though the contrary desire, love of pleasure, serves the purpose of encouraging us to live. The wrongness of

231

suicide, as opposed to its folly, is not easily proved. Is it clear that an atheist should not kill himself, if he wants to and has no special duties to others? Or, on grounds of theism, is it clear that God wants us to suffer needlessly? It would seem that in any case the question can hardly be discussed without reference to God and his will. The test of universalization merely forbids us to kill ourselves in situations where we would regard it as wrong for others to kill themselves.

The perfect duty to others chosen by Kant to illustrate the first formulation of the categorical imperative is the duty of not giving a false promise. For example, we are forbidden to borrow money which we know that we will be unable to repay. Can I, in such a case, will the maxim of my conduct to be a universal law? As we have already noted, a maxim which told us that we could give a false promise whenever it was in our interest to do so would render it impossible for us to promise, as no one would have any faith in our word. Such a maxim is therefore self-destructive. Kant does not consider the case where a promise has been extorted from us by threat of violence. His argument would imply that all promises are valid. But if we are to distinguish between valid and invalid promises and suppose Kant to mean that we may violate our promise in all cases where we would be willing that any one should violate his promise, we have gone back to the anarchic authority of the individual conscience. It is true that if we are to promise we must at least pretend to take promising seriously; still, we could probably gain some aid from others even if we were known only to keep our word in most cases. International treaties are not deemed worthless even though it is suspected that the contracting powers will repudiate the treaty under certain circumstances. A promise may have some binding force without being regarded as *absolutely* sacred.

232

The imperfect duty to one's self cited by Kant was the duty of developing one's talents. The question is whether we shall give ourselves over to luxury and idleness and permit our talents to rust or whether we shall develop these talents. Here again Kant cites the purposes of nature (our talents have been "given" to us for all sorts of purposes) and declares that as rational beings we could not will it to be a universal law that no one should develop his talents. But the argument is not clear. The man who fails to develop his talents runs not only the risk of poverty but also that of boredom. There is an impulse of self-expression found in most people; they will feel a sense of frustration if they are unable to do anything or say anything or be anything which will be admired by at least a few other people. In short, hedonism itself would demand that we make an effort to utilize whatever talents we may possess. Furthermore, there is a difficulty in the notion of duty to oneself. If a man prefers to be idle and finds such a life more enjoyable and does not fall short in his duties to others, how has he failed in his duty? Should one sacrifice himself to develop his talents even if these talents are of no use to others? Kant admits that life would be possible even if this duty were neglected. It seems that he is implicitly appealing to a common utilitarian consideration, namely, that it is actually for the greater happiness of both the individual and society for as many as possible to develop to the full whatever talents they may happen to possess.

The example given by Kant of a duty to others which is "imperfect" is that of assisting the needy. The human race could continue to exist even if each looked out only for himself, provided that no one violated the natural rights of others. But although such a mode of life is physically possible, we cannot will that it be universally practiced. For any man might himself on occasion need the help of others and to will that selfishness should be the only rule would be for the will to be in conflict with itself. Kant's thought is not that it is imprudent never to give to charity, since we might sometime need help ourselves, but rather that it is *absurd* never to give to charity, since we know that *we* would welcome aid under certain non-existent but always possible conditions. With regard to this generally recognized duty, we may say that it too can easily be explained from the standpoint of a utilitarianism based on sympathy. Looking out on society, we see that it is for the general good that the more fortunate should assist the needy. It is true that if we ourselves belonged to the necessitous we should especially want to be helped. Approval and disapproval, according to this school, is based on sympathy. In this case we sympathize with ourselves; we imaginatively identify ourselves with ourselves in a possible condition of need and feel resentment against those who deny all assistance.

Kant's four examples are well-chosen cases of generally accepted duties and might even be regarded as a convenient summary of morality in general. We are forbidden to commit suicide and to give false promises and we are positively commanded, but with a degree of free-play, to develop our talents and to give to charity. But the four duties can easily be explained from the point of view of the emotive theory; the non-performance of these acts awakens resentment when we look at them as impartial observers who sympathize with the strivings of all the persons involved. The deduction of the four duties from the principle of universalization remains unconvincing. It would be generally accepted, however, that the principle of universalization is both true and useful. We *should* only do those things which we would be willing for all to do in the same circumstances. This is because the idea of right, whether in the sense of the permissible or of the obligatory, always implies a certain indifference to persons. Right

234

claims to be something objective and therefore not dependent on our private desires. We may use the test of universalization to discover whether we are truly impartial. On the other hand, this "form" of rationality seems to be given content by our emotions. We are always concerned for others and for ourselves; if we were totally indifferent there would be no restriction on what we could will to be a universal law.

The second formulation of the categorical imperative bids us always treat mankind (and any other rational beings we may chance upon) as ends, never merely as means. The use of the word *end* is clearly metaphorical. Health is an end to which exercise is a means; in short, an end is something which we seek to bring into existence or to continue in existence. But I need not seek to bring myself or my associates into existence, since we already exist. What did Kant mean? His examples imply that I am to treat myself and other humans with respect; I am not to degrade myself nor invade the rights of others. "Rational nature exists as an end in itself." [5] The formula may be taken as a command to respect personality in the sense of not depriving people of their lives, their liberty or their property and at the same time preserving and developing my own existence. We are to adopt the point of view of a universal spectator who identifies himself with the wish, which each of us has, to be respected in his basic rights and to realize his highest capacities.

It is clear that this principle is not identical with the principle of universalization, since the latter may cover a duty of not being cruel to animals, while the new principle is concerned only with humans. The latter envisages a society of men and grants them rights along with a duty of self-realization. The same four examples were used by Kant in connection with the second formulation as were used in connection with the first.

235

(1) The would-be suicide is told that he may not use mankind in his own person merely as a means. The argument is decidedly weak. Why should a being who can grandly say "I am an end in myself" consent to continue a troublesome existence which benefits no one? If he must preserve his life merely as an example to others, he is using himself as a means, not as an end. Suicide is a difficult problem in any ethical system.

(2) The second example of perfect obligation is the prohibition of false promise. This is connected by Kant with attacks on the freedom and property of others. In all these cases I am using others merely as a means; he whom I propose to use in this manner cannot assent to my action. This rule of conduct comes back to what Hume called justice, that is, promises and property, in other words, our basic rights. We regard ourselves as members of some group and as possessing equal rights with all members of that group.

(3) We must develop our talents. Not to do so does not literally conflict with humanity in our person; at the same time, it does not harmonize with it.

> "There are capacities for greater perfection which belong to the end of nature with respect to humanity in our own person." [6]

Kant was, in his way, a "self-realizationist," a "perfectionist." A minor perplexity is connected with the fact that this duty and the following one are described by Kant as *meritorious;* this would imply that failure to develop our talents is not blameworthy, although to develop them is praiseworthy. It cannot be said that Kant was clear on this subject.

(4) We must practice charity also, although the world could exist without it. Still our lives are in positive harmony with the conception of mankind as an end if the ends of any other person are, as

far as possible, our ends also. This comes down to saying that we are to regard others with sympathy. Kant does not consider the arguments which can be brought against charity; it is after all possible that it would be better for the race in the long run were charity entirely suppressed. The point can be made with regard to charity that Kant, as a teacher of orthodox morality, accepted the common assumption, which is after all empirical in character, that we add to the sum total of happiness in the world by giving to charity; if the opposite were known to be the case, the principle of respecting mankind as an end would oblige us to seek to eliminate the needy rather than to assist them. It is obvious, however, that suffering naturally prompts us to come to the aid of the sufferers and there is no way in which we *could* know that a total suppression of charity was really for the universal happiness.

On the whole, Kant's second formulation must be accepted as an orthodox "summary of ethics." Those who believe in the emotional theory of ethics would regard it as a formulation of the moral emotions when we adopt the standpoint of an impartial observer and look out over mankind as a whole. In practice human beings are sometimes dealt with merely as means. One race may condemn another to slavery or serfdom. The rulers of society may decide that it is for the general good to sacrifice a larger or smaller segment of the population; it may be said that as long as the basic consideration was impartial (or might have been impartial, had any consideration taken place) this fact itself constitutes a due respect for personality. The doctrine of treating mankind as an end merely affirms a humanitarian point of view against an attitude of universal sympathy which would demand that we consider all living beings as ends in themselves.

The first formulation of the categorical imperative tells us that we must act so that we can will the "maxim" of our conduct to be a universal law. What is a "maxim"? Why does my conduct have to have a maxim? Let us attempt an answer in terms of everyday experience in an effort to avoid Kantian jargon as much as possible. A maxim is some statement which gives a justification of our conduct, as when we say, on some occasion, that we believe in saving for a rainy day or that we believe that one should have some concern for others. This justifying saying or "principle," however, would have no effect unless it applied to everyone in the same situation. It must, therefore, be a statement which we think valid for any one in the same situation. A "maxim" in short is a justifying statement which claims to be valid for everyone. The categorical imperative may be interpreted as saying that we should act only according to principles which are universally valid. The meaning would be: Act according to maxims which you can *rightly* will to be universal. It follows that the principle of universalization does not enable us to define the word *right*; it rather presupposes that it is already understood. The categorical imperative, one may say, is an analytic elaboration of something implied in the idea of right conduct as such.

The second formulation told us that we were to treat mankind always as an end, never merely as a means. As explained by Kant, the second formulation contains two ideas, the idea of rights and the idea of self-realization. The first formulation had brought out the concept of universality which is implied in any ethical principle. The second applies this to those rights which we claim for ourselves and tells us that we must grant the same rights to others. This reasoning is merely an application of something contained in the idea of rights. What is added in the second formulation is the thought of the respect due to personality as such and this leads to a prohibition of suicide and a slothful life as well as of an invasion of the rights of others with regard to property, life or liberty. The second formulation is more concrete than the first; it is summed up in the traditional phrase "respect for the dignity of the individual." But Kant was not content with merely two "formulations" but felt that he had to lay down a third statement. We must act as legislative members of a universal kingdom of ends. It is difficult to see that this statement adds anything to the first two formulations; it may be regarded as a mere combination of the two. When one acts, one may regard oneself as a legislator thereby enacting a certain principle, that is, making it a universal law. If one is not willing that his principle should be a universal law, he thereby acknowledges that his action was a wrongful one. Thus if one lies one seems to justify lying in general or at least lying in all similar situations. A clever man will generally find some way of justifying any action but this consideration does not impugn the general validity of the Kantian law.

A further elaboration of the Kantian ethical theory is found in the definition of morality as autonomy. Man's nature, Kant thinks, is two-fold; in part, the human being illustrates reason, for the rest, he has an empirical or animal nature. Since his sensuous desires tempt him to act contrary to ethical reason, he is aware of a sense of *ought* or duty; this would be unknown to him were he purely rational. We may suppose that God knows what is fitting without a sense of struggle derived from overcoming sensuous temptation; we humans know what is fitting but also experience a sense of constraint. Kant draws the conclusion that to act in accordance with practical reason is true freedom. Thus Kant reaches the conclusion that I am free when I am not doing what I wish to do but am following the dictates of pure reason. One may criticize Kant as follows. Autonomy means self-rule, but no one naturally identifies his self with the single faculty of practical reason. On the other hand, it is natural to speak of an "ethical" self or a "higher" self having a natural right to rule. A self implies a rational faculty combined with emotion. Thus a man's higher self is simply his self wishing for the social good and recognizing that this good would be promoted were all, including oneself, to follow certain rules. To call one's ethical self his *real* self is both flattering and edifying in that it tends to encourage us in ethical practice. The fact seems to be that the description of either the higher self or the lower self as the *real* self is meaningless, since both are equally real. Doing one's duty is autonomy only on the assumption that the ethical self is the real self and the self of sensuous impulses not the real self. But if we choose to regard man's animal nature as his real self then vice is autonomy and virtue heteronomy. Nevertheless, the Kantian doctrine of autonomy may be accepted by the follower of the emotive theory to the extent of recognizing that the virtuous man follows a law imposed on himself by his own emotions, namely, by his sympathetic disposition which enables him to identify himself with society or even with humanity in general.

Kant undertakes to show that the false systems of ethics rest on heteronomy. This cannot be a difficult assignment since, according to Kant, morality is the rule of *a priori* ethical reason and every other explanation of ethics must mean the dominance of some phase of man's lower nature. Empiricism is especially to be condemned, since it cannot establish any principle of universal validity. "The principle of one's own happiness is the most objectionable of all." [7] Experience fails to show that happiness is proportional to good conduct and, furthermore, to make a man prudent is very different from making him virtuous. This principle robs morality of its sublimity and puts the motives of virtue and of vice in the same class.[8] We need not discuss at this point the possibility of an egoistic grounding of morals or attempt to explain how it can be rational for an individual to sacrifice his happiness or his life because of the decrees of *a priori* ethical reason. Spinoza, as we have seen, introduced rather abruptly the notion that the "free man" always acts honorably, while Locke, following religious orthodoxy, established what may be called theological egoism; God was regarded as enforcing the moral law with supernatural rewards and punishments. Kant proclaimed the primacy of practical reason, but felt it necessary to add that the existence of God and the immortality of the soul were necessary postulates of morality. In insisting that self-sacrifice is *sublime,* Kant seems to admit that the apprehension of ethical value is a matter of emotion and beyond the reach of either empirical verification or rational deduction.

Hutcheson's doctrine of a moral sense, since it fails to recognize the sovereignty of *a priori* reason, is also brought under the heading of heteronomy. Kant says sarcastically that "those who cannot think expect help from feeling." [9] Feelings differ indefinitely and so cannot furnish a single standard; furthermore, one cannot validly judge for others by means of his own feeling. Nevertheless, says Kant, the theory of a moral sense esteems morality for its own sake and does not tell her to her face that we are attached to her only by our own advantage and not by her beauty. In the *Critique of Practical Reason* the doctrine of the moral sense is again condemned. There the moral sense is taken by Kant primarily as a rewarding and punishing agent, rather than as telling us what we ought to do; everything is reduced to a desire for happiness. We are to do what is right under the influence of the rewards and punishments of the moral sense. As Kant points out, this presupposes that we have already a consciousness of duty; he would agree that it is our duty to cultivate a feeling of satisfaction in doing our duty and a contrary feeling in case of failing to do our duty. With reference to the charge of heteronomy, it may be said that a man

241

who acts under the guidance of disinterested benevolence according to the dictates of Hutcheson's moral sense illustrates autonomy in the sense of being free from slavery to egoism. With regard to the complaint that we cannot validly judge others by our own feelings, one may postulate an identical moral sense in all men. One may argue, in defense of Hutcheson, that an identical moral sense in all humans is not a more difficult assumption than an identical faculty of pure reason. Kant himself seems to assume an identical human nature in that we are all supposed to be (more or less) responsive to the law of duty and to moral goodness in the sense of the morally admirable. Kant's basic criticism of the theory of the moral sense as telling us what we ought to do is that it failed to realize the importance of the "form of universality" contained in such ideas as right and duty. Against all forms of heteronomy Kant points out that, starting from some end to be realized, and relying on experience, we can reach no exceptionless rules. He assumes that the true rules of morality must admit of no exception. This, however, is not wholly in accordance with common sense. Many people would think it right to lie or to give a false promise if threatened by a brutal robber and murderer. In war, deception is a legitimate weapon and detectives are not blamed for using trickery in capturing criminals. In short, it is difficult to find a rule which common sense would regard as holding in every single case. The doctrine of acting so that you can will the maxim of your conduct to be a universal law can be given a much more liberal interpretation than Kant would have accepted, namely, act in a manner which you would think right for anyone under the circumstances. The fact is, however, that this rule gives little guidance; it is fortunate that we have more specific principles (such as tell the truth, keep your word, respect the property of others) which cover almost all cases which arise in life. A person who followed only the Kantian imperative would be indistinguishable from a person who followed only his own conscience and would, in practice, be quite unreliable. The details of right and wrong and especially of property are settled in every society by law and custom. The follower of Kantian rigorism would never tell a lie, never violate a promise and always respect the property rights of others. However, we know that there may be a revolution and property may be redistributed by the sovereign people or their representatives. It is not to be denied that such a revolution, if ethical, will seek to realize conditions of ultimate equality and a maximum of self-realization.

Kant also mentions certain rational principles of morality, such as perfection and the divine will. The idea of achieving perfection is indefinite as well as circular, since it presupposes that we already know what moral perfection is, while the divine will, taken apart from the concepts of morality, would be merely God's desire for glory and power and could only be the basis of a system of ethics contrary to true morality. The will of God by itself produces only servility and fear and constitutes the system of heteronomy *par excellence*. As a system of heteronomy it proposes individual happiness as an end and tells us to act in a certain way to achieve this end. Theological ethics, in so far as it is based on egoism, is overthrown when we doubt the existence of God. The ethics of autonomy, Kant tells us, obliges us to will in a certain way without regard to our individual happiness; the existence of God, which is beyond the reach of theoretical proof, turns out to be involved in the moral will.

There is a passage in the *Critique of Practical Reason* [10] in which Kant touches on the idea that the happiness of others might provide a criterion of right conduct. The happiness of others, he tells us, may be an object of a rational will but gives rise to no categorical imperative, since I may or may not happen to be concerned with the welfare of others. But if I start with the fact that I desire my own happiness, my pursuit of my own happiness can become an objective practical law only if "I include within it the happiness of others." Kant concludes that the principle that we should further the happiness of others arises from the form of universality. It cannot depend upon our possessing a sympathetic disposition, since the obligation is binding upon all without regard to what their empirical constitution happens to be. It is possible to understand Kant's argument in this passage in the sense of universalistic hedonism. Since each seeks his own happiness and is bound by the principle of universalization to consider the happiness of others, the indicated course would be to follow rules which tend to the greatest happiness of the greatest number. These rules would include a recognition of the rights of individuals. It is probable, however, that Kant would have rejected this suggestion since it would not have yielded the rigorism of particular moral rules which he regarded as essential.

Kant's argument against egoism as the basis of morals is effective. Thus if a man attempts to justify himself for having borne false witness by appealing to his duty to his own happiness, we are indeed likely to shrink from him in disgust. And assuredly we shall not be eager to engage as a steward a man who is unscrupulous in the use of other people's money. We know that egoism or prudence can only be accepted as a principle of conduct if it is combined with a recognition of the sacredness of the rights of others. One might add that in practice these rights are determined by law and custom and cannot be ascertained by *a priori* reasoning. It is true that prudence merely advises and morality commands; this is something which is involved in the ethical concepts as such and does not contradict the thought that morality is in fact the voice of society. Nevertheless, Kant's statement that "what duty is, is plain of itself to everyone" is not always true. In cases of social conflict, civil wars, revolutions and the like, the path of duty may be far from clear. On the other hand, Kant's instance of the gambler who wins by cheating and who must inwardly admit his moral worthlessness no matter how much he may have filled his purse is sufficient proof that unlimited egoism cannot be the principle of morality.

Kant, like Adam Smith, upheld the retributive theory of punishment. The essence of punishment is harm; this may be combined with benevolence toward the culprit but the essential thing is justice; the wrong-doer, if rational, will acknowledge the justice of his punishment even though it is not mitigated by a kindly purpose. Kant refers to the serpent-windings of the happiness-theory (which we have come to know as utilitarianism) which he connects with the pharisaical saying that it is better that one man should die than that the whole people perish. According to Kant, the basis of punishment is that the criminal has been guilty of a wrongful act and deserves to suffer. The point may be made that Kant's theory of punishment tends to confirm the view that practical reason is closely connected with the retributive emotions, in other words, with our natural feelings of resentment toward those whose actions tend to tear down the institutions of society which we believe make for the general good. In criticism of the retributive theory one may reflect that human authorities are not in a position to dispense what may be called ultimate justice; only God could know all the circumstances and the precise degree of guilt of each individual.

We must now consider the Kantian postulate of the freedom of the will. His reasoning is founded on the thought that freedom is presupposed in the moral law. This means more than the mere fact of choice between alternatives both of which are based on sensuous desires; it is assumed that we are to do right because it is right; ethical reason makes demands on us which cannot be explained without taking into account man's dual nature. As a denizen of the empirical world, he is subject to various sensuous desires, but as a "thing-in-itself" he acknowledges the commands of *a priori* reason. The Kantian theory of freedom is a metaphysical topic which has been discussed countless times. One question which may be asked is whether man alone has a noumenal side or whether all the objects of experience also are rooted in the realm of things-in-themselves. Do rocks and trees have a metaphysical side just as man has? If we follow out this suggestion, we arrive at Schopenhauer's doctrine of a metaphysical world-will as a universal thing-in-itself. Or perhaps we reach the thought of Aristotle according to which whatever exists has an essence which it strives to realize.

According to Kant, human action is subject to the law of cause and effect and we do not find in nature any absolute beginning such as an act of free will is supposed to be. On the other hand, the moral law presupposes freedom in some sense. The point has often been made that man needs the freedom which is involved in the moral law in the phenomenal world where he is called upon to do his duty rather than in some mysterious realm of things-in-themselves. In general, it seems, man's actions are expressions of his desires. Desires are not events and, therefore, are not causes in the sense of events connected with other events by some law of nature. A desire is similar to such a force as gravitation which only comes into action when an occasion is given. Strictly speaking, desires, like forces, are unobservable. The force of gravity may be regarded as a fictitious entity, which is postulated as a way of expressing concisely a great number of hypothetical truths such as "if some event X occurs, then such and such a motion will also occur." In a similar way, I may say that a given desire, *e.g.* ambition or greed is merely a fictitious entity which summarizes a large number of truths to the effect that under such and such circumstances a given individual will act in such and such ways. Character may also be regarded as a similar fictitious entity, which expresses the entire complex of desires found in a given individual. However, force, desire and character are "fictitious" entities merely from a point of view, which may be called "eventism," which would exclude the existence even of such continuants as selves or "things" in general. It would be difficult to discuss ethical theory in terms of a strict "eventism." It is more natural to think of desires as really existent tensions in a really existent self and as expressing themselves in the decisions of this self.

Kant does not discuss the question of free will in all its aspects as a separate problem; he rather propounds a general doctrine of freedom as an essential part of the critical philosophy, which, above all, hinges on the distinction between the world of phenomena in space and time, which is subject to a strict determinism, and, on the other hand, an unknowable realm of things-in-themselves. It is clear that free will, in some sense, is presupposed in everyday praise and blame and legal punishments; on the other hand, it is not clear that the free will involved is really contrary to the law of cause and effect or that it involves any consideration of noumena as opposed to phenomena. Kant was determined to make a metaphysical mystery out of morality in general and free will in particular. Nature, including man, was to be assigned to mechanistically-minded scientists, but religion was given an unchallengable field in the region beyond space, time and causation, which was accessible only to faith.

In the *Grundlegung zur Metaphysik der Sitten* we are told that will is a "kind of causality of living

247

beings as far as they are rational" and that "freedom is a property of this causality by which it can be effective independently of foreign causes determining it." [11] In comment, we note that the word *will* has many meanings; here emphasis is placed on rational beings as causes. A living and rational being is assuredly not an event; he is rather an agent which exerts an influence on other beings. But irrational beings are determined to activity always by external causes. A rational being, apparently, may spontaneously exert itself and so be a genuine free cause, or better, a free causal agency. However, even an inanimate object has certain indwelling energies, such as gravity, inertia, electrical and magnetic powers and the like, which are released by changing circumstances. In the same way we may think of the rational being as having a certain dynamic constitution made up of habits and instincts, that is, of desires, which express themselves in various choices. A being subject to praise and blame, reward and punishment, must have a faculty of choice, but it does not follow that choice is not always under the sway of innate or acquired desires. In fact, it would indeed be strange if a rational being should choose one alternative in preference to another without a reason, that is, without some desire which led him to make that choice. The determining desire might be a unique sort of desire, namely, the desire to do what the individual regarded as right. But in any case Kant's basic division between determination by foreign causes and non-determination by foreign causes is open to criticism since there may be determination by desire and desire is not rightly described as a foreign cause. There must also be an occasion or situation which demands a choice. In both inanimate objects and rational beings, there is an interplay between internal potentialities and the external situation. Kant, however, proceeds to tell us that non-determination by foreign causes does not give us the essence of freedom, since it is a negative definition; he then gives us a positive definition of freedom, which is that it is the self-determination of the will, that is, a determination by non-natural and immutable laws imposed by the will on itself. Positive freedom is, therefore, identical with morality. If we start with the concept of free will, says Kant, we find that it analytically contains the categorical imperative.

But how can the concept of freedom give us a moral law? Even if we are prepared to consider the possibility of wholly spontaneous action which is not an expression of internal tensions or desires, still nothing follows from this concept with regard to how one *ought* to act. Kant says that it would be absurd to be determined by no law at all; however, if there is an absurdity, it is in the original assumption of un-caused action. It is evident that an *ought* proposition cannot be inferred from an *is* proposition, although it is true that a denial of freedom does entail a denial of duty. But we have a feeling that Kant is making a significant statement when he tells us that morality, *i.e.*, ethical rationality, is true freedom. We feel that we are, in some sense, following a self-imposed law in being moral and that we are doing what we really want to do. Freedom is a word which may be used in different senses; it may be a synonym for a kind of virtue or, again, it may stand for a power of choice which, although a precondition of virtue, is itself neutral. Choice itself is an undeniable fact of life; we could not understand the word if it did not corre-spond to an actual experience. On the other hand, we commonly think that our choices are determined by our desires and that we necessarily choose accord-ing to our strongest desire, although we are willing to grant that we cannot tell which desire is the strongest until after we have chosen. But even if virtue is, in some sense, self-rule, it does not seem to be identical with the rule of *a priori* reason, but rather with the rule of our selves in so far as we have made the will of society our own will.

Kant asserts that

> "freedom is a mere idea, the objective reality of which can in no way be shown according to natural laws or in any possible experience. Since no example in accordance with any analogy can support it, it can never be comprehended or even imagined. It holds only as the necessary presupposition of reason in a being that believes itself conscious of a will, i.e. of a faculty different from the mere faculty of desire, or a faculty of determining itself to act as intelligence and thus according to the laws of reason independently of all natural instincts." [12]

Free will, therefore, is a power of self-determination, apart from and even against our natural inclinations. It is not identical with the freedom of action asserted by Hobbes, Locke and Hume in the physical sense of "you can if you choose." Choice may belong to a mere animal and of an animal one can say that there are certain things which it could do if it chose as well as others which it could not do if it chose. Kant explains that truly moral action is prompted not by desire but by *respect* for the moral law, which is a unique feeling, connected with the moral law by an *a priori* necessity. The point may be made that a feeling is a self-contained entity and that it has no tendency to produce action. If respect or any other feeling does tend to influence choice it does so by producing a desire, else it may be considered to be itself a desire. If respect for the moral law, or for human personality, does influence our behavior it may be considered one desire along with others, differing from them only in its object. It is in short the desire to do what is right. The moral law, according to Kant, tends to awaken this feeling or desire, but nevertheless we are likely not to obey this law of reason; we are led astray by our sensuous desires. It is, however, our faculty of free will which enables us spontaneously to decide whether we shall yield to sensuous desire or to our "respect" for the ethical imperative.

The reality of freedom is confirmed by Kant by means of two examples.[13] A man says that his lust is irresistible when opportunity offers. But this man, if threatened with hanging immediately after satisfying his lust, would nevertheless refrain. In this case, one sensuous impulse, the will to live, overcomes another, namely, lust. In this case transcendental freedom does not come into play. But in the next case we are asked to consider a man who is commanded by his sovereign, under threat of the death penalty, to bear false witness against an honorable man. This individual, whatever he may actually do, is conscious that he could (and should) sacrifice his life for truth and justice, even going against the command of his king. This is the consciousness of absolute freedom, which is implicit in the moral law itself. It is a freedom which enables us to choose to do what we think is right even at the cost of our lives; it is, in short, a freedom to sacrifice ourselves.

Kant specifically argues against those who seek to explain freedom on an empirical basis and thus attempt to deprive us of the "great revelation" of an intelligible world. In order to show the impossibility of freedom in an empirical world, Kant cites the fact that according to the law of causality (as he understands it) the present is determined by the past, so that even if my whole life were self-determined, still I could never be free, since my present deed would be determined by my past experiences and decisions. But this doctrine of determination by the past is very much open to criticism. One can understand the principle of causation, that is, of determinism, in quite a different way. Each thing, we may say, including under this term, animals and persons as well as plants and inanimate objects, acts according to its nature and the circumstances it is in at the moment. There is really no determination by the past, although, knowing the past, we may infer the future, on the principle that things of the same character placed in the same circumstances, must act in the same way. But the past is, at the moment of action, non-existent and cannot determine what happens in the present. In a similar way, events are not determined by laws, which are mere descriptive formulae, telling us what does happen on certain specified occasions. The world, in short, is a system of interacting things, each of which acts according to its nature. The Kantian doctrine of determination by the past is an application of eventism, according to which phenomenal reality consists of a series of events connected by laws. Against this one may suggest the more substantialistic view of "things" acting according to their respective natures. Let us say that each "thing" acts spontaneously, with reference to its circumstances and in accordance with certain laws of nature; it is therefore always "free," even though its actions are predictable to minds which are cognizant of how things of this character have behaved in the past. To say that each thing acts according to its nature is to say something which is very obvious when we reflect that the nature of a thing is simply the totality of laws according to which it acts. It is also to be noted that we only learn the natures of things empirically and that we often revise our opinions of the natures of the various inanimate objects and living beings with which we deal.

According to the view which we have just outlined all things act freely but also in accordance with certain laws; all things are characterized by self-determination. It is obvious that freedom in this sense does not establish moral responsibility, since it is much too broad. Moral censure is limited to beings who are capable of choice and who have a sufficient degree of intelligence to be influenced by praise and blame. Nevertheless, we may defend the thesis that even in what Kant calls the phenomenal world there is always spontaneity in the sense of self-determination along with a limited predictability. Kant has by no means established the view that in the so-called phenomenal world there can be only determination by a past which stretches back either indefinitely or to a first beginning. There is rather, we may say, only determination by what exists *now*, which includes thought of what may exist in the future.

As we have seen, Kant specifically rejects the "self-determination" theory of freedom. Our actions may be determined by psychological rather than by physical causes; nevertheless, we still illustrate determination in time and we have not escaped from fatalism. This can be done, he thinks, only by the concept of transcendental freedom. It matters not whether we are to be regarded as *automata materiale* or *automata spirituale* (as Leibniz supposed) we have still only the freedom of a turnspit "which, once wound up, carries out its motions of itself." [14] The Kantian doctrine is that as "things-in-ourselves" we are outside of time and therefore free from causality. As ethical beings we are conscious of our existence in the intelligible world. We can say of any wrong action which we have done, even if as a phenomenal event it was causally necessitated, that we could still have left it undone, since it is a phenomenal manifestation of a character which we ourselves create. It is our metaphysical or intelligible character which is free from both time and causality; this expresses itself in our empirical character and its deeds. Our awareness of our unchanging metaphysical character is seen in our inescapable feelings of guilt and repentance in connection with our past misdeeds, even though we know that in the temporal sequence of events there

253

was a strict causal necessity which rendered those deeds inevitable.

Since the metaphysical character is outside of time, it cannot change and this fact seems to entail a new form of fatalism. Kant asserts that if it were possible for us to have a sufficiently deep insight into a man's character we could predict his actions as surely as we can predict a solar or lunar eclipse. In comment one may say that a series of past deeds, empirically observed, would only establish the likelihood of similar actions in the future, never a certainty. Furthermore, the notion of an intelligible character seems to be a form of the fallacy of an individual essence. A thing has an essence, in the proper sense of the word, as belonging to a certain class. Thus all red things must participate in redness; all wooden things in the essence of woodenness, whatever it may be. But an individual entity, considered as such, has only a proper name and an indefinitely extended list of properties; it has no essence, unless we call its entire destiny its essence. Thus, in retrospect, it belongs to the essence of Julius Caesar to cross the Rubicon, but this detail of his biography could not have been deduced with certainty from the earlier incidents of his life, even though it may have come about *necessarily*, in view of the circumstances, from some philosophical point of view. We cannot say that the deeds and experiences of a man flow from his individual essence, since an individual essence, if the expression is to be tolerated at all, is merely a collective term for all that happens to an individual viewed retrospectively. The fatalism implicit in the Kantian doctrine of an intelligible character is seen in his statement that some men are born villains and are incapable of any improvement of character. Such men show an increasing depravity from childhood on, in spite of the advantages of education; they themselves must acknowledge their badness, which is an expression of a vicious quality which is all the more culpable because it is a result of freely assumed evil principles. Against this, one may say that there is no evidence for the existence of such an unchanging metaphysical character. No one can know how good or bad a given individual is until all his deeds have been done. It is only a postulated supra-temporal divine mind which might know an individual essence, which would be all the incidents of a life seen in a single comprehensive glance. It would be rash, therefore, to assume with regard to an individual that he possessed either an unchangeably good or an unchangeably evil metaphysical character.

Kant felt that the true doctrine of transcendental freedom was threatened not only by the false notion of empirical self-determination but also by the idea of God as the first cause and as, therefore, the cause of the existence and properties of each finite substance. The actions of a man seem to be completely determined by something much greater than himself. He is a marionette or automaton; self-consciousness makes him a thinking automaton but the consciousness of his spontaneity is a mere illusion. We can remove this difficulty, Kant thinks, with the familiar distinction between phenomena and things-in-themselves. If we fail to recognize the ideality of space and time, we are led to Spinozism, which, he says, regards time and space as attributes of the first cause and all finite beings as mere accidents inhering in an infinite self-existent substance. This view is incompatible with individual freedom. The creation theory leads to the same result, namely, the total dependence of finite substances on the Creator. Kant takes the position that creation refers to us only as noumena and that, as phenomena, although we are entangled in the universal causal nexus, we are not deprived of our freedom because of our dependence on God. This argument is manifestly a very weak one. Kant himself says "The solution . . . here given . . . will be said to have so much difficulty in it, that it is hardly susceptible of a lucid presentation." [15] He then asks whether any other solution is better. The reconciliation of divine omnipotence and human freedom may be considered as a challenge to the theologian rather than to the moralist. Kant has by no means removed the difficulty since, if our phenomenal characters are the manifestation in space and time of our noumenal selves, which in turn are creatures of God, it appears that God is responsible for all our deeds, good and bad alike. We cannot sin, since, whatever we do, it is still God's will. The fact seems to be that the ethical judgment does not go back of the deeds and characters of individuals. How this character came into being is irrelevant; it is either good or bad when measured by certain standards. God chooses to confer existence upon us; we must have some innate character or disposition to start with. We may not infer that all characters are good because all have been created by God. The question why God creates evil is one which theology must answer if it can but is irrelevant to moral judgment.

We may translate Kant's theory of an intelligible character out of its metaphysical context. He does not assert the existence of a phenomenal indeterminism. Our noumenal freedom may be taken to mean that our actions are expressions of what we inwardly are. Our inner nature is difficult to discover since what we are as adults is largely a result of childhood training and example. Ordinary moral judgment pronounces a man to be good or bad without attempting to distinguish between the respective contributions of heredity and environment. However, in so far as we reflectively excuse people's conduct by taking account of their bad environments, we are vaguely considering what they are in themselves. We are seeking to form an idea of their innate character, which must always be indefinite, since innate character can only manifest itself in interaction with environment. It cannot be said that all innate characters

are the same since some men remain perversely selfish, in spite of good environments, while others,
brought up in surroundings counted evil, nevertheless display traits of nobility. We are therefore led
to admit that some innate characters are better than
others. Innate character cannot be changed. One may
cite the possibility of reform through training or example, etc. However, it is to be noted that if reformation takes place, there must have been an innate
susceptibility to reform; a person may chance to
have been born with a character incorrigibly bad. Or,
at any rate, some people are less reformable than
others. It is certain that a person does not choose his
innate character, although he always acts in accordance with it. In thinking of people and their actions
we may, if we choose, adopt a "psychological" attitude in which we seek merely to *understand*, as
Spinoza said, without praise or blame. In this frame
of reference there is no "arbitrary free-will" but only
necessary self-determination, since a person acts as
he must act, being the kind of person he is, in the
kind of situation he happens to be in. The moral
judgment, on the other hand, is always in some sense
practical, that is, directed on changing people's characters into patterns conducive to the general good by
means of reward and punishment, praise and blame.
One need not assume that choice is free in any metaphysical sense but only in the empirical sense of
"you can if you choose." Choice may be regarded as
determined by our present character, which in turn
is a resultant of our innate character and our past
decisions and experiences. There is a *de facto* unpredictability of human choice, which does not differ
from the unpredictability which is found in all material things, including sub-atomic particles. The sense
of "I could have done otherwise," according to this
doctrine of "moderate determinism," is simply that
there is unpredictability based on an irremovable in-
adequacy of our knowledge. We choose as we must

choose being the kind of persons we are. The conclusion may be drawn that it is unwise to torment ourselves with self-blame with regard to our past transgressions, save in so far as such self-blame tends to prevent future misdeeds. The Kantian doctrine of an unchangeable intelligible character deserving of everlasting blame for being what it is opens up a cruel prospect of endless self-torture, which is, after all, quite uncalled for since no one can help being the kind of person he is.

The postulates of practical reason include, in addition to the freedom of the will, the immortality of the soul and the existence of God. Virtue, that is, good will, is the highest good but the complete good includes happiness. Happiness, Kant tells us, may be regarded as, either, in some mysterious way, identical with virtue or else as synthetically connected with it. The Epicurean reduces virtue to mere prudence; in what way this makes prudence the *same* as happiness, Kant does not explain. The Stoic, says Kant, holds that virtue is the highest good and happiness is the consciousness of the possession of this good; this is the doctrine of the identity of happiness and virtue. But the doctrine of the identity of the two is, according to Kant, not defensible. It may be true, as a matter of fact, that only the virtuous are happy or perhaps even that only the happy are virtuous, still the terms do not mean the same. It is at least theoretically possible to be virtuous without being happy or vice versa and common experience thoroughly familiarizes us with the possibility of one condition without the other. The virtuous person is "morally admirable" while the happy person, as far as one can see from mere consideration of the concepts, may be morally despicable. The highest good, says Kant, must be the union of happiness and virtue; this is a synthesis of predicates, the possibility and necessity of which are known *a priori*. The ultimate

258

distribution of happiness in accordance with merit can only be conceived, Kant maintains, by means of the postulates of the existence of God and the immortality of the soul.

The Kantian doctrine strongly suggests the familiar thought that the teachings of religion are necessary for the upholding of law and order and that we should simply accept them, outwardly if not inwardly, without closely questioning them. This may be called the pragmatic attitude and is probably the most widely accepted position. However, the Kantian formulation may be regarded as addressed by a man to himself. We find that we are unable to sacrifice ourselves to duty unless we believe that we are to be compensated for our trouble in another life. This argument is dubious, since we may believe that if we do what we think is wrong we shall suffer so greatly from remorse in this life that we should be the losers, no matter how much we gained materially by our transgression. It cannot be said therefore, that the transcendental postulates are strictly demanded; it is also difficult to say with what degree of literalness the doctrines are really believed by persons who perform noble actions. A person professing belief in God and a future life may be speaking in a poetic or symbolic manner; he may merely have faith in human nature, which convinces him of the unprofitableness of dishonesty. There is also the possibility that these persons may understand the ethical imperative to be truly unconditional and therefore as not implying any thought of future compensation, either in this life or in any future life.

Reward and punishment after death, if regulated by justice, would be of only finite duration and would therefore not entail an infinite future duration for the soul. This was probably the reason why Kant, in the *Critique of Practical Reason*, defended the postulate of immortality by means of a quite different argument. Emphasis is placed on the thought that we need an infinite future for gaining moral perfection, which Kant identifies with holiness, which is, in turn, defined as the complete accordance between the desires and the imperative of ethical reason. Without the postulate of immortality we are likely to fall into despair and thus into a lax moral attitude. Kant further complicates matters by telling us that the infinite being, God, is above time. He sees the series which for us is endless as "a whole conformable to the moral law." [16] However, the conception of a single intellectual intuition which is to encompass the existence of all rational beings and to see each participating in the highest good according to its deserts is highly problematic. Did Kant mean that even now, as we follow our endless destiny in time, we are also in eternity enjoying our just deserts? Still, we may ask whether the proposed timeless vision of justice enjoyed by God is relevant to our problems. We are doomed to continue forever in our struggle for moral perfection; that which comes at the end of an infinite series *never* comes. It follows that we may as well relax in our efforts to overcome our selfish desires, since we are never to reach perfection. The fact is that the prospect of endless moral struggle, that is, of endless war with ourselves, is terrifying. Do we not hope for some condition of ultimate rest?

The postulate of the existence of God is defended by Kant by the thought that only the existence of God can render intelligible the existence of a moral order which guarantees that righteousness must ultimately triumph. With regard to the ultimate harmony of morality and happiness Kant says that

"Reason cannot objectively decide whether it (comes about) by universal laws of nature without a wise Author presiding over nature or only on the assumption of such an Author." [17]

We choose theism in response to a "free interest of pure practical reason." Belief in God, says Kant, is not commanded. "Faith that is commanded is an absurdity." [18] The moral will finds that it must postulate a moral order and that it can comprehend this moral order only by the idea of God. The attributes ascribed to God are the traditional ones of omnipotence, omniscience, omnipresence, etc. The primary attributes, Kant says, are holiness, blessedness and wisdom. By virtue of these he is the holy lawgiver, the beneficent ruler and the just judge. It would seem that the last attribute is the most essential one since his existence is postulated primarily in order to enforce the moral law. The essential point is that moral action can take place only on the basis of *faith* in a moral order which brings it about that we shall not lose by sacrificing ourselves to duty. If this faith were *knowledge* our actions would be merely prudent and, although right, they would cease to be "morally admirable." It is possible to interpret this faith in terms of humanism, that is to say, in terms of faith in the ethical tendencies of human nature which bring it about that we cannot achieve happiness by actions which go against our moral convictions. Kant cannot be called a humanist in the modern sense, but if we strip off all reference to the transcendent, we are left with a mere faith in the goodness of human nature.

In dealing with the subject of moral education, Kant seems to admit the necessity for faith in the goodness of man. How can we instill morality? This is indeed a very difficult problem. It is one thing to induce the young to do and not to do certain things by threats and bribes; it is another thing altogether to induce them to sacrifice themselves for the sake of honesty and justice. Kant defends the thesis that moral education is best advanced by presenting the moral law in its purity. Emphasis upon practical advantages can produce a mere legality of actions but not a true "morality of intentions." Kant did not clearly distinguish between intention and motive; he is actually speaking of motives and means to assert (1) that we are truly moral only when we act for the sake of the moral law and (2) that human nature is so constituted that it is greatly stirred by the thought of action inspired by no thought of gain but solely by the idea of rightness. He points out that people in general are keenly interested in subtle moral arguments, especially as bearing on the motives of the characters of history. A man's own character is revealed in his judgments of others; some are always engaged in attacking the alleged disinterestedness of famous men, while others exercise themselves to remove any blemish suspected in the great, fearing that if all examples are disputed doubt will arise as to the possibility of virtue. Moral education, Kant thought, might be conducted by considering the story of an honest man who refuses to join the calumniators of an innocent but powerless person, in spite of every sort of bribe and threat. The young listener will be led from approval to admiration and eventually to veneration and a lively wish to be such a man (although not in his circumstances). The motive must be duty, not any pretension to greatness of mind or noble sentiment. In short, moral education, Kant thinks will be more effective in proportion as it emphasizes duty as a motive. His attack is especially directed against those who teach morality by the flattering device of regarding certain actions as "noble." Kant offers certain examples. In the case of a man who sacrifices his life in an effort to save others in a ship-wreck, the action may be counted as duty but our esteem for it as meritorious is weakened by the thought that duty to self has been infringed. By Kant's own admission our duty in such a case is unclear; whether or not the action is meritorious would seem to depend on our feelings as we view the action in various lights. Similar uncertainty is expressed by Kant with regard to sacrificing ourselves for our country apart from some specific call of duty. But Kant was also convinced that there may be an "inexorable duty, transgression against which violates of itself the moral law without respect to human welfare." [19] This is commonly considered to be duty to God; it may demand the sacrifice of all our inclinations; the thought of it strengthens and elevates the soul. It is illustrated by Kant by a quotation from Juvenal in which we are bidden to be stout soldiers, faithful guardians and incorruptible judges and we are especially forbidden to bear false witness. It is clear enough, no matter how we interpret the categorical imperative, that only individual conscience can decide what duties fall in this inviolable class. But we may understand Kant's point here to be that if we are strictly moral we shall do nothing in order to do a noble deed. We must rather make up our minds concerning our duty and proceed to do it. In so far as there is an element of self-sacrifice, that is, of going against our natural inclinations, the action will be meritorious as well as merely right. It would be blamable to seek primarily to do a meritorious or noble action rather than seeking to do our duty, whether this duty happens to involve self-sacrifice or not. Asceticism may be understood as an attempt to practice self-sacrifice for its own sake and as such is open to condemnation.

We have already seen that rewards and punishments in moral education can only produce an external rightness of conduct rather than an inner goodness. In actual practice, we seek to influence the young by examples from religious and secular history; we also seek to communicate to them our emotions, so that they will admire what we admire and despise what we despise. It is necessary that they believe in our sincerity, and, therefore, the accordance of our actions and our words is of utmost importance. The young person must form an idea of what sort of a world it is in which he finds himself. If he believes that he is surrounded by ruthless and unscrupulous persons, he will also adopt egoism as his sole guide; on the other hand, if he has reason to believe in the goodness of human nature he will be inspired to deeds involving self-sacrifice. In the process of moral education, we seek to put the young person into a state of mind in which he will feel that he really wants to do his duty, no matter what the evil consequences to him may be. We seek to instill good habits in the thought that the individual will, as it were, be carried along by them, even in the unusual situations where telling the truth, etc., is disadvantageous to him personally. What we seek is essentially to cause the young to share our emotions of approval and disapproval.[20] This, as a matter of fact, includes causing our children to adopt as their own even our prejudices.

The topic of moral education brings us to the thought that morality, whether or not it involves faith in the transcendental postulates, does presuppose faith in the goodness of human nature. Thus a man who feels that those with whom he associates are conscienceless egoists is not likely to practice strict veracity and fidelity. This, in fact, is the point of the Hobbesian doctrine of the *bellum omnium contra omnes* and his belief that morality apart from the sanctions of the state is necessarily inoperative. The follower of Hobbes may say that he is quite willing to obey the maxims of fidelity and veracity in situations where others are willing to do the same, but that he refuses to be the only one to sacrifice himself for ideal moral standards; furthermore, he is quite ready to universalize his attitude and to refrain from blaming others who likewise dispense with morality. The conclusion to be drawn is that in order to carry out moral education we must be able to instill the belief that human nature is predominantly good. Morality cannot be based entirely on *a priori* reason but involves beliefs concerning matter of fact, namely, human nature. The matter of the interpretation of the motives of religious and political leaders is, therefore, important; it is also true that decision concerning the reason why a certain historical figure did a certain thing must always be problematic and, to a certain extent, arbitrary. The humanist would admit that there must be a certain "leap of faith," in which we overcome our suspicions, and, believing ourselves to be dealing with honorable men, dare to act honorably ourselves.

NOTES

CHAPTER I

HOBBES (1588-1679)

1. *Leviathan, or the Matter, Forme and Power of a Commonwealth, ecclesiastical and civil*, 1651, Part I, Ch. 11.
2. *idem*
3. *idem*
4. *ibid*, Part I, Ch. 13
5. *ibid*, Ch. 15
6. *ibid*, Part I, Ch. 20
7. *ibid*, Part II, Ch. 31
8. *ibid*, Part II, Ch. 21
9. *idem*.

CHAPTER II

SPINOZA (1632-1677)

1. *Ethics,* Part 4, Prop. 18, note.
2. *ibid,* Part 3, Prop. 39, note.
3. *ibid,* Part 3, Prop. 9.
4. *ibid,* Part 4, Prop. 18, note.
5. *idem.*
6. *ibid,* Part 4, Prop. 72.
7. *ibid,* Part 4, Prop. 63, corollary.
8. *idem.*

CHAPTER III

LOCKE (1632-1704)

1. *Essay concerning Human Understanding*, 1690. Here reference is made to the edition published by the Oxford University Press, in 1894, Vol. I, p. 303.
2. *ibid*, Vol. I, p. 474.
3. *ibid*, Vol. I, p. 70.
4. *Essay concerning Civil Government* (1689) Chapter 2, Section 6.
5. *Essay*, Vol. I, p. 329.
6. *Essay*, Vol. I, p. 328.
7. *Essay*, Vol. I, p. 341.
8. *Essay*, Vol. I. p. 342.

CHAPTER IV

CUDWORTH, CLARKE AND WOLLASTON

Cudworth, 1617-1688, Samuel Clarke, 1675-1729, Wollaston, 1659-1724. Cudworth, Ralph, *A Treatise concerning Eternal and Immutable Morality*, 1731; Clarke, Samuel, *Discourse concerning the Unchangable Obligations of Natural Religion*, 1705; Wollaston, William, *The Religion of Nature delineated*, 1722.

1. Selby-Bigge, *British Moralists*, Oxford University Press, 1897, Vol. II, p. 247.
2. *ibid*, p. 250
3. *ibid*, p. 250
4. *ibid*, p. 260
5. *ibid*, p. 257
6. *ibid*, p. 3
7. *ibid*, p. 9
8. *ibid*, p. 15
9. *ibid*, p. 16
10. *ibid*, p. 18
11. *ibid*, p. 23
12. *ibid*, p. 23
13. *ibid*, p. 25
14. *ibid*, p. 25
15. *ibid*, p. 27
16. *ibid*, p. 26
17. *ibid*, p. 28

18. *ibid*, p. 29
19. *ibid*, p. 31
20. *ibid*, p. 363
21. *ibid*, p. 371
22. *ibid*, p. 202
23. *ibid*, p. 369

CHAPTER V

SHAFTESBURY (1671-1713)

1. Selby-Bigge, *British Moralists*, Vol. I, p. 9
2. *ibid*, p. 12
3. *ibid*, p. 15
4. *ibid*, p. 13
5. *idem*
6. *ibid*, p. 20
7. *ibid*, p. 20
8. *ibid*, p. 18
9. W. T. Stace, in *The Concept of Morals*.
10. *ibid*, p. 38
11. *ibid*, p. 39
12. *ibid*, p. 46
13. *ibid*, p. 47
14. *ibid*, p. 48
15. John Brown, 1715-1766, Vicar of St. Nicholas, Newcastle, author of *Essays on the Characteristics*, 1751.
16. Selby-Bigge, *British Moralists*, Vol. II, p. 220

CHAPTER VI

MANDEVILLE AND HUTCHESON

(Mandeville, 1670-1733, Hutcheson, 1694-1746)

1. Selby-Bigge, *British Moralists*, Vol. II, p. 353
2. *op. cit.*, Vol. I, p. 75
3. *ibid*, p. 120
4. *ibid*, p. 125
5. *ibid*, p. 103
6. *ibid*, p. 84
7. *ibid*, p. 91
8. *ibid*, p. 93
9. *ibid*, p. 101
10. *ibid*, p. 113
11. *ibid*, p. 106
12. *ibid*, p. 395
13. *ibid*, p. 396
14. *ibid*, p. 397
15. *ibid*, p. 410
16. *ibid*, p. 423
17. Clarke, John, *The Foundation of Morality in Theory and Practice*, 1730, see Selby-Bigge, Vol. II, p. 221 ff.
18. Selby-Bigge, Vol. II, p. 222 ff.
19. *ibid*, p. 224
20. *ibid*, p. 225

CHAPTER VII

BUTLER (1692-1752)

1. Selby-Bigge, *British Moralists*, Vol. I, p. 246
2. *ibid*, p. 193
3. *ibid*, p. 225
4. *ibid*, p. 240
5. *ibid*, p. 240
6. *ibid*, p. 199
7. *ibid*, p. 221
8. *idem*
9. *ibid*, p. 235
10. *ibid*, p. 243
11. *ibid*, p. 253
12. *ibid*, p. 246

CHAPTER VIII

BALGUY AND PRICE

1. John Balguy, 1686-1748, Richard Price, 1723-1791. Price is of interest to the student of the American Revolution. See Cone, Carl B., *Torchbearer of Freedom,* University of Kentucky Press, 1952.
2. *ibid,* p. 64
3. *idem*
4. *ibid,* p. 66
5. *ibid,* p. 90
6. *ibid,* p. 86
7. Price's *Review of the Principal Questions in Morals* was re-published by the Oxford University Press (1948) edited by D. Daiches Raphael. All references are to this edition. Cf. Rashdall, Hastings, *Theory of Good and Evil,* Second Edition, Vol. I, p. 81.
8. *op. cit.,* p. 45
9. *ibid,* p. 50
10. *ibid,* p. 59
11. *ibid,* p. 62
12. *ibid,* p. 70
13. *ibid,* p. 74
14. Cf. Spinoza's *Ethics,* Part III, Prop. LIX.
15. Price, *op. cit.,* p. 76
16. *idem*

17. *ibid*, p. 125
18. *idem*
19. *ibid*, p. 126
20. *ibid*, p. 154
21. *ibid*, p. 151
22. *idem*.
23. *ibid*, p. 152
24. *ibid*, p. 164
25. *ibid*, p. 153; Cf. Ross, W. D., *The Right and the Good*, Oxford, 1930, p. 19 ff.
26. *ibid*, p. 172
27. *ibid*, p. 174
28. *ibid*, p. 178
29. *ibid*, p. 179
30. *ibid*, p. 180
31. *ibid*, p. 184
32. *ibid*, p. 186
33. *ibid*, p. 228

CHAPTER IX

HUME (1711-1776)

Hume, David, *A Treatise of Human Nature*, 1739-40. Page references are given to the one-volume edition reprinted by the Clarendon Press, Oxford, 1949.

1. Bk. II, Pt. III, Sect. 1, p. 402
2. Bk. II, Pt. II, Sect. 9, p. 439
3. Bk. II, Pt. III, Sect. 3, p. 417
4. Bk. II, Pt. II, Sect. 8, p. 376
5. Bk. II, Pt. III, Sect. 3, p. 415
6. *ibid*, p. 414
7. *ibid*, p. 416
8. Selby-Bigge, *British Moralists*, Vol. I, p. 240
9. *Treatise*, Book III, Pt. I, Sect. 1, p. 469
10. *idem*
11. *idem*
12. *idem*
13. *ibid*, Bk. III, Pt. II, Sect. 2, p. 472
14. *ibid*, Bk. III, Pt. II, Sect. 1, p. 478
15. Bk. III, Pt. II, Sect. 1, p. 478
16. Bk. III, Pt. II, Sect. 2, p. 491
17. Bk. III, Pt. II, Sect. 2, p. 487
18. *idem*, p. 489
19. *idem*, p. 497
20. Bk. III, Pt. II, Sect. 3, p. 503
21. *idem*, p. 509

22. Bk. III, Pt. II, Sect. 5, p. 522
23. *idem*, p. 521
24. Bk. III, Pt. II, Sect. 10, p. 588
25. *idem*
26. Bk. III, Pt. II, Sect. 11, p. 568
27. *idem*, p. 569
28. Bk. III, Pt. III, Sect. 1, p. 579
29. *idem*, p. 582
30. *idem*, p. 583
31. *idem*, Bk. III, Pt. III, Sect. 1, p. 587
32. *idem*
33. *idem*, p. 606
34. *Enquiry concerning Morals*, 1751, Sect. I, p. 455
35. *Treatise*, Bk. II, Pt. I, Sect. 1
36. *Enquiry*, Sect. 1
37. *Enquiry*, Appendix I
38. *Enquiry*, Sect. 3

CHAPTER X

ADAM SMITH (1723-1790)

1. Westermarck, Edward, *Ethical Relativity*, New York, 1932, p. 70
2. Adam Smith's *Theory of Moral Sentiments* was first published in 1759. See Schneider, *Adam Smith's Moral and Political Philosophy*, Hafner Publishing Co., New York, 1948, p. xvi.
3. Hume, *Treatise of Human Nature*, Bk. II, Pt. II, Sect. 5
4. *idem*
5. Hume, *Treatise*, Book III, Pt. III, Sect. 1
6. Adam Smith, ed. by Schneider, p. 75
7. *ibid*, p. 74
8. *ibid*, p. 76
9. *ibid*, p. 77
10. *ibid*, p. 78
11. *ibid*, p. 27
12. *idem*
13. *idem*
14. *ibid*, p. 156
15. *ibid*, p. 157
16. *ibid*, p. 103
17. *ibid*, p. 268
18. *ibid*, p. 112
19. *ibid*, p. 114
20. *ibid*, p. 128

21. *ibid*, p. 130
22. *ibid*, p. 125
23. *ibid*, p. 163
24. *ibid*, p. 166
25. *ibid*, p. 181
26. *ibid*, p. 182
27. *ibid*, p. 194
28. *ibid*, p. 214
29. *ibid*, p. 215
30. *idem*
31. *ibid*, p. 242
32. *ibid*, p. 243
33. *ibid*, p. 259

CHAPTER XI

BENTHAM (1748-1832)

An Introduction to the Principles of Morals and Legislation (first printed, 1780, first published, 1789). Reference is here made to the Oxford edition of 1907.

1. *op. cit.*, p. 1, note.
2. *ibid*, p. 16
3. *ibid*, p. 336
4. *ibid*, p. 195
5. *ibid*, p. 98
6. *ibid*, p. 102
7. *ibid*, p. 122
8. *ibid*, p. 131
9. *ibid*, p. 150

CHAPTER XII

KANT (1724-1804)

The *Grundlegung zur Metaphysik der Sitten* was published in 1785 and the *Kritik der praktischen Vernunft* in 1785. Reference is made to the *Foundations of the Metaphysics of Morals* and the *Critique of Practical Reason*, translated by Lewis White Beck, published by the Liberal Arts Press, New York, 1959. The passages are reprinted by permission of the publishers. The following references are to the edition of these translations published by the University of Chicago Press, 1949.

1. *op. cit.*, p. 55
2. *idem*
3. *ibid*, p. 169
4. *ibid*, p. 88
5. *ibid*, p. 87
6. *ibid*, p. 88
7. *ibid*, p. 99
8. *idem*
9. *ibid*, p. 99
10. *ibid*, p. 145
11. *ibid*, p. 101
12. *ibid*, p. 113
13. *ibid*, p. 141
14. *ibid*, p. 203

15. *ibid*, p. 208
16. *ibid*, p. 226
17. *ibid*, p. 246
18. *ibid*, p. 245
19. *ibid*, p. 255
20. *Cf.* Ewing, *The Definition of Good*, New York, 1947, p. 182

INDEX